# 48th Annual Meeting of the Association for Computational Linguistics 2010 (ACL 2010)

# Student Research Workshop



## Uppsala, Sweden
## 13 July 2010

ISBN: 978-1-61738-826-2

**Printed from e-media with permission by:**

Curran Associates, Inc.
57 Morehouse Lane
Red Hook, NY 12571

**Some format issues inherent in the e-media version may also appear in this print version.**



Printed by Curran Associates, Inc. (2010)

For permission requests, please contact the Association for Computational Linguistics at the address below.

Association for Computational Linguistics
209 N. Eighth Street
Stroudsburg, Pennsylvania 18360

Phone: 1-570-476-8006
Fax: 1-570-476-0860

acl@aclweb.org

**Additional copies of this publication are available from:**

Curran Associates, Inc.
57 Morehouse Lane
Red Hook, NY 12571 USA
Phone: 845-758-0400
Fax: 845-758-2634
Email: curran@proceedings.com
Web: www.proceedings.com

# Introduction

We are pleased to present the papers accepted for presentation at the Student Research Workshop of the 48th Annual Meeting of the Association for Computational Linguistics held in Uppsala, Sweden, July 11-16, 2010. The Student Research Workshop, an established tradition at the annual meetings of ACL, offers students the opportunity to present their work in a setting embedded in the main conference and features ACL's efforts to invest in young researchers who will be a part of the research community in Computational Linguistics, Natural Language Processing and related fields in the near future. The workshop aimed at enabling students to exchange ideas with other researchers and experts and to receive useful feedback and directions for future research in an early stage of their work.

We are indebted to many people who contributed to the organization of the ACL 2010 Student Research Workshop. A total of 54 students and senior researchers agreed to serve on the program committee, of which 21 were from North America, 24 were from Europe, 2 were from Middle East, and 7 were from Asia/Pacific regions. The committee members, who represented various areas of NLP and computational linguistics research, well understood the spirit of the Student Research Workshop and provided high-quality, constructive, and elaborate reviews to all students who submitted their work. We are thankful to the members of the program committee for the time they spent reading and reviewing the papers.

We received 37 submissions from all over the world. Each submission was assigned to 3 reviewers, at least one of which was a senior researcher. We accepted 7 submissions for oral and poster presentation and 12 submissions for only poster presentation during a parallel session with the main conference. The presentation format was assigned based on the suggestions of the reviewers about how the work could be presented best, and does not indicate a quality difference among accepted papers. We would like to thank all students who contributed to the success of this years Student Research Workshop by submitting their research papers from a wide range of topics.

We are very grateful to Tomek Strzalkowski and Marketa Lopatkova, our tireless faculty advisors, for their advice, constant support, and obtaining funding. We also would like to thank the conference organizers of ACL'2010: the general chair, Jan Hajic, the program chairs, Sandra Carberry and Stephen Clark, the publications chairs Jing-Shin Chang and Philipp Koehn, and the local organization committee in particular Joakim Nivre, and Priscilla Rasmussen.

Finally, we wish to thank the U.S. National Science Foundation (NSF), The Don and Betty Walker Student Scholarship Fund of the Association for Computational Linguistics, and European Chapter of the ACL (EACL) for generously sponsoring this workshop by offering grants to assist presenters in covering their registration, accommodation, and travel costs.

The ACL 2010 Student Research Workshop Co-Chairs
Seniz Demir, Nils Reiter, Jan Raab

**Faculty Advisors:**

Marketa Lopatkova
Charles University
Prague, Czech Republic

Tomek Strzalkowski
State University of New York (SUNY)
Albany, NY, USA

**Chairs:**

Seniz Demir
University of Delaware
Newark, DE, USA

Jan Raab
Charles University
Prague, Czech Republic

Nils Reiter
Heidelberg University
Germany

**Program Committee:**

Eneko Agirre, University of the Basque Country, Spain
Regina Barzilay, MIT, USA
Fadi Biadsy, Columbia University, USA
Johan Bos, Italy
Razvan Bunescu, Ohio University, USA
Richard Burns, University of Delaware, USA
Aoife Cahill, University of Stuttgart, Germany
Bethold Crysmann, Saarland University, Germany
Micha Elsner, Brown University, USA
Alex Gruenstein, Google, USA
Tunga Gungor, Bogazici University, Turkey
Aria Haghighi, UC Berkeley, USA
Dilek Hakkani-Tur, International Computer Science Institute (ICSI) - Berkeley, USA
Ilana Heintz, Ohio State University, USA
Julia Hockenmaier, University of Illinois at Urbana-Champaign, USA
Alexander Koller, Saarland University, Germany
Udo Kruschwitz, University of Essex, UK
Cheongjae Lee, Pohang University of Science and Engineering, Korea
Wei-Hao Lin, Google, USA
Yang Liu, University of Texas at Dallas, USA

Daniel Marcu, Information Sciences Institute (ISI) - USC, USA
Philippe Martin, University of Toronto, Canada
Sameer Maskey, IBM, USA
Diana Maynard, University of Sheffield, UK
David McDonald, BBN Technologies, USA
Timothy Miller, University of MinnesotaTwin Cities, USA
Jeremy Nicholson, University of Melbourne, Australia
Kemal Oflazer, Carnegie Mellon University in Qatar, Qatar
Rainer Osswald, Distance University of Hagen, Germany
You Ouyang, Hong Kong Polytechnic University, Hong Kong
Sebastian Pado, University of Stuttgart, Germany
Katerina Pastra, Institute for Language and Speech Processing, Greece
Paul Piwek, The Open University, UK
Jan Ptacek, Charles University in Prague, Czech Republic
Verena Rieser, University of Edinburgh, UK
Jan Romportl, University of West Bohemia, Czech Republic
Helmut Schmid, University of Stuttgart, Germany
Sabine Schulte im Walde, University of Stuttgart, Germany
Samira Shaikh, University at Albany - SUNY, NY, USA
Drahomira Spoustova, Charles University in Prague, Czech Republic
Xu Sun, University of Tokyo, Japan
Idan Szpektor, Bar Ilan University, Israel
Ahmet Cuneyd Tantug, Istanbul Technical University, Turkey
Keith Trnka, University of Delaware, USA
Ming-Feng Tsai, National University of Singapore, Singapore
Bonnie Webber, University of Edinburgh, UK
Furu Wei, IBM, China
Michael White, Ohio State University, USA
Yorick Wilks, University of Sheffield, UK
Emine Yilmaz, Microsoft, UK
Zdenek Zabokrtsky, Charles University in Prague, Czech Republic
Daniel Zeman, Charles University in Prague, Czech Republic
Guodong Zhou, Soochow University, China
Xiaodan Zhu, University of Toronto, Canada

# Table of Contents

# Conference Program

**Tuesday, July 13, 2010**

**Oral Session (10:30–11:45)**

*Chaired by Jan Raab*

10:30–10:40 *Non-Cooperation in Dialogue*
Brian Plüss

10:40–10:50 *Towards Relational POMDPs for Adaptive Dialogue Management*
Pierre Lison

10:50–11:00 *WSD as a Distributed Constraint Optimization Problem*
Siva Reddy and Abhilash Inumella

11:00–11:10 *A Probabilistic Generative Model for an Intermediate Constituency-Dependency Representation*
Federico Sangati

11:10–11:20 *Sentiment Translation through Lexicon Induction*
Christian Scheible

11:20–11:30 *Unsupervised Search for the Optimal Segmentation for Statistical Machine Translation*
Coşkun Mermer and Ahmet Afşın Akın

11:30–11:40 *How Spoken Language Corpora Can Refine Current Speech Motor Training Methodologies*
Daniil Umanski and Federico Sangati

11:55–13:15 Each talk is accompanied by a poster presentation

**Tuesday, July 13, 2010 (continued)**

**Poster Session (11:55–13:15)**

*Mood Patterns and Affective Lexicon Access in Weblogs*
Thin Nguyen

*Growing Related Words from Seed via User Behaviors: A Re-Ranking Based Approach*
Yabin Zheng, Zhiyuan Liu and Lixing Xie

*Transition-Based Parsing with Confidence-Weighted Classification*
Martin Haulrich

*Expanding Verb Coverage in Cyc with VerbNet*
Clifton McFate

*A Framework for Figurative Language Detection Based on Sense Differentiation*
Daria Bogdanova

*Automatic Selectional Preference Acquisition for Latin Verbs*
Barbara McGillivray

*Edit Tree Distance Alignments for Semantic Role Labelling*
Hector-Hugo Franco-Penya

*Automatic Sanskrit Segmentizer Using Finite State Transducers*
Vipul Mittal

*Adapting Self-Training for Semantic Role Labeling*
Rasoul Samad Zadeh Kaljahi

*Weakly Supervised Learning of Presupposition Relations between Verbs*
Galina Tremper

*Importance of Linguistic Constraints in Statistical Dependency Parsing*
Bharat Ram Ambati

*The Use of Formal Language Models in the Typology of the Morphology of Amerindian Languages*
Andres Osvaldo Porta

# Non-Cooperation in Dialogue

**Brian Plüss**
Centre for Research in Computing
The Open University
Milton Keynes, UK
b.pluss@open.ac.uk

## Abstract

This paper presents ongoing research on computational models for non-cooperative dialogue. We start by analysing different levels of cooperation in conversation. Then, inspired by findings from an empirical study, we propose a technique for measuring non-cooperation in political interviews. Finally, we describe a research programme towards obtaining a suitable model and discuss previous accounts for conflictive dialogue, identifying the differences with our work.

## 1 Introduction

Most approaches to modeling conversation are based on a strong notion of cooperation between the dialogue participants (DPs). Traditional models using intentions (Cohen and Levesque, 1991), dialogue games (Power, 1979), shared plans (Grosz and Sidner, 1990) or collaborative problem-solving (Blaylock and Allen, 2005) explain dialogue situations in which DPs recognise each other's intentions and, at least to a certain extent, accept each other's goals when deciding on their actions. These assumptions are theoretically grounded, as most work in linguistics has considered situations in which DPs share a common goal and cooperate to achieve it by means of conversation (Grice, 1975; Clark and Schaefer, 1989). They are also practically sound: dialogue models are usually implemented in the form of dialogue systems, built for the purpose of providing a service to their users (e.g., TRAINS (Allen and Schubert, 1991)). In this scenario, failure to cooperate, either on the side of the system or of the user, is against the premises on which the system is conceived and used.

In everyday conversation, however, a great many situations escape the arguments above. Consider the following example[1]:

(1) PAXMAN [1]: (interrupting) Did you threaten to overrule him?
HOWARD [2]: I, I, was not entitled to *instruct* Derek Lewis, and I did not instruct him.
PAXMAN [3]: Did you threaten to overrule him?
HOWARD [4]: The truth of the matter is that Mr. Marriott was not suspended. I...
PAXMAN [5]: (overlappling) Did you threaten to overrule him?
HOWARD [6]: ...did not overrule Derek Lewis.
PAXMAN [7]: Did you *threaten* to overrule him?
HOWARD [8]: I took advice on what I could or could not do...
PAXMAN [9]: (overlappling) Did you threaten to overrule him, Mr. Howard?
HOWARD[10]: ...and I acted scrupulously in accordance with that advice, I did *not* overrule Derek Lewis...
PAXMAN[11]: (overlapping) Did you threaten to overrule him?
HOWARD[12]: ...Mr. Marriott was *not* suspended.
PAXMAN[13]: Did you threaten to overrule him?
HOWARD[14]: (pauses) I have accounted for my decision to dismiss Derek Lewis...
PAXMAN[15]: (overlapping) Did you threaten to overrule him?
HOWARD[16]: in great detail, before the House of Commons.
PAXMAN[17]: I note that you're not answering the question of whether you *threatened* to overrule him.

(*Newsnight*, BBC, 1997)

We take it for granted that, at some level, Paxman and Howard are sharing a goal, for otherwise they would not be having an interview. Still, the exchange is clearly conflictive, to the point that their behaviour compromises the flow of the conversation.

Heritage (1998) analyses the distinctive roles of DPs in news interviews:

[1]BBC presenter Jeremy Paxman questions former UK Home Secretary Michael Howard with respect to a meeting in 1995 between Howard and the head of the Prison Service, Derek Lewis, about the dismissal of the governor of Parkhurst Prison, John Marriott, due to repeated security failures. The case was given considerable attention in the media, as a result of accusations by Lewis that Howard had instructed him, thus exceeding the powers of his office.



*Proceedings of the ACL 2010 Student Research Workshop*, pages 1–6,
Uppsala, Sweden, 13 July 2010. 

"the participants -IRs [=interviewers] and IEs [=interviewees]- exclude themselves from a wide variety of actions that they are normally free to do in the give and take of ordinary conversation. If IRs restrict themselves to asking questions, then they cannot - at least overtly - express opinions, or argue with, debate or criticize the interviewees' positions nor, conversely, agree with, support or defend them. Correspondingly, if IEs restrict themselves to answers (or responses) to questions, then they cannot ask questions (of IRs or other IEs), nor make unsolicited comments on previous remarks, initiate changes of topic, or divert the discussion into criticisms of the IR or the broadcasting organization."

(Heritage, 1998, p.8)

Now, consider the fragment below[2]:

(2) PAXMAN[1]: Can you clear up whether or not you did threaten to overrule Derek Lewis when you were Home Secretary?
HOWARD[2]: Oh, come on, Jeremy, you are really going to go back over that again? As...
PAXMAN[3]: (overlapping) You've had seven years to think about it!
HOWARD[4]: (overlapping)... as, as it happens, I didn't. Are you satisfied now?
PAXMAN[5]: Thank you. Why didn't you say that at the time?
HOWARD[6]: I, well, we've been over this many, many times. I, I, I knew that everyone was crawling over every syllable I said about that, and I wanted to check very carefully what I said before answering your question.

(*Newsnight*, BBC, 2004)

On this occasion, Howard provides an answer almost immediately and the flow of the conversation contrasts noticeably with that in (1). The investigation reported in this article aims at shedding light on the nature of non-cooperation in dialogue, by capturing the intuitions that allow us to differentiate between both conversations in terms of participant behaviour.

Dialogue games supporters could say that there is a game that describes the interaction in the first example. While this might be true, such an approach would force us, in the limit, to define one game for each possible conversation that would not fit a certain standard. Walton and Krabbe (1995) attempt a game-based approach in their study of natural argumentation. They claim that a rigorous model of conversational interaction is useful, but accept that most of the huge variety of everyday conversation escapes it. Dialogue games are based on strict rules that capture typical dialogue situations while leaving out considerable detail. As example (1) shows, DPs behaviour can divert from the typical case in unexpected ways, falling outside the characterisation[3].

Nevertheless, the rules and patterns captured by game models are useful, as they describe the expected behaviour of the DPs under a certain conversational scenario. In our research, we aim at reconciling two worlds, using the insights from dialogue games to provide a description of expected behaviour in the form of social obligations, but looking at naturally occurring cases that deviate from the norm. This, in turn, calls for a technique to measure non-cooperation in dialogue and in this paper we provide one that is theoretically sound and supported by empirical evidence.

The following section discusses levels of cooperation in dialogue; Section 3 presents an empirical study and a practical measure of non-cooperation in political interviews; in Section 4 we discuss related work, our working hypothesis and a methodology; and Section 5 has the conclusions.

## 2 Linguistic and Non-Linguistic Cooperation

Cooperation in dialogue can happen at different levels. In most cases, conversation supports a social activity that constrains the behaviour acceptable or expected from the participants. In addition, conversational behaviour determines how cooperatively participants engage in a social activity. However, cooperation at the conversational level does not necessarily translate to the social level. Consider, for instance, a witness under interrogation in a U.S. trial refusing to answer a question by appealing to the Fifth Amendment of the Constitution[4]. Such behaviour will be accepted in the conversational setting as established by law, although it is not cooperative in relation with the goals of the trial. Non-cooperation at the conversational level, on the other hand, usually results in lack of cooperation at the social level. Take as an example, the same witness remaining silent, rather than answering or appealing to the Fifth Amendment.

To illustrate further, consider a fictional alternative to (1), where Howard replies by saying "I will not answer that question, as it is not relevant to whether I exceeded the powers of my office".

[2]This exchange took place seven years after (1), when public awareness of the 1995 affair had dissipated.

[3]Consider, for instance, Giznburg's QUD model (Ginzburg, 1996) when applied to dialogue (1), in which Howard repeatedly fails to either accept or reject Paxman's question.

[4]"*No person shall (...) be compelled in any criminal case to be a witness against himself*".

This is not cooperative for the interview, but it is so at the linguistic level. It would help in preserving the flow of the conversation, e.g., by triggering a sub-dialogue to solve the disagreement.

The distinction between linguistic and non-linguistic (also called task-related, high-level or social) cooperation has been addressed before. Attardo (1997) revisits Gricean pragmatics, relating non-linguistic cooperation to participants' behaviour towards realising task-related goals, and linguistic cooperation to assumptions on their respective behaviour in order to encode and decode intended meaning. From a computational perspective, Bunt (1994) relies on a similar distinction for defining dialogue acts. Also, Traum and Allen (1994) introduce discourse obligations as an alternative to joint intentions and shared plans, to allow for models of dialogues in which participants do not share the same high-level goals and where behaviour is also determined by "a sense of obligation to behave within limits set by the society" (Traum and Allen, 1994, p.2).

Walton and Krabbe (1995) proposed a typology of dialogue based on the initial situation triggering the exchange and participants' shared aims and individual goals. Based on their work, Reed and Long (1997) distinguish cases where participants follow a common set of dialogue rules and stay within a mutually acknowledged framework from a stronger notion in which their individual goals are in the same direction. Borrowing from the latter, in the rest of the paper, we will speak of *collaboration* when DPs share the same task-level goals, and use *cooperation* when participants follow the conversational obligations imposed by the social activity (i.e., linguistic cooperation as discussed above). We will not deal with collaboration here, though, as our focus is on non-cooperation.

## 3 An Empirical Study

In this section, we describe an empirical pilot study aimed at identifying a set of features that distinguish cooperative from non-cooperative conversational behaviour and at establishing a suitable domain in which to focus our work.

### 3.1 The Corpus

We collected the transcripts of 10 adversarial dialogues: 4 political interviews, 2 entertainment interviews, 1 parliamentary inquiry, 1 courtroom confrontation, 1 courtroom interrogation and 1 dispute. The corpus includes 2 collaborative political interviews for result comparison and is nearly 14,500 words long[5].

In a first analysis, we identified those surface features that characterised each conversation as conflictive: e.g., interruptions, short turns, unfinished adjacency pairs, verbatim repetition. Next, looking for a better understanding, we preformed an in-depth case study of one of the examples, approaching the analysis from different angles.

By studying, e.g., the observance of turn-taking rules, the implicatures of the participants and, more extensively, how the case fitted within the normative framework proposed by Walton and Krabbe (1995), we were able to better identify the nature of non-cooperative features present in the dialogue and establish a formalisable framework for approaching non-cooperative dialogue.

As for the domain, the wealth of interesting conversational situations that arise in political interviews make a suitable context for this research. In the English-speaking world, journalists are well-known for their incisive approach to public servants. At the same time, politicians are usually well trained to deliver a set of key messages when speaking in public, and to avoid issues unfavorable to their image. We will only consider naturally occurring (i.e. non-scripted) two-party interviews.

### 3.2 Degrees of Non-Cooperation

Based on the analysis described above, we propose a technique for measuring non-cooperation in political interviews using a set of non-cooperative features (NCFs). The number of occurrences of these features will determine the degree of non-cooperation (DNC) of an exchange.

We grouped NCFs following three aspects of conversation: turn-taking, grounding and speech acts (see Table 1 for a complete list).

Turn-taking rules (Sacks et al., 1974) establish that speakers make their contributions at adequate places and in particular ways. Interlocutors in a political interview are expected to respect transition-relevance places, openings and closings according to social conventions. Failing to do so (e.g., by interrupting each other) constitutes a non-cooperative feature.

Grounding (Clark and Schaefer, 1989) refers to participants' acknowledgement of each other's

[5]These resources are available at `http://www.open.ac.uk/blogs/brianpluss/pilot-study/`.

| Turn-Taking | For both speakers:<br>• interrupting<br>• overlapping<br>• ending the exchange abruptly |
|---|---|
| **Grounding** | Interviewer fails to either:<br>• ask next relevant question<br>• move to next topical issue<br>• state irrelevance of answer<br>Interviewee fails to either:<br>• give relevant answer<br>• reject question |
| **Speech Acts** | Interviewer either:<br>• expresses personal opinion<br>• argues, debates with or criticises interviewee's position subjectively<br>• agrees with, supports or defends interviewee's position subjectively<br>Interviewee either:<br>• asks (non-CR) question<br>• makes irrelevant comment<br>• initiates change of topic<br>• criticises interviewer |

Table 1: NCFs for political interviews

contributions by providing evidence of understanding (e.g, continued attention, relevant next contribution). In political interviews a question is acknowledged by rejecting it or by providing a direct answer. Likewise, answers are acknowledged by rejecting their relevance, by asking a next relevant question or by moving on to a new topical issue. Failing to provide sufficient evidence of understanding is also a non-cooperative feature.

Speech Act theory (Searle, 1979) classifies utterances according to their associated force and propositional content. Going back to Heritage's comment, in a political interview participants can fail to restrict their speech acts to the force and content expected for their role. Non-cooperative features related to speech acts include the interviewer expressing a personal opinion or criticising subjectively the interviewee's positions and the interviewee asking questions (except for clarification requests) or making irrelevant comments.

We define the degree of non-cooperation (DNC) of a dialogue as the proportion of utterances with one of more occurrences of these non-cooperative features[6]. Furthermore, the DNC could be thus computed for the whole conversation and also for each participant, by counting only occurrences of features and utterances from each DP.

As an example, consider an extended fragment of (1) annotated with non-cooperative features (**O**: overlap; **GF**: grounding failure; **UC**: unsolicited comment; **I**: interruption; **TC**: topic change):

| | | | |
|---|---|---|---|
| (3) | P[11] : Uir.1 | (overlapping) Did you threaten to overrule him? | **O** |
| | H[12] : Uie.1 | ... Mr. Marriot was *not* suspended. | **GF** |
| | P[13] : Uir.2 | Did you threaten to overrule him? | **GF** |
| | H[14] : Uie.2 | (pauses) I have accounted for my decision to dismiss Derek Lewis... | |
| | P[15] : Uir.3 | (overlapping) Did you threaten to overrule him? | **O** |
| | H[16] : Uie.2 | ... in great detail before the House of Commons. | **UC** |
| | P[17] : Uir.4 | I note that you're not answering the question whether you *threatened* to overrule him. | |
| | H[18] : Uie.3 | Well, the important aspect of this which it's very clear to bear in mind... | **GF** |
| | P[19] : Uir.5 | (interrupting) I'm sorry, I'm going to be frightfully rude but... | **I** |
| | H[20] : Uie.4 | Yes, you can... | |
| | P[21] : Uir.6 | (overlapping) I'm sorry... | **O** |
| | H[22] : Uie.4 | (overlapping) ...you can put the question and I will give you, I will give you an answer. | **O** |
| | P[23] : Uir.7 | ...it's a straight yes-or-no question and a straight yes-or-no answer: | |
| | Uir.8 | did you threaten to overrule him? | |
| | H[24] : Uie.5 | I discussed the matter with Derek Lewis. | |
| | Uie.6 | I gave him the benefit of my opinion. | |
| | Uie.7 | I gave him the benefit of my opinion in strong language, but I did not instruct him because I was not, er, entitled to instruct him. | **UC** |
| | Uie.8 | I was entitled to express my opinion and that is what I did. | **UC** |
| | P[25] : Uir.9 | With respect, that is not answering the question of whether you threatened to overrule him. | |
| | H[26] : Uie.9 | It's dealing with the relevant point which was what I was entitled to do and what I was not entitled to do, | **TC** |
| | Uie.10 | and I have dealt with this in detail before the House of Commons and before the select committee. | **UC** |

Table 2 summarises non-cooperative features, utterances and the degree of non-cooperation for each participant and for the whole fragment.

| | P (ir) | H (ie) | Fragment |
|---|---|---|---|
| Interruptions | 1 | 0 | 1 |
| Overlaps | 3 | 1 | 4 |
| Grounding Failure | 1 | 2 | 3 |
| Unsolicited Comments | 0 | 4 | 4 |
| Topic Change | 0 | 1 | 1 |
| Total NCFs | 5 | 8 | 13 |
| Utterances | 9 | 10 | 19 |
| **DNC** | **0.56** | **0.80** | **0.68** |

Table 2: Computing the DNC for dialogue (3)

The DNC was computed for all the political interviews in the corpus. Table 3 shows the val-

[6]At this stage, all NCFs are weighted equally. This is a simplifying assumption we will remove in the future so that, e.g., an interviewee attempting a change of topic has a stronger impact on the DNC than, say, one interrupting.

| | Dialogue | Utterances | NCF | DNC |
|---|---|---|---|---|
| Adversarial Dialogues | 1. Paxman v. Howard | 54 | 30 | **0.56** |
| | Paxman (IR) | 24 | 13 | **0.54** |
| | Howard (IE) | 30 | 17 | **0.57** |
| | 2. Paxman v. Galloway | 48 | 15 | **0.31** |
| | Paxman (IR) | 19 | 7 | **0.37** |
| | Galloway (IE) | 29 | 8 | **0.28** |
| | 4. O'Reilly v. Hartman | 36 | 9 | **0.25** |
| | O'Reilly (IR) | 15 | 4 | **0.27** |
| | Hartman (IE) | 21 | 5 | **0.24** |
| | 8. Rather v. Bush (Turns 107-133) | 40 | 19 | **0.48** |
| | Rather (IR) | 18 | 8 | **0.44** |
| | Bush (IE) | 22 | 11 | **0.5** |
| Cooperative Dialogues | 7. Keating v. Thatcher | 57 | 0 | **0** |
| | Keating (IR) | 12 | 0 | **0** |
| | Thatcher (IE) | 45 | 0 | **0** |
| | 8. Brodie v. Blair (Turns 7-20) | 31 | 2 | **0.06** |
| | Brodie (IR) | 9 | 1 | **0.11** |
| | Blair (IE) | 22 | 1 | **0.05** |

Table 3: DNC of political interviews in the corpus

ues obtained. Adversarial interviews have a large number of NCFs, thus a high value for the DNC. On the other hand, collaborative exchanges have low occurrence of NCFs (or none at all)[7].

## 4 Discussion

There have been previous approaches to modeling dialogue on the basis that participants are not always fully cooperative. Jameson (1989) presents an extensive study for modeling bias, individual goals, projected image and belief ascription in conversation. User-model approaches are flexible to account for intricate situations but, as noted by Taylor et al. (1996), can lead to problems like infinite regress in nested beliefs. Taylor (1994) addressed non-cooperative dialogue behaviour by implementing CYNIC, a dialogue system able to generate and recognise deception; a notion of non-cooperation weaker than the one we address.

More recently, Traum (2008) brought attention to the need for computational accounts of dialogue situations in which a broader notion of cooperation is not assumed: e.g., intelligent tutoring systems, bargaining agents, role-playing training agents[8]. Traum's work on conflictive dialogue is mainly aimed at creating virtual humans with abilities to engage in adversarial dialogue. Traum et al. (2008) present a model of conversation strategies for negotiation, that includes variables representing trust, politeness and emotions, and a set of conversational strategies. Despite being adversarial in nature, the conversational scenarios are modeled by means of rules, that are followed by the interlocutors, according to the values of some of the variables. Hence, the dialogues are adversarial, but cooperative under our characterisation of linguistic non-cooperation, and it is not clear how effectively the model accounts for cases in which participants fail to follow the rules of a scenario.

### 4.1 Working Hypothesis

Finding a suitable model of non-cooperative dialogue involves bridging the gap between the theoretical aspects mentioned so far and the evidence in the empirical data of the previous section. Following Traum and Allen (1994), we base on the hypothesis that non-cooperative features result from decisions that participants make during the conversation, by considering the obligations imposed by the social activity and their individual goals, with an adequate configuration of the priorities for goals and obligations.

Thus, a participant with high priorities for individual goals might compromise the workings of a conversation by choosing contributions that go against the norms of the social activity. On the other hand, participants with higher priorities associated with obligations will favour contributions consistent with the rules of the social activity.

### 4.2 Research Methodology

For the next steps of the project, we will construct a model based on the hypothesis and test it by means of simulation[9].

The construction of the model is a formalization of the working hypothesis, including rules for political interviews, goals, obligations, priorities and a dialogue management component. At the

[7]These results and the validity of DNC measure need further evaluation. We are currently performing two studies: one to determine inter-annotator agreement of the coding scheme for NCFs, and another to test how NCFs correlate to human judgements of non-cooperative conversational behaviour.

[8]Traum also provides a list of "behaviours of interest", along the lines of the NCFs we identified above: e.g., unilateral topic shifts or topic maintenance, unhelpful criticism, withholding of information, lying, deception, antagonism.

[9]The use of simulation in dialogue modeling was pioneered by Power (1979). It suits our project better than alternatives (e.g., Wizard-of-Oz, dialogue systems), by making it easier to introduce modifications, do re-runs, and generate a large number of cases with different parameter settings.

moment of writing, we are investigating the line of research on obligation-driven dialogue modeling, initiated by Traum and Allen (1994) and developed further by Poesio and Traum (1998) and Kreutel and Matheson (2003).

For the simulation, DPs will be autonomous conversational agents with a cognitive state consisting of goals, a notion of their expected behaviour in a political interview, priorities, and some knowledge of the world. We are currently implementing a prototype based on EDIS (Matheson et al., 2000).

## 5 Conclusions

In this paper we presented an attempt to shed light on non-cooperation in dialogue by proposing a practical measure of the degree of linguistic non-cooperation in political interviews and a methodology towards a suitable computational model.


## Acknowledgments

We would like to thank the NLG group at The Open University (especially Paul Piwek, Richard Power and Sandra Williams) for helpful discussion and comments on previous versions of this paper; and three anonymous reviewers for thoughtful feedback and suggestions.


## References


J.F. Allen and L.K. Schubert. 1991. The TRAINS project. TRAINS Technical Note 91-1. *Computer Science Dept. University of Rochester.*

S. Attardo. 1997. Locutionary and perlocutionary cooperation: The perlocutionary cooperative principle. *Journal of Pragmatics*, 27(6):753–779.

N. Blaylock and J. Allen. 2005. A collaborative problem-solving model of dialogue. In *Proceedings of the 6th SIGdial Workshop on Discourse and Dialogue*, pages 200–211, Lisbon, Portugal.

Harry Bunt. 1994. Context and dialogue control. *THINK Quarterly*, 3.

H.H. Clark and E.F. Schaefer. 1989. Contributing to discourse. *Cognitive science*, 13(2):259–294.

P.R. Cohen and H.J. Levesque. 1991. Confirmations and joint action. In *Proceedings of the 12 th International Joint Conference on Artificial Intelligence*, pages 951–957.

J. Ginzburg. 1996. Interrogatives: Questions, facts and dialogue. *The handbook of contemporary semantic theory*, 5:359–423.

H. P. Grice. 1975. Logic and conversation. *Syntax and Semantics*, 3:41–58.

B.J. Grosz and C.L. Sidner. 1990. Plans for discourse. *Intentions in communication*, pages 417–444.

J. Heritage. 1998. Conversation analysis and institutional talk. Analyzing distinctive turn-taking systems. In *Proceedings of the 6th International Congress of IADA, Tubingen, Niemeyer.*

A. Jameson. 1989. But what will the listener think? Belief ascription and image maintenance in dialog. *User Models in Dialog Systems. Springer-Verlag*, pages 255–312.

J. Kreutel and C. Matheson. 2003. Incremental information state updates in an obligation-driven dialogue model. *Logic Journal of IGPL*, 11(4):485.

C. Matheson, M. Poesio, and D. Traum. 2000. Modelling grounding and discourse obligations using update rules. In *Proceedings of the 1st NAACL conference*, pages 1–8, San Francisco, CA, USA.

M. Poesio and D. Traum. 1998. Towards an axiomatization of dialogue acts. In *Proceedings of the Twente Workshop on the Formal Semantics and Pragmatics of Dialogues*, pages 207–222.

R. Power. 1979. The organisation of purposeful dialogues. *Linguistics*, 17:107–152.

C. Reed and D. Long. 1997. Collaboration, cooperation and dialogue classification. *Working Notes of the IJCAI97 Workshop on Collaboration, Cooperation and Conflict in Dialogue Systems, IJCAI 97*, pages 73–78.

H. Sacks, E.A. Schegloff, and G. Jefferson. 1974. A simplest systematics for the organization of turn-taking for conversation. *Language*, pages 696–735.

J.R. Searle. 1979. A Taxonomy of Illocutionary Acts. *Expression and meaning: studies in the theory of speech acts*, pages 1–29.

J. A. Taylor, J. Carletta, and C. Mellish. 1996. Requirements for belief models in cooperative dialogue. *User Modeling and User-Adapted Interaction*, 6(1):23–68.

J.A. Taylor. 1994. *A multi-agent planner for modelling dialogue*. Ph.D. Thesis, School of Cognitive and Computing Sciences, University of Sussex.

D.R. Traum and J.F. Allen. 1994. Discourse obligations in dialogue processing. In *Proceedings of the 32nd annual meeting of ACL*, pages 1–8. Morristown, NJ, USA.

D. Traum, W. Swartout, J. Gratch, and S. Marsella. 2008. A virtual human dialogue model for non-team interaction. *Recent Trends in Discourse and Dialogue. Springer.*

D. Traum. 2008. Extended Abstract: Computational Models of Non-cooperative dialogue. In *Proceedings of LONDIAL 2008, the 12th Workshop on the Semantics and Pragmatics of Dialogue*, pages 11–14, London, UK.

D. Walton and E. Krabbe. 1995. *Commitment in dialogue: Basic concepts of interpersonal reasoning*. State University of New York Press.

# Towards Relational POMDPs for Adaptive Dialogue Management

**Pierre Lison**
Language Technology Lab
German Research Centre for Artificial Intelligence (DFKI GmbH)
Saarbrücken, Germany

**Abstract**

Open-ended spoken interactions are typically characterised by both structural complexity and high levels of uncertainty, making dialogue management in such settings a particularly challenging problem. Traditional approaches have focused on providing theoretical accounts for either the uncertainty or the complexity of spoken dialogue, but rarely considered the two issues simultaneously. This paper describes ongoing work on a new approach to dialogue management which attempts to fill this gap. We represent the interaction as a Partially Observable Markov Decision Process (POMDP) over a rich state space incorporating both dialogue, user, and environment models. The tractability of the resulting POMDP can be preserved using a mechanism for dynamically constraining the action space based on prior knowledge over locally relevant dialogue structures. These constraints are encoded in a small set of general rules expressed as a Markov Logic network. The first-order expressivity of Markov Logic enables us to leverage the rich relational structure of the problem and efficiently abstract over large regions of the state and action spaces.

## 1 Introduction

The development of spoken dialogue systems for rich, open-ended interactions raises a number of challenges, one of which is dialogue management. The role of dialogue management is to determine which communicative actions to take (i.e. what to say) given a goal and particular observations about the interaction and the current situation.

Dialogue managers have to face several issues. First, spoken dialogue systems must usually deal with high levels of noise and uncertainty. These uncertainties may arise from speech recognition errors, limited grammar coverage, or from various linguistic and pragmatic ambiguities.

Second, open-ended dialogue is characteristically complex, and exhibits rich relational structures. Natural interactions should be adaptive to a variety of factors dependent on the interaction history, the general context, and the user preferences. As a consequence, the state space necessary to model the dynamics of the environment tends to be large and sparsely populated.

These two problems have typically been addressed separately in the literature. On the one hand, the issue of uncertainty in speech understanding is usually dealt using a range of probabilistic models combined with decision-theoretic planning. Among these, *Partially Observable Markov Decision Process* (POMDP) models have recently emerged as a unifying mathematical framework for dialogue management (Williams and Young, 2007; Lemon and Pietquin, 2007). POMDPs provide an explicit account for a wide range of uncertainties related to partial observability (noisy, incomplete spoken inputs) and stochastic action effects (the world may evolve in unpredictable ways after executing an action).

On the other hand, structural complexity is typically addressed with logic-based approaches. Some investigated topics in this paradigm are pragmatic interpretation (Thomason et al., 2006), dialogue structure (Asher and Lascarides, 2003), or collaborative planning (Kruijff et al., 2008). These approaches are able to model sophisticated dialogue behaviours, but at the expense of robustness and adaptivity. They generally assume complete observability and provide only a very limited account (if any) of uncertainties.

We are currently developing an hybrid approach which *simultaneously* tackles the uncertainty and complexity of dialogue management, based on a



*Proceedings of the ACL 2010 Student Research Workshop*, pages 7–12,
Uppsala, Sweden, 13 July 2010. 

POMDP framework. We present here our ongoing work on this issue. In this paper, we more specifically describe a new mechanism for dynamically constraining the space of possible actions available at a given time. Our aim is to use such mechanism to significantly reduce the search space and therefore make the planning problem globally more tractable. This is performed in two consecutive steps. We first structure the state space using *Markov Logic Networks*, a first-order probabilistic language. Prior pragmatic knowledge about dialogue structure is then exploited to derive the set of dialogue actions which are locally admissible or relevant, and prune all irrelevant ones. The first-order expressivity of Markov Logic Networks allows us to easily specify the constraints via a small set of general rules which abstract over large regions of the state and action spaces.

Our long-term goal is to develop an unified framework for adaptive dialogue management in rich, open-ended interactional settings.

This paper is structured as follows. Section 2 lays down the formal foundations of our work, by describing dialogue management as a POMDP problem. We then describe in Section 3 our approach to POMDP planning with control knowledge using Markov Logic rules. Section 4 discusses some further aspects of our approach and its relation to existing work, followed by the conclusion in Section 5.

## 2 Background

### 2.1 Partially Observable Markov Decision Processes (POMDPs)

POMDPs are a mathematical model for sequential decision-making in partially observable environments. It provides a powerful framework for control problems which combine partial observability, uncertain action effects, incomplete knowledge of the environment dynamics and multiple, potentially conflicting objectives.

Via reinforcement learning, it is possible to automatically *learn* near-optimal action policies given a POMDP model combined with real or simulated user data (Schatzmann et al., 2007).

#### 2.1.1 Formal definition

A POMDP is a tuple $\langle \mathcal{S}, \mathcal{A}, \mathcal{Z}, T, \Omega, R \rangle$, where:

- $\mathcal{S}$ is the **state space**, which is the model of the world from the agent's viewpoint. It is defined as a set of mutually exclusive states.

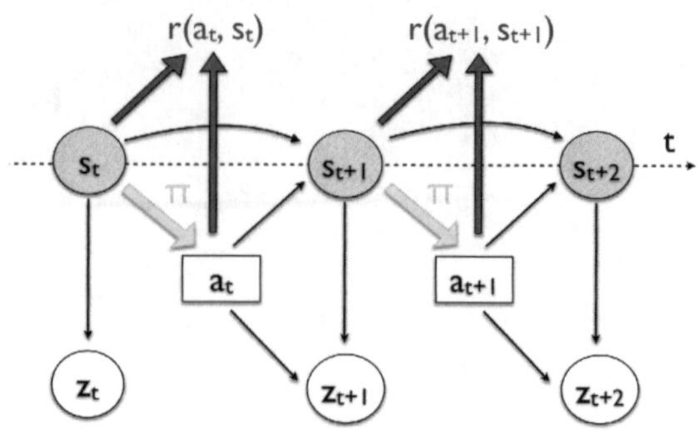


Figure 1: *Bayesian decision network* corresponding to the POMDP model. Hidden variables are greyed. Actions are represented as rectangles to stress that they are system actions rather than observed variables. Arcs into circular nodes express influence, whereas arcs into squared nodes are informational. For readability, only one state is shown at each time step, but it should be noted that the policy $\pi$ is function of the full belief state rather than a single (unobservable) state.

- $\mathcal{A}$ is the **action space**: the set of possible actions at the disposal of the agent.
- $\mathcal{Z}$ is the **observation space**: the set of observations which can be captured by the agent. They correspond to features of the environment which can be directly perceived by the agent's sensors.
- $T$ is the **transition function**, defined as $T : \mathcal{S} \times \mathcal{A} \times \mathcal{S} \rightarrow [0,1]$, where $T(s,a,s') = P(s'|s,a)$ is the probability of reaching state $s'$ from state $s$ if action $a$ is performed.
- $\Omega$ is the **observation function**, defined as $\Omega : \mathcal{Z} \times \mathcal{A} \times \mathcal{S} \rightarrow [0,1]$, with $\Omega(z,a,s') = P(z|a,s')$, i.e. the probability of observing $z$ after performing $a$ and being now in state $s'$.
- $R$ is the **reward function**, defined as $R : \mathcal{S} \times \mathcal{A} \rightarrow \Re$, $R(s,a)$ encodes the utility for the agent to perform the action $a$ while in state $s$. It is therefore a model for the goals or preferences of the agent.

A graphical illustration of a POMDP model as a Bayesian decision network is provided in Fig. 1.

In addition, a POMDP can include additional parameters such as the horizon of the agent (number of look-ahead steps), and the discount factor (weighting scheme for non-immediate rewards).

#### 2.1.2 Beliefs and belief update

A key idea of POMDP is the assumption that the state of the world is not directly accessible, and can only be inferred via observation. Such uncertainty is expressed in the **belief state** $b$, which is a probability distribution over possible states, that is: $b : \mathcal{S} \rightarrow [0, 1]$. The belief state for a state space of cardinality $n$ is therefore represented in a real-valued simplex of dimension $(n-1)$.

This belief state is dynamically updated before executing each action. The belief state update operates as follows. At a given time step $t$, the agent is in some unobserved state $s_t = s \in \mathcal{S}$. The probability of being in state $s$ at time $t$ is written as $b_t(s)$. Based on the current belief state $b_t$, the agent selects an action $a_t$, receives a reward $R(s, a_t)$ and transitions to a new (unobserved) state $s_{t+1} = s'$, where $s_{t+1}$ depends only on $s_t$ and $a_t$. The agent then receives a new observation $o_{t+1}$ which is dependent on $s_{t+1}$ and $a_t$.

Finally, the belief distribution $b_t$ is updated, based on $o_{t+1}$ and $a_t$ as follows[1].

$$b_{t+1}(s') = P(s'|o_{t+1}, a_t, b_t) \tag{1}$$

$$= \frac{P(o_{t+1}|s', a_t, b_t)P(s'|a_t, b_t)}{P(o_{t+1}|a_t, b_t)} \tag{2}$$

$$= \frac{P(o_{t+1}|s', a_t) \sum_{s \in \mathcal{S}} P(s'|a_t, s)P(s|a_t, b_t)}{P(o_{t+1}|a_t, b_t)} \tag{3}$$

$$= \alpha\, \Omega(o_{t+1}, s', a_t) \sum_{s \in \mathcal{S}} T(s, a_t, s')b_t(s) \tag{4}$$

where $\alpha$ is a normalisation constant. An initial belief state $b_0$ must be specified at runtime as a POMDP parameter when initialising the system.

#### 2.1.3 POMDP policies

Given a POMDP model $\langle \mathcal{S}, \mathcal{A}, \mathcal{Z}, T, Z, R \rangle$, the agent should execute at each time-step the action which maximises its expected cumulative reward over the horizon. The function $\pi : \mathcal{B} \rightarrow \mathcal{A}$ defines a *policy*, which determines the action to perform for each point of the belief space.

The expected reward for policy $\pi$ starting from belief $b$ is defined as:

$$J^{\pi}(b) = E\Big[\sum_{t=0}^{h} \gamma^t R(s_t, a_t) \mid b, \pi\Big] \tag{5}$$

[1]As a notational shorthand, we write $P(s_t{=}s)$ as $P(s)$ and $P(s_{t+1}{=}s')$ as $P(s')$.

The optimal policy $\pi^*$ is then obtained by optimizing the long-term reward, starting from $b_0$:

$$\pi^* = \underset{\pi}{\text{argmax}}\ J^{\pi}(b_0) \tag{6}$$

The optimal policy $\pi^*$ yields the highest expected reward value for each possible belief state. This value is compactly represented by the optimal value function, noted $V^*$, which is a solution to the Bellman optimality equation (Bellman, 1957).

Numerous algorithms for (offline) policy optimisation and (online) planning are available. For large spaces, exact optimisation is impossible and approximate methods must be used, see for instance grid-based (Thomson and Young, 2009) or point-based (Pineau et al., 2006) techniques.

### 2.2 POMDP-based dialogue management

Dialogue management can be easily cast as a POMDP problem, with the *state space* being a compact representation of the interaction, the *action space* being a set of dialogue moves, the *observation space* representing speech recognition hypotheses, the *transition function* defining the dynamics of the interaction (which user reaction is to be expected after a particular dialogue move), and the *observation function* describing a "sensor model" between observed speech recognition hypotheses and actual utterances. Finally, the *reward function* encodes the utility of dialogue policies – it typically assigns a big positive reward if a long-term goal has been reached (e.g. the retrieval of some important information), and small negative rewards for minor "inconveniences" (e.g. prompting the user to repeat or asking for confirmations).

Our long-term aim is to apply such POMDP framework to a rich dialogue domain for human-robot interaction (Kruijff et al., 2010). These interactions are typically open-ended, relatively long, include high levels of noise, and require complex state and action spaces. Furthemore, the dialogue system also needs to be *adaptive* to its user (attributed beliefs and intentions, attitude, attentional state) and to the current situation (currently perceived entities and events).

As a consequence, the state space must be expanded to include these knowledge sources. Belief monitoring is then used to continuously update the belief state based on perceptual inputs (see also (Bohus and Horvitz, 2009) for an overview of techniques to extract such information). These requirements can only be fullfilled if we address the "curse of dimensionality" characteristic of traditional POMDP models. The next section provides a tentative answer.

## 3 Approach

### 3.1 Control knowledge

Classical approaches to POMDP planning operate directly on the full action space and select the next action to perform based on the maximisation of the expected cumulative reward over the specified horizon. Such approaches can be used in small-scale domains with a limited action space, but quickly become intractable for larger ones, as the planning time increases exponentially with the size of the action space. Significant planning time is therefore spend on actions which should be directly discarded as irrelevant[2]. Dismissing these actions *before* planning could therefore provide important computational gains.

Instead of a direct policy optimisation over the full action space, our approach formalises action selection as a *two-step* process. As a first step, a set of *relevant dialogue moves* is constructed from the full action space. The POMDP planner then computes the optimal (highest-reward) action on this reduced action space in a second step.

Such an approach is able to significantly reduce the dimensionality of the dialogue management problem by taking advantage of prior knowledge about the expected relational structure of spoken dialogue. This prior knowledge is to be encoded in a set of general rules describing the admissible dialogue moves in a particular situation.

How can we express such rules? POMDPs are usually modeled with Bayesian networks which are inherently propositional. Encoding such rules in a propositional framework requires a distinct rule for every possible state and action instance. This is not a feasible approach. We therefore need a first order (probabilistic) language able to express generalities over large regions of the state action spaces. Markov Logic is such a language.

### 3.2 Markov Logic Networks (MLNs)

Markov Logic combines first-order logic and probabilistic graphical models in a unified representation (Richardson and Domingos, 2006). A Markov Logic Network $L$ is a set of pairs $(F_i, w_i)$, where $F_i$ is a formula in first-order logic and $w_i$ is a real number representing the formula weight.

A Markov Logic Network $L$ can be seen as a *template* for constructing markov networks[3]. To construct a markov network from $L$, one has to provide an additional set of constants $C = \{c_1, c_2, ..., c_{|C|}\}$. The resulting markov network is called a *ground markov network* and is written $M_{L,C}$. The ground markov network contains one feature for each possible grounding of a first-order formula in $L$, with the corresponding weight. The technical details of the construction of $M_{L,C}$ from the two sets $L$ and $C$ is explained in several papers, see e.g. (Richardson and Domingos, 2006).

Once the markov network $M_{L,C}$ is constructed, it can be exploited to perform *inference* over arbitrary queries. Efficient probabilistic inference algorithms such as Markov Chain Monte Carlo (MCMC) or other sampling techniques can then be used to this end (Poon and Domingos, 2006).

### 3.3 States and actions as relational structures

The specification of Markov Logic rules applying over complete regions of the state and action spaces (instead of over single instances) requires an explicit relational structure over these spaces.

This is realised by factoring the state and action spaces into a set of distinct, conditionally independent features. A state $s$ can be expanded into a tuple $\langle f_1, f_2, ...f_n \rangle$, where each sub-state $f_i$ is assigned a value from a set $\{v_1, v_2, ...v_m\}$. Such structure can be expressed in first-order logic with a binary predicate $f_i(s, v_j)$ for each sub-state $f_i$, where $v_j$ is the value of the sub-state $f_i$ in $s$. The same type of structure can be defined over actions. This factoring leads to a relational structure of arbitrary complexity, compactly represented by a set of unary and binary predicates.

For instance, (Young et al., 2010) factors each dialogue state into three independent parts $s = \langle s_u, a_u, s_d \rangle$, where $s_u$ is the user goal, $a_u$ the last user move, and $s_d$ the dialogue history. These can be expressed in Markov Logic with predicates such as $\texttt{UserGoal}(\texttt{s}, \texttt{s}_\texttt{u})$, $\texttt{LastUserMove}(\texttt{s}, \texttt{a}_\texttt{u})$, or $\texttt{History}(\texttt{s}, \texttt{s}_\texttt{d})$.

[2]For instance, an agent hearing a user command such as "Please take the mug on your left" might spent a lot of planning time calculating the expected future reward of dialogue moves such as "Is the box green?" or "Your name is John", which are irrelevant to the situation.

[3]Markov networks are undirected graphical models.

### 3.4 Relevant action space

For a given state $s$, the relevant action space $RelMoves(\mathcal{A}, s)$ is defined as:

$$\{a_m : a_m \in \mathcal{A} \wedge \texttt{RelevantMove}(\texttt{a}_\texttt{m}, \texttt{s})\} \quad (7)$$

The truth-value of the predicate $\texttt{RelevantMove}(\texttt{a}_\texttt{m}, \texttt{s})$ is determined using a set of Markov Logic rules dependent on both the state $s$ and the action $a_m$. For a given state $s$, the relevant action space is constructed via probabilistic inference, by estimating the probability $P(\texttt{RelevantMove}(\texttt{a}_\texttt{m}, \texttt{s}))$ for each action $a_m$, and selecting the subset of actions for which the probability is above a given threshold.

Eq. 8 provides a simple example of such Markov Logic rule:

$$\texttt{LastUserMove}(\texttt{s}, \texttt{a}_\texttt{u}) \wedge \texttt{PolarQuestion}(\texttt{a}_\texttt{u}) \wedge \texttt{YesNoAnswer}(\texttt{a}_\texttt{m}) \rightarrow \texttt{RelevantMove}(\texttt{a}_\texttt{m}, \texttt{s}) \quad (8)$$

It defines an admissible dialogue move for a situation where the user asks a polar question to the agent (e.g. "do you see my hand?"). The rule specifies that, if a state $s$ contains $a_u$ as last user move, and if $a_u$ is a polar question, then an answer $a_m$ of type yes-no is a relevant dialogue move for the agent. This rule is (implicitly) universally quantified over $s$, $a_u$ and $a_m$.

Each of these Markov Logic rules has a weight attached to it, expressing the strength of the implication. A rule with infinite weight and satisfied premises will lead to a relevant move with probability 1. Softer weights can be used to describe moves which are less relevant but still possible in a particular context. These weights can either be encoded by hand or learned from data (how to perform this efficiently remains an open question).

### 3.5 Rules application on POMDP belief state

The previous section assumed that the state $s$ is known. But the real state of a POMDP is never directly accessible. The rules we just described must therefore be applied on the belief state. Ultimately, we want to define a function $Rel : \Re^n \rightarrow \mathcal{P}(\mathcal{A})$, which takes as input a point in the belief space and outputs a set of relevant moves. For efficiency reasons, this function can be precomputed offline, by segmenting the state space into distinct regions and assigning a set of relevant moves to each region. The function can then be directly called at runtime by the planning algorithm.

Due to the high dimensionality of the belief space, the above function must be approximated to remain tractable. One way to perform this approximation is to extract, for belief state $b$, a set $S_m$ of $m$ most likely states, and compute the set of relevant moves for each of them. We then define the global probability estimate of $a$ being a relevant move given $b$ as such:

$$P(\texttt{RelevantMove(a)} \mid b, a) \approx \sum_{s \in S_m} P(\texttt{RelevantMove(a, s)} \mid s, a) \times b(s) \quad (9)$$

In the limit where $m \rightarrow |S|$, the error margin on the approximation tends to zero.

## 4 Discussion

### 4.1 General comments

It is worth noting that the mechanism we just outlined does not intend to *replace* the existing POMDP planning and optimisation algorithms, but rather *complements* them. Each step serves a different purpose: the action space reduction provides an answer to the question "Is this action relevant?", while the policy optimisation seeks to answer "Is this action useful?". We believe that such distinction between relevance and usefulness is important and will prove to be beneficial in terms of tractability.

It is also useful to notice that the Markov Logic rules we described provides a "positive" definition of the action space. The rules were applied to produce an exhaustive list of all admissible actions given a state, all actions outside this list being *de facto* labelled as non-admissible. But the rules can also provide a "negative" definition of the action space. That is, instead of generating an exhaustive list of possible actions, the dialogue system can initially consider all actions as admissible, and the rules can then be used to prune this action space by removing irrelevant moves.

The choice of action filter depends mainly on the size of the dialogue domain and the availability of prior domain knowledge. A "positive" filter is a necessity for large dialogue domains, as the action space is likely to grow exponentially with the domain size and become untractable. But the positive definition of the action space is also significantly more expensive for the dialogue developer. There is therefore a trade-off between the costs of tractability issues, and the costs of dialogue domain modelling.

### 4.2 Related Work

There is a substantial body of existing work in the POMDP literature about the exploitation of the problem structure to tackle the curse of dimensionality (Poupart, 2005; Young et al., 2010), but the vast majority of these approaches retain a propositional structure. A few more theoretical papers also describe first-order MDPs (Wang et al., 2007), and recent work on Markov Logic has extended the MLN formalism to include some decision-theoretic concepts (Nath and Domingos, 2009). To the author's knowledge, none of these ideas have been applied to dialogue management.

## 5 Conclusions

This paper described a new approach to exploit relational models of dialogue structure for controlling the action space in POMDPs. This approach is part of an ongoing work to develop a unified framework for adaptive dialogue management in rich, open-ended interactional settings. The dialogue manager is being implemented as part of a larger cognitive architecture for talking robots.

Besides the implementation, future work will focus on refining the theoretical foundations of relational POMDPs for dialogue (including how to specify the transition, observation and reward functions in such a relational framework), as well as investigating the use of reinforcement learning for policy optimisation based on simulated data.

## References


N. Asher and A. Lascarides. 2003. *Logics of Conversation*. Cambridge University Press.

R. Bellman. 1957. *Dynamic Programming*. Princeton University Press.

Dan Bohus and Eric Horvitz. 2009. Dialog in the open world: platform and applications. In *ICMI-MLMI '09: Proceedings of the 2009 international conference on Multimodal interfaces*, pages 31–38, New York, NY, USA. ACM.

G.J.M. Kruijff, M. Brenner, and N.A. Hawes. 2008. Continual planning for cross-modal situated clarification in human-robot interaction. In *Proceedings of the 17th International Symposium on Robot and Human Interactive Communication (RO-MAN 2008)*, Munich, Germany.

G.-J. M. Kruijff, P. Lison, T. Benjamin, H. Jacobsson, H. Zender, and I. Kruijff-Korbayova. 2010. Situated dialogue processing for human-robot interaction. In H. I. Christensen, A. Sloman, G.-J. M. Kruijff, and J. Wyatt, editors, *Cognitive Systems*. Springer Verlag. (in press).

O. Lemon and O. Pietquin. 2007. Machine learning for spoken dialogue systems. In *Proceedings of the European Conference on Speech Communication and Technologies (Interspeech'07)*, pages 2685–2688, Anvers (Belgium), August.

A. Nath and P. Domingos. 2009. A language for relational decision theory. In *Proceedings of the International Workshop on Statistical Relational Learning*.

J. Pineau, G. Gordon, and S. Thrun. 2006. Anytime point-based approximations for large pomdps. *Artificial Intelligence Research*, 27(1):335–380.

H. Poon and P. Domingos. 2006. Sound and efficient inference with probabilistic and deterministic dependencies. In *AAAI'06: Proceedings of the 21st national conference on Artificial intelligence*, pages 458–463. AAAI Press.

P. Poupart. 2005. *Exploiting structure to efficiently solve large scale partially observable markov decision processes*. Ph.D. thesis, University of Toronto, Toronto, Canada.

M. Richardson and P. Domingos. 2006. Markov logic networks. *Machine Learning*, 62(1-2):107–136.

Jost Schatzmann, Blaise Thomson, Karl Weilhammer, Hui Ye, and Steve Young. 2007. Agenda-based user simulation for bootstrapping a POMDP dialogue system. In *HLT '07: Proceedings of the 45th Annual Meeting of the Association for Computational Linguistics on Human Language Technologies*, pages 149–152, Rochester, New York, April. Association for Computational Linguistics.

R. Thomason, M. Stone, and D. DeVault. 2006. Enlightened update: A computational architecture for presupposition and other pragmatic phenomena. In Donna Byron, Craige Roberts, and Scott Schwenter, editors, *Presupposition Accommodation*. Ohio State Pragmatics Initiative.

B. Thomson and S. Young. 2009. Bayesian update of dialogue state: A pomdp framework for spoken dialogue systems. *Computer Speech & Language*, August.

Ch. Wang, S. Joshi, and R. Khardon. 2007. First order decision diagrams for relational mdps. In *IJCAI'07: Proceedings of the 20th international joint conference on Artifical intelligence*, pages 1095–1100, San Francisco, CA, USA. Morgan Kaufmann Publishers Inc.

J. Williams and S. Young. 2007. Partially observable markov decision processes for spoken dialog systems. *Computer Speech and Language*, 21(2):231–422.

S. Young, M. Gašić, S. Keizer, F. Mairesse, J. Schatzmann, B. Thomson, and K. Yu. 2010. The hidden information state model: A practical framework for pomdp-based spoken dialogue management. *Computer Speech & Language*, 24(2):150–174.

# WSD as a Distributed Constraint Optimization Problem

**Siva Reddy**
IIIT Hyderabad
India
gvsreddy@students.iiit.ac.in

**Abhilash Inumella**
IIIT Hyderabad
India
abhilashi@students.iiit.ac.in

## Abstract

This work models Word Sense Disambiguation (WSD) problem as a Distributed Constraint Optimization Problem (DCOP). To model WSD as a DCOP, we view information from various knowledge sources as constraints. DCOP algorithms have the remarkable property to jointly maximize over a wide range of utility functions associated with these constraints. We show how utility functions can be designed for various knowledge sources. For the purpose of evaluation, we modelled all words WSD as a simple DCOP problem. The results are competitive with state-of-art knowledge based systems.

## 1 Introduction

Words in a language may carry more than one sense. The correct sense of a word can be identified based on the context in which it occurs. In the sentence, *He took all his money from the bank*, *bank* refers to *a financial institution* sense instead of other possibilities like *the edge of river* sense. Given a word and its possible senses, as defined by a dictionary, the problem of Word Sense Disambiguation (WSD) can be defined as the task of assigning the most appropriate sense to the word within a given context.

WSD is one of the oldest problems in computational linguistics which dates back to early 1950's. A range of knowledge sources have been found to be useful for WSD. (Agirre and Stevenson, 2006; Agirre and Martínez, 2001; McRoy, 1992; Hirst, 1987) highlight the importance of various knowledge sources like part of speech, morphology, collocations, lexical knowledge base (sense taxonomy, gloss), sub-categorization, semantic word associations, selectional preferences, semantic roles, domain, topical word associations, frequency of senses, collocations, domain knowledge. etc. Methods for WSD exploit information from one or more of these knowledge sources.

Supervised approaches like (Yarowsky and Florian, 2002; Lee and Ng, 2002; Martínez et al., 2002; Stevenson and Wilks, 2001) used collective information from various knowledge sources to perform disambiguation. Information from various knowledge sources is encoded in the form of a feature vector and models were built by training on sense-tagged corpora. These approaches pose WSD as a classification problem. They crucially rely on hand-tagged sense corpora which is hard to obtain. Systems that do not need hand-tagging have also been proposed. Agirre and Martinez (Agirre and Martínez, 2001) evaluated the contribution of each knowledge source separately. However, this does not combine information from more than one knowledge source.

In any case, little effort has been made in formalizing the way in which information from various knowledge sources can be collectively used within a single framework: a framework that allows interaction of evidence from various knowledge sources to arrive at a global optimal solution.

Here we present a way for modelling information from various knowledge sources in a multi agent setting called distributed constraint optimization problem (DCOP). In DCOP, agents have constraints on their values and each constraint has a utility associated with it. The agents communicate with each other and choose values such that a global optimum solution (maximum utility) is attained. We aim to solve WSD by modelling it as a DCOP.

To the best of our knowledge, ours is the first attempt to model WSD as a DCOP. In DCOP framework, information from various knowledge sources can be used combinedly to perform WSD.

In section 2, we give a brief introduction of



*Proceedings of the ACL 2010 Student Research Workshop*, pages 13–18,
Uppsala, Sweden, 13 July 2010. 

DCOP. Section 3 describes modelling WSD as a DCOP. Utility functions for various knowledge sources are described in section 4. In section 5, we conduct a simple experiment by modelling all-words WSD problem as a DCOP and perform disambiguation on Senseval-2 (Cotton et al., 2001) and Senseval-3 (Mihalcea and Edmonds, 2004) data-set of all-words task. Next follow the sections on related work, discussion, future work and conclusion.

## 2 Distributed Constraint Optimization Problem (DCOP)

A DCOP (Modi, 2003; Modi et al., 2004) consists of n variables $V = x_1, x_2, ...x_n$ each assigned to an agent, where the values of the variables are taken from finite, discrete domains $D_1, D_2, ..., D_n$ respectively. Only the agent has knowledge and control over values assigned to variables associated to it. The goal for the agents is to choose values for variables such that a given global objective function is maximized. The objective function is described as the summation over a set of utility functions.

DCOP can be formalized as a tuple (A, V, D, C, F) where

- A = $\{a_1, a_2, \dots a_n\}$ is a set of $n$ agents,
- V = $\{x_1, x_2, \dots x_n\}$ is a set of $n$ variables, each one associated to an agent,
- D = $\{D_1, D_2, \dots D_n\}$ is a set of finite and discrete domains each one associated to the corresponding variable,
- C = $\{f_k : D_i \times D_j \times \dots D_m \to \Re\}$ is a set of constraints described by various utility functions $f_k$. The utility function $f_k$ is defined over a subset of variables $V$. The domain of $f_k$ represent the constraints $C_{f_k}$ and $f_k(c)$ represents the utility associated with the constraint $c$, where $c \in C_{f_k}$.
- F = $\sum_k z_k \cdot f_k$ is the objective function to be maximized where $z_k$ is the weight of the corresponding utility function $f_k$

An agent is allowed to communicate only with its neighbours. Agents communicate with each other to agree upon a solution which maximizes the objective function.

## 3 WSD as a DCOP

Given a sequence of words W= $\{w_1, w_2, \dots w_n\}$ with corresponding admissible senses $D_{w_i} = \{s^1_{w_i}, s^2_{w_i} \dots\}$, we model WSD as DCOP as follows.

### 3.1 Agents

Each word $w_i$ is treated as an agent. The agent (word) has knowledge and control of its values (senses).

### 3.2 Variables

Sense of a word varies and it is the one to be determined. We define the sense of a word as its variable. Each agent $w_i$ is associated with the variable $s_{w_i}$. The value assigned to this variable indicates the sense assigned by the algorithm.

### 3.3 Domains

Senses of a word are finite in number. The set of senses $D_{w_i}$, is the domain of the variable $s_{w_i}$.

### 3.4 Constraints

A constraint specifies a particular configuration of the agents involved in its definition and has a utility associated with it. For e.g. If $c_{ij}$ is a constraint defined on agents $w_i$ and $w_j$, then $c_{ij}$ refers to a particular instantiation of $w_i$ and $w_j$, say $w_i = s^p_{w_i}$ and $w_j = s^q_{w_j}$.

A utility function $f_k : C_{f_k} \to \Re$ denote a set of constraints $C_{f_k} = \{D_{w_i} \times D_{w_j} \dots D_{w_m}\}$, defined on the agents $w_i, w_j \dots w_m$ and also the utilities associated with the constraints. We model information from each knowledge source as a utility function. In section 4, we describe in detail about this modelling.

### 3.5 Objective function

As already stated, various knowledge sources are identified to be useful for WSD. It is desirable to use information from these sources collectively, to perform disambiguation. DCOP provides such framework where an objective function is defined over all the knowledge sources ($f_k$) as below

$$F = \sum_k z_k \cdot f_k$$

where $F$ denotes the total utility associated with a solution and $z_k$ is the weight given to a knowledge source i.e. information from various sources can be weighted. (Note: It is desirable to normalize utility functions of different knowledge sources in order to compare them.)

Every agent (word) choose its value (sense) in a such a way that the objective function (global solution) is maximized. This way an agent is assigned a best value which is the target sense in our case.

## 4 Modelling information from various knowledge sources

In this section, we discuss the modelling of information from various knowledge sources.

### 4.1 Part-of-speech (POS)

Consider the word *play*. It has 47 senses out of which only 17 senses correspond to *noun* category. Based on the POS information of a word $w_i$, its domain $D_{w_i}$ is restricted accordingly.

### 4.2 Morphology

Noun *orange* has at least two senses, one corresponding to *a color* and other to *a fruit*. But plural form of this word *oranges* can only be used in the *fruit* sense. Depending upon the morphological information of a word $w_i$, its domain $D_{w_i}$ can be restricted.

### 4.3 Domain information

In the sports domain, *cricket* likely refers to *a game* than *an insect*. Such information can be captured using a unary utility function defined for every word. If the sense distributions of a word $w_i$ are known, a function $f : D_{w_i} \rightarrow \Re$ is defined which return higher utility for the senses favoured by the domain than to the other senses.

### 4.4 Sense Relatedness

Sense relatedness between senses of two words $w_i, w_j$ is captured by a function $f : D_{w_i} \times D_{w_j} \rightarrow \Re$ where $f$ returns sense relatedness (utility) between senses based on sense taxonomy and gloss overlaps.

### 4.5 Discourse

Discourse constraints can be modelled using a n-ary function. For instance, to the extent one sense per discourse (Gale et al., 1992) holds true, higher utility can be returned to the solutions which favour same sense to all the occurrences of a word in a given discourse. This information can be modeled as follows: If $w_i, w_j, \ldots w_m$ are the occurrences of a same word, a function $f : D_i \times D_j \times \ldots D_m \rightarrow \Re$ is defined which returns higher utility when $s_{w_i} = s_{w_j} = \ldots s_{w_m}$ and for the rest of the combinations it returns lower utility.

### 4.6 Collocations

Collocations of a word are known to provide strong evidence for identifying correct sense of the word. For example: if in a given context *bank* co-occur with *money*, it is likely that *bank* refers to *financial institution* sense rather than *the edge of a river* sense. The word *cancer* has at least two senses, one corresponding to the astrological sign and the other a disease. But its derived form *cancerous* can only be used in disease sense. When the words *cancer* and *cancerous* co-occur in a discourse, it is likely that the word *cancer* refers to *disease sense*.

Most supervised systems work through collocations to identify correct sense of a word. If a word $w_i$ co-occurs with its collocate *v*, collocational information from $v$ can be modeled by using the following function

$$coll\_infrm\_v_{w_i} : D_{w_i} \rightarrow \Re$$

where $coll\_infrm\_v_{w_i}$ returns high utility to collocationally preferred senses of $w_i$ than other senses.

Collocations can also be modeled by assigning more than one variable to the agents or by adding a dummy agent which gives collocational information but in view of simplicity we do not go into those details.

Topical word associations, semantic word associations, selectional preferences can also be modeled similar to collocations. Complex information involving more than two entities can be modelled by using n-ary utility functions.

## 5 Experiment: DCOP based All Words WSD

We carried out a simple experiment to test the effectiveness of DCOP algorithm. We conducted our experiment in an all words setting and used only WordNet (Fellbaum, 1998) based relatedness measures as knowledge source so that results can be compared with earlier state-of-art knowledge-based WSD systems like (Agirre and Soroa, 2009; Sinha and Mihalcea, 2007) which used similar knowledge sources as ours.

Our method performs disambiguation on sentence by sentence basis. A utility function based on semantic relatedness is defined for every pair of words falling in a particular window size. Restricting utility functions to a window size reduces the number of constraints. An objective function is defined as sum of these restricted utility functions over the entire sentence and thus allowing information flow across all the words. Hence, a DCOP algorithm which aims to maximize this objective function leads to a globally optimal solution.

In our experiments, we used the best similarity measure settings of (Sinha and Mihalcea, 2007) which is a sum of normalized similarity measures jcn, lch and lesk. We used used Distributed Pseudotree Optimization Procedure (DPOP) algorithm (Petcu and Faltings, 2005), which solves DCOP using linear number of messages among agents. The implementation provided with the open source toolkit FRODO[1] (Léauté et al., 2009) is used.

### 5.1 Data

To compare our results, we ran our experiments on SENSEVAL-2 and SENSEVAL -3 English all-words data sets.

### 5.2 Results

Table 1 shows results of our experiments. All these results are carried out using a window size of four. Ideally, precision and recall values are expected to be equal in our setting. But in certain cases, the tool we used, FRODO, failed to find a solution with the available memory resources.

Results show that our system performs consistently better than (Sinha and Mihalcea, 2007) which uses exactly same knowledge sources as used by us (with an exception of adverbs in Senseval-2). This shows that DCOP algorithm perform better than page-rank algorithm used in their graph based setting. Thus, for knowledge-based WSD, DCOP framework is a potential alternative to graph based models.

Table 1 also shows the system (Agirre and Soroa, 2009), which obtained best results for knowledge based WSD. A direct comparison between this and our system is not quantitative since they used additional knowledge such as extended WordNet relations (Mihalcea and Moldovan, 2001) and sense disambiguated gloss present in WordNet3.0.

| | noun | verb | adj | adv | all |
|---|---|---|---|---|---|
| Senseval-2 All Words data set | | | | | |
| P_dcop | 67.85 | 37.37 | **62.72** | 56.87 | 58.63 |
| R_dcop | 66.44 | 35.47 | 61.28 | 56.65 | 57.09 |
| F_dcop | 67.14 | 36.39 | **61.99** | 56.76 | 57.85 |
| P_Sinha07 | 67.73 | 36.05 | 62.21 | 60.47 | **58.83** |
| R_Sinha07 | 65.63 | 32.20 | **61.42** | 60.23 | 56.37 |
| F_Sinha07 | 66.24 | 34.07 | 61.81 | 60.35 | 57.57 |
| Agirre09 | **70.40** | **38.90** | 58.30 | **70.1** | **58.6** |
| MFS | 71.2 | 39.0 | 61.1 | 75.4 | 60.1 |
| Senseval-3 All Words data set | | | | | |
| P_dcop | 62.31 | 43.48 | 57.14 | **100** | 54.68 |
| R_dcop | 60.97 | 42.81 | 55.17 | **100** | 53.51 |
| F_dcop | 61.63 | 43.14 | 56.14 | **100** | 54.09 |
| P_Sinha07 | 61.22 | 45.18 | 54.79 | **100** | 54.86 |
| R_Sinha07 | 60.45 | 40.57 | 54.14 | **100** | 52.40 |
| F_Sinha07 | 60.83 | 42.75 | 54.46 | **100** | 53.60 |
| Agirre09 | **64.1** | **46.9** | **62.6** | 92.9 | **57.4** |
| MFS | 69.3 | 53.6 | 63.7 | 92.9 | 62.3 |

Table 1: Evaluation results on Senseval-2 and Senseval-3 data-set of all words task.

### 5.3 Performance analysis

We conducted our experiment on a computer with two 2.94 GHz process and 2 GB memory. Our algorithm just took 5 minutes 31 seconds on Senseval-2 data set, and 5 minutes 19 seconds on Senseval-3 data set. This is a singable reduction compared to execution time of page rank algorithms employed in both Sinha07 and Agirre09. In Agirre09, it falls in the range 30 to 180 minutes on much powerful system with 16 GB memory having four 2.66 GHz processors. On our system, time taken by the page rank algorithm in (Sinha and Mihalcea, 2007) is 11 minutes when executed on Senseval-2 data set.

Since DCOP algorithms are truly distributed in nature the execution times can be further reduced by running them parallely on multiple processors.

## 6 Related work

Earlier approaches to WSD which encoded information from variety of knowledge sources can be classified as follows:

- Supervised approaches: Most of the supervised systems (Yarowsky and Florian, 2002;

[1] http://liawww.epfl.ch/frodo/

Lee and Ng, 2002; Martínez et al., 2002; Stevenson and Wilks, 2001) rely on the sense tagged data. These are mainly discriminative or aggregative models which essentially pose WSD a classification problem. Discriminative models aim to identify the most informative feature and aggregative models make their decisions by combining all features. They disambiguate word by word and do not collectively disambiguate whole context and thereby do not capture all the relationships (e.g sense relatedness) among all the words. Further, they lack the ability to directly represent constraints like one sense per discourse.

- Graph based approaches: These approaches crucially rely on lexical knowledge base. Graph-based WSD approaches (Agirre and Soroa, 2009; Sinha and Mihalcea, 2007) perform disambiguation over a graph composed of senses (nodes) and relations between pairs of senses (edges). The edge weights encode information from a lexical knowledge base but lack an efficient way of modelling information from other knowledge sources like collocational information, selectional preferences, domain information, discourse. Also, the edges represent binary utility functions defined over two entities which lacks the ability to encode ternary, and in general, any N-ary utility functions.

## 7 Discussion

This framework provides a convenient way of integrating information from various knowledge sources by defining their utility functions. Information from different knowledge sources can be weighed based on the setting at hand. For example, in a domain specific WSD setting, sense distributions play a crucial role. The utility function corresponding to the sense distributions can be weighed higher in order to take advantage of domain information. Also, different combination of weights can be tried out for a given setting. Thus for a given WSD setting, this framework allows us to find 1) the impact of each knowledge source individually 2) the best combination of knowledge sources.

*Limitations of DCOP algorithms*: Solving DCOPs is NP-hard. A variety of search algorithms have therefore been developed to solve DCOPs (Mailler and Lesser, 2004; Modi et al., 2004; Petcu and Faltings, 2005) . As the number of constraints or words increase, the search space increases thereby increasing the time and memory bounds to solve them. Also DCOP algorithms exhibit a trade-off between memory used and number of messages communicated between agents. DPOP (Petcu and Faltings, 2005) use linear number of messages but requires exponential memory whereas ADOPT (Modi et al., 2004) exhibits linear memory complexity but exchange exponential number of messages. So it is crucial to choose a suitable algorithm based on the problem at hand.

## 8 Future Work

In our experiment, we only used relatedness based utility functions derived from WordNet. Effect of other knowledge sources remains to be evaluated individually and in combination. The best possible combination of weights of knowledge sources is yet to be engineered. Which DCOP algorithm performs better WSD and when has to be explored.

## 9 Conclusion

We initiated a new line of investigation into WSD by modelling it in a distributed constraint optimization framework. We showed that this framework is powerful enough to encode information from various knowledge sources. Our experimental results show that a simple DCOP based model encoding just word similarity constraints performs comparably with the state-of-the-art knowledge based WSD systems.

## Acknowledgement

We would like to thank *Prof. Rajeev Sangal* and *Asrar Ahmed* for their support in coming up with this work.

## References

Eneko Agirre and David Martínez. 2001. Knowledge sources for word sense disambiguation. In *Text, Speech and Dialogue, 4th International Conference, TSD 2001, Zelezna Ruda, Czech Republic, September 11-13, 2001*, Lecture Notes in Computer Science, pages 1–10. Springer.

Eneko Agirre and Aitor Soroa. 2009. Personalizing pagerank for word sense disambiguation. In *EACL '09: Proceedings of the 12th Conference of the European Chapter of the Association for Computational Linguistics*, pages 33–41, Morristown, NJ, USA. Association for Computational Linguistics.

Eneko Agirre and Mark Stevenson. 2006. Knowledge sources for wsd. In *Word Sense Disambiguation: Algorithms and Applications*, volume 33 of *Text, Speech and Language Technology*, pages 217–252. Springer, Dordrecht, The Netherlands.

Scott Cotton, Phil Edmonds, Adam Kilgarriff, and Martha Palmer. 2001. Senseval-2. `http://www.sle.sharp.co.uk/senseval2`.

Christiane Fellbaum, editor. 1998. *WordNet An Electronic Lexical Database*. The MIT Press, Cambridge, MA ; London, May.

William A. Gale, Kenneth W. Church, and David Yarowsky. 1992. One sense per discourse. In *HLT '91: Proceedings of the workshop on Speech and Natural Language*, pages 233–237, Morristown, NJ, USA. Association for Computational Linguistics.

Graeme Hirst. 1987. *Semantic interpretation and the resolution of ambiguity*. Cambridge University Press, New York, NY, USA.

Thomas Léauté, Brammert Ottens, and Radoslaw Szymanek. 2009. FRODO 2.0: An open-source framework for distributed constraint optimization. In *Proceedings of the IJCAI'09 Distributed Constraint Reasoning Workshop (DCR'09)*, pages 160–164, Pasadena, California, USA, July 13. `http://liawww.epfl.ch/frodo/`.

Yoong Keok Lee and Hwee Tou Ng. 2002. An empirical evaluation of knowledge sources and learning algorithms for word sense disambiguation. In *EMNLP '02: Proceedings of the ACL-02 conference on Empirical methods in natural language processing*, pages 41–48, Morristown, NJ, USA. Association for Computational Linguistics.

Roger Mailler and Victor Lesser. 2004. Solving distributed constraint optimization problems using cooperative mediation. In *AAMAS '04: Proceedings of the Third International Joint Conference on Autonomous Agents and Multiagent Systems*, pages 438–445, Washington, DC, USA. IEEE Computer Society.

David Martínez, Eneko Agirre, and Lluís Màrquez. 2002. Syntactic features for high precision word sense disambiguation. In *COLING*.

Susan W. McRoy. 1992. Using multiple knowledge sources for word sense discrimination. *COMPUTATIONAL LINGUISTICS*, 18:1–30.

Rada Mihalcea and Phil Edmonds, editors. 2004. *Proceedings Senseval-3 3rd International Workshop on Evaluating Word Sense Disambiguation Systems*. ACL, Barcelona, Spain.

Rada Mihalcea and Dan I. Moldovan. 2001. extended wordnet: progress report. In *in Proceedings of NAACL Workshop on WordNet and Other Lexical Resources*, pages 95–100.

Pragnesh Jay Modi, Wei-Min Shen, Milind Tambe, and Makoto Yokoo. 2004. Adopt: Asynchronous distributed constraint optimization with quality guarantees. *Artificial Intelligence*, 161:149–180.

Pragnesh Jay Modi. 2003. Distributed constraint optimization for multiagent systems. *PhD Thesis*.

Adrian Petcu and Boi Faltings. 2005. A scalable method for multiagent constraint optimization. In *IJCAI'05: Proceedings of the 19th international joint conference on Artificial intelligence*, pages 266–271, San Francisco, CA, USA. Morgan Kaufmann Publishers Inc.

Ravi Sinha and Rada Mihalcea. 2007. Unsupervised graph-basedword sense disambiguation using measures of word semantic similarity. In *ICSC '07: Proceedings of the International Conference on Semantic Computing*, pages 363–369, Washington, DC, USA. IEEE Computer Society.

Mark Stevenson and Yorick Wilks. 2001. The interaction of knowledge sources in word sense disambiguation. *Comput. Linguist.*, 27(3):321–349.

David Yarowsky and Radu Florian. 2002. Evaluating sense disambiguation across diverse parameter spaces. *Natural Language Engineering*, 8:2002.

# A probabilistic generative model for an intermediate constituency-dependency representation

**Federico Sangati**
Institute for Logic, Language and Computation
University of Amsterdam, the Netherlands
f.sangati@uva.nl

**Abstract**

We present a probabilistic model extension to the Tesnière Dependency Structure (TDS) framework formulated in (Sangati and Mazza, 2009). This representation incorporates aspects from both constituency and dependency theory. In addition, it makes use of *junction* structures to handle coordination constructions. We test our model on parsing the English Penn WSJ treebank using a re-ranking framework. This technique allows us to efficiently test our model without needing a specialized parser, and to use the standard evaluation metric on the original Phrase Structure version of the treebank. We obtain encouraging results: we achieve a small improvement over state-of-the-art results when re-ranking a small number of candidate structures, on all the evaluation metrics except for chunking.

## 1 Introduction

Since its origin, computational linguistics has been dominated by Constituency/Phrase Structure (PS) representation of sentence structure. However, recently, we observe a steady increase in popularity of Dependency Structure (DS) formalisms. Several researchers have compared the two alternatives, in terms of linguistic adequacy (Nivre, 2005; Schneider, 2008), practical applications (Ding and Palmer, 2005), and evaluations (Lin, 1995).

Dependency theory is historically accredited to Lucien Tesnière (1959), although the relation of dependency between words was only one of the various key elements proposed to represent sentence structures. In fact, the original formulation incorporates the notion of *chunk*, as well as a special type of structure to represent *coordination*.

The Tesnière Dependency Structure (TDS) representation we propose in (Sangati and Mazza, 2009), is an attempt to formalize the original work of Tesnière, with the intention to develop a simple but consistent representation which combines constituencies and dependencies. As part of this work, we have implemented an automatic conversion[1] of the English Penn Wall Street Journal (WSJ) treebank into the new annotation scheme.

In the current work, after introducing the key elements of TDS (section 2), we describe a first probabilistic extension to this framework, which aims at modeling the different levels of the representation (section 3). We test our model on parsing the WSJ treebank using a re-ranking framework. This technique allows us to efficiently test our system without needing a specialized parser, and to use the standard evaluation metric on the original PS version of the treebank. In section 3.4 we also introduce new evaluation schemes on specific aspects of the new TDS representation which we will include in the results presented in section 3.4.

## 2 TDS representation

It is beyond the scope of this paper to provide an exhaustive description of the TDS representation of the WSJ. It is nevertheless important to give the reader a brief summary of its key elements, and compare it with some of the other representations of the WSJ which have been proposed. Figure 1 shows the original PS of a WSJ tree (a), together with 3 other representations: (b) TDS, (c) DS[2], and (d) CCG (Hockenmaier and Steedman, 2007).

[1] staff.science.uva.nl/~fsangati/TDS

[2] The DS representation is taken from the conversion procedure used in the CoNLL 2007 Shared Task on dependency parsing (Nivre et al., 2007). Although more elaborate representation have been proposed (de Marneffe and Manning, 2008; Cinková et al., 2009) we have chosen this DS representation because it is one of the most commonly used within the CL community, given that it relies on a fully automatic conversion procedure.



*Proceedings of the ACL 2010 Student Research Workshop*, pages 19–24,
Uppsala, Sweden, 13 July 2010. 

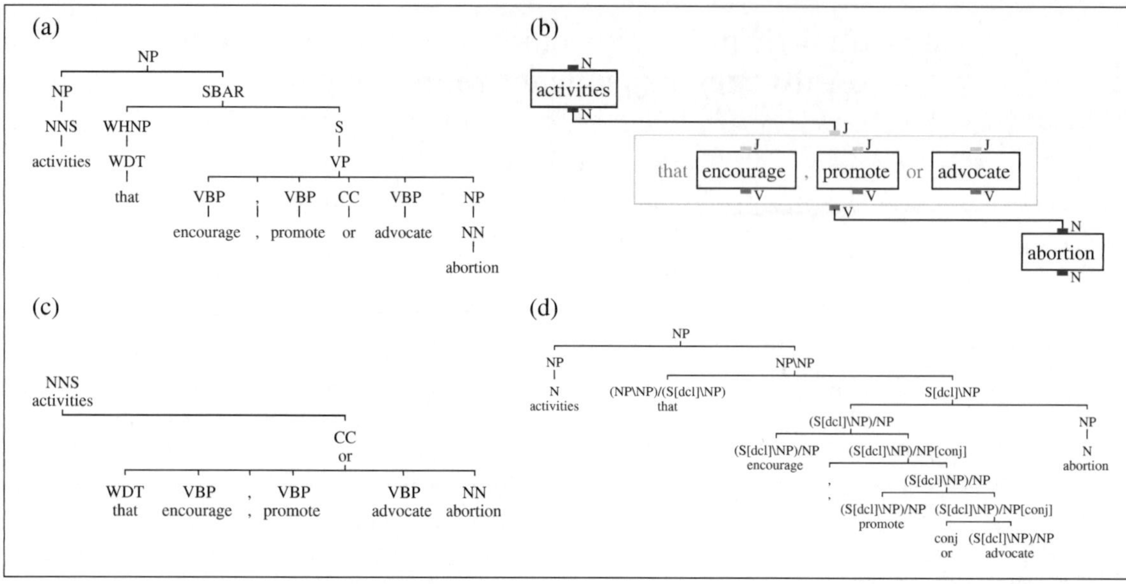


Figure 1: Four different structure representations, derived from a sentence of the WSJ treebank (section 00, #977). (a) PS (original), (b) CCG, (c) DS, (d) TDS.

**Words and Blocks** In TDS, words are divided in *functional* words (determiners, prepositions, etc.) and *content* words (verbs, nouns, etc.). *Blocks* are the basic elements (chunks) of a structure, which can be combined either via the dependency relation or the junction operation. Blocks can be of two types: *standard* and *junction* blocks. Both types may contain any sequence of functional words. Standard blocks (depicted as black boxes) represent the elementary chunks of the original PS, and include exactly one content word.

**Coordination** Junction blocks (depicted as yellow boxes) are used to represent coordinated structures. They contain two or more blocks (conjuncts) possibly coordinated by means of functional words (conjunctions). In Figure 1(d) the yellow junction block contains three separate standard blocks. This representation allows to capture the fact that these conjuncts occupy the same role: they all share the relativizer 'that', they all depend on the noun 'activities', and they all govern the noun 'abortion'. In Figure 1(a,c), we can notice that both PS and DS do not adequately represent coordination structures: the PS annotation is rather flat, avoiding to group the three verbs in a unique unit, while in the DS the last noun 'abortion' is at the same level of the verbs it should be a dependent of. On the other hand, the CCG structure of Figure 1(d), properly represents the coordination. It does so by grouping the first three verbs in a unique constituent which is in turn binarized in a right-branching structure. One of the strongest advantages of the CCG formalism, is that every structure can be automatically mapped to a logical-form representation. This is one reason why it needs to handle coordinations properly. Nevertheless, we conjecture that this representation of coordination might introduce some difficulties for parsing: it is very hard to capture the relation between 'advocate' and 'abortion' since they are several levels away in the structure.

**Categories and Transference** There are 4 different block categories, which are indicated with little colored bricks (as well as one-letter abbreviation) on top and at the bottom of the corresponding blocks: verbs (red, V), nouns (blue, N), adverbs (yellow, A), and adjectives (green, J). Every block displays at the bottom the *original category* determined by the content word (or the original category of the conjuncts if it is a junction structure), and at the top, the *derived category* which relates to the grammatical role of the whole block in relation to the governing block. In several cases we can observe a shift in the categories of a block, from the original to the derived category. This phenomenon is called *transference* and often occurs by means of functional words in the block. In Figure 1(b) we can observe the transference of the junction block, which has the original category of a verb, but takes the role of an adjective (through the relativizer 'that') in modifying the noun 'activities'.

$$P(S) = P_{BGM}(S) \cdot P_{BEM}(S) \cdot P_{WFM}(S) \quad (1)$$

$$P_{BGM}(S) = \prod_{B \in dependentBlocks(S)} P(B|parent(B), direction(B), leftSibling(B)) \quad (2)$$

$$P_{BEM}(S) = \prod_{B \in blocks(S)} P(elements(B)|derivedCat(B)) \quad (3)$$

$$P_{WFM}(S) = \prod_{B \in standardBlocks(S)} P(cw(B)|cw(parent(B)), cats(B), fw(B), context(B)) \quad (4)$$

Table 1: Equation (1) gives the likelihood of a structure $S$ as the product of the likelihoods of generating three aspects of the structure, according to the three models (BGM, BEM, WFM) specified in equations (2-4) and explained in the main text.

## 3 A probabilistic Model for TDS

This section describes the probabilistic generative model which was implemented in order to disambiguate TDS structures. We have chosen the same strategy we have described in (Sangati et al., 2009). The idea consists of utilizing a state of the art parser to compute a list of $k$-best candidates of a test sentence, and evaluate the new model by using it as a reranker. How well does it select the most probable structure among the given candidates? Since no parser currently exists for the TDS representation, we utilize a state of the art parser for PS trees (Charniak, 1999), and transform each candidate to TDS. This strategy can be considered a first step to efficiently test and compare different models before implementing a full-fledged parser.

### 3.1 Model description

In order to compute the probability of a given TDS structure, we make use of three separate probabilistic generative models, each responsible for a specific aspect of the structure being generated. The probability of a TDS structure is obtained by multiplying its probabilities in the three models, as reported in the first equation of Table 2.

The first model (equation 2) is the **Block Generation Model (BGM)**. It describes the event of generating a block $B$ as a dependent of its parent block (governor). The dependent block B is identified with its categories (both original and derived), and its functional words, while the parent block is characterized by the original category only. Moreover, in the conditioning context we specify the direction of the dependent with respect to the parent[3], and its adjacent left sister (*null* if not present) specified with the same level of details of B. The model applies only to dependent blocks[4].

The second model (equation 3) is the **Block Expansion Model (BEM)**. It computes the probability of a generic block $B$ of known derived category, to expand to the list of elements it is composed of. The list includes the category of the content word, in case the expansion leads to a standard block. In case of a junction structure, it contains the conjunctions and the conjunct blocks (each identified with its categories and its functional words) in the order they appear. Moreover, all functional words in the block are added to the list[5]. The model applies to all blocks.

The third model (equation 4) is the **Word Filling Model (WFM)**, which applies to each standard block B of the structure. It models the event of filling $B$ with a content word ($cw$), given the content word of the governing block, the categories ($cats$) and functional words ($fw$) of $B$, and further information about the context[6] in which $B$ occurs. This model becomes particularly interest-

[3]A dependent block can have three different positions with respect to the parent block: left, right, inner. The first two are self-explanatory. The *inner* case occurs when the dependent block starts after the beginning of the parent block but ends before it (e.g. *a nice dog*).

[4]A block is a dependent block if it is not a conjunct. In other words, it must be connected with a line to its governor.

[5]The attentive reader might notice that the functional words are generated twice (in BGM and BEM). This decision, although not fully justified from a statistical viewpoint, seems to drive the model towards a better disambiguation.

[6]$context(B)$ comprises information about the grandparent block (original category), the adjacent left sibling block (derived category), the direction of the content word with respect to its governor (in this case only left and right), and the absolute distance between the two words.

ing when a standard block is a dependent of a junction block (such as 'abortion' in Figure 1(d)). In this case, the model needs to capture the dependency relation between the content word of the dependent block and each of the content words belonging to the junction block[7].

### 3.2 Smoothing

In all the three models we have adopted a smoothing techniques based on back-off level estimation as proposed by Collins (1999). The different back-off estimates, which are listed in decreasing levels of details, are interpolated with confidence weights[8] derived from the training corpus.

The first two models are implemented with two levels of back-off, in which the last is a constant value ($10^{-6}$) to make the overall probability small but not zero, for unknown events.

The third model is implemented with three levels of back-off: the last is set to the same constant value ($10^{-6}$), the first encodes the dependency event using both pos-tags and lexical information of the governor and the dependent word, while the second specifies only pos-tags.

### 3.3 Experiment Setup

We have tested our model on the WSJ section of Penn Treebank (Marcus et al., 1993), using sections 02-21 as training and section 22 for testing. We employ the Max-Ent parser, implemented by Charniak (1999), to generate a list of $k$-best PS candidates for the test sentences, which are then converted into TDS representation.

Instead of using Charniak's parser in its original settings, we train it on a version of the corpus in which we add a special suffix to constituents which have circumstantial role[9]. This decision is based on the observation that the TDS formalism well captures the argument structure of verbs, and we believe that this additional information might benefit our model.

We then applied our probabilistic model to re-rank the list of available $k$-best TDS, and evaluate the selected candidates using several metrics which will be introduced next.

### 3.4 Evaluation Metrics for TDS

The re-ranking framework described above, allows us to keep track of the original PS of each TDS candidate. This provides an implicit advantage for evaluating our system, viz. it allows us to evaluate the re-ranked structures both in terms of the standard evaluation benchmark on the original PS (F-score) as well as on more refined metrics derived from the converted TDS representation. In addition, the specific head assignment that the TDS conversion procedure performs on the original PS, allows us to convert every PS candidate to a standard projective DS, and from this representation we can in turn compute the standard benchmark evaluation for DS, i.e. unlabeled attachment score[10] (UAS) (Lin, 1995; Nivre et al., 2007).

Concerning the TDS representation, we have formulated 3 evaluation metrics which reflect the accuracy of the chosen structure with respect to the gold structure (the one derived from the manually annotated PS), regarding the different components of the representation:

**Block Detection Score (BDS)**: the accuracy of detecting the correct boundaries of the blocks in the structure[11].

**Block Attachment Score (BAS)**: the accuracy of detecting the correct governing block of each block in the structure[12].

**Junction Detection Score (JDS)**: the accuracy of detecting the correct list of content-words composing each junction block in the structure[13].

[7]In order to derive the probability of this multi-event we compute the average between the probabilities of the single events which compose it.

[8]Each back-off level obtains a confidence weight which decreases with the increase of the *diversity of the context* ($\theta(C_i)$), which is the number of separate events occurring with the same context ($C_i$). More formally if $f(C_i)$ is the frequency of the conditioning context of the current event, the weight is obtained as $f(C_i)/(f(C_i) \cdot \mu \cdot \theta(C_i))$; see also (Bikel, 2004). In our model we have chosen $\mu$ to be 5 for the first model, and 50 for the second and the third.

[9]Those which have certain function tags (e.g. ADV, LOC, TMP). The full list is reported in (Sangati and Mazza, 2009). It was surprising to notice that the performance of this slightly modified parser (in terms of F-score) is only slightly lower than how it performs out-of-the-box (0.13%).

[10]UAS measures the percentage of words (excluding punctuation) having the correct governing word.

[11]It is calculated as the harmonic mean between recall and precision between the test and gold set of blocks, where each block is identified with two numerical values representing the start and the end position (punctuation words are discarded).

[12]It is computed as the percentage of words (both functional and content words, excluding punctuation) having the correct governing block. The governing block of a word, is defined as the governor of the block it belongs to. If the block is a conjunct, its governing block is computed recursively as the governing block of the junction block it belongs to.

[13]It is calculated as the harmonic mean between recall and precision between the test and gold set of junction blocks expansions, where each expansion is identified with the list of content words belonging to the junction block. A recursive junction structure expands to a list of lists of content-words.

| | F-Score | UAS | BDS | BAS | JDS |
|---|---|---|---|---|---|
| Charniak ($k = 1$) | 89.41 | 92.24 | 94.82 | 89.29 | 75.82 |
| Oracle Best F-Score ($k = 1000$) | 97.47 | 96.98 | 97.03 | 95.79 | 82.26 |
| Oracle Worst F-Score ($k = 1000$) | 57.04 | 77.04 | 84.71 | 70.10 | 43.01 |
| Oracle Best JDS ($k = 1000$) | 90.54 | 93.77 | 96.20 | 90.57 | 93.55 |
| PCFG-reranker ($k = 5$) | 89.03 | 92.12 | **94.86** | 88.94 | **75.88** |
| PCFG-reranker ($k = 1000$) | 83.52 | 87.04 | 92.07 | 82.32 | 69.17 |
| TDS-reranker ($k = 5$) | **89.65** | **92.33** | 94.77 | **89.35** | **76.23** |
| TDS-reranker ($k = 10$) | 89.10 | 92.11 | 94.58 | 88.94 | 75.47 |
| TDS-reranker ($k = 100$) | 86.64 | 90.24 | 93.11 | 86.34 | 69.60 |
| TDS-reranker ($k = 500$) | 84.94 | 88.62 | 91.97 | 84.43 | 65.30 |
| TDS-reranker ($k = 1000$) | 84.31 | 87.89 | 91.42 | 83.69 | 63.65 |

Table 2: Results of Charniak's parser, the TDS-reranker, and the PCFG-reranker according to several evaluation metrics, when the number $k$ of best-candidates increases.

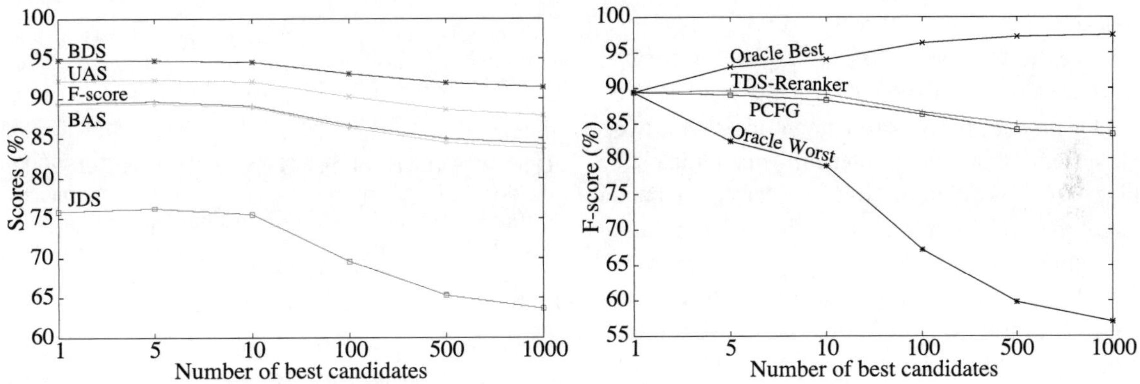


Figure 2: **Left**: results of the TDS-reranking model according to several evaluation metrics as in Table 2. **Right:** comparison between the F-scores of the TDS-reranker and a vanilla PCFG-reranker (together with the lower and the upper bound), with the increase of the number of best candidates.

### 3.5 Results

Table 2 reports the results we obtain when re-ranking with our model an increasing number of $k$-best candidates provided by Charniak's parser (the same results are shown in the left graph of Figure 2). We also report the results relative to a PCFG-reranker obtained by computing the probability of the $k$-best candidates using a standard vanilla-PCFG model derived from the same training corpus. Moreover, we evaluate, by means of an oracle, the upper and lower bound of the F-Score and JDS metric, by selecting the structures which maximizes/minimizes the results.

Our re-ranking model performs rather well for a limited number of candidate structures, and outperforms Charniak's model when $k = 5$. In this case we observe a small boost in performance for the detection of junction structures, as well as for all other evaluation metrics, except for the BDS.

The right graph in Figure 2 compares the F-score performance of the TDS-reranker against the PCFG-reranker. Our system consistently outperforms the PCFG model on this metric, as for UAS, and BAS. Concerning the other metrics, as the number of $k$-best candidates increases, the PCFG model outperforms the TDS-reranker both according to the BDS and the JDS.

Unfortunately, the performance of the re-ranking model worsens progressively with the increase of $k$. We find that this is primarily due to the lack of robustness of the model in detecting the block boundaries. This suggests that the system might benefit from a separate preprocessing step which could chunk the input sentence with higher accuracy (Sang et al., 2000). In addition the same module could detect local (intra-clausal) coordinations, as illustrated by (Marinčič et al., 2009).

## 4 Conclusions

In this paper, we have presented a probabilistic generative model for parsing TDS syntactic representation of English sentences. We have given evidence for the usefulness of this formalism: we consider it a valid alternative to commonly used PS and DS representations, since it incorporates the most relevant features of both notations; in addition, it makes use of junction structures to represent coordination, a linguistic phenomena highly abundant in natural language production, but often neglected when it comes to evaluating parsing resources. We have therefore proposed a special evaluation metrics for junction detection, with the hope that other researchers might benefit from it in the future. Remarkably, Charniak's parser performs extremely well in all the evaluation metrics besides the one related to coordination.

Our parsing results are encouraging: the overall system, although only when the candidates are highly reliable, can improve on Charniak's parser on all the evaluation metrics with the exception of chunking score (BDS). The weakness on performing chunking is the major factor responsible for the lack of robustness of our system. We are considering to use a dedicated pre-processing module to perform this step with higher accuracy.

**Acknowledgments** The author gratefully acknowledge funding by the Netherlands Organization for Scientific Research (NWO): this work is funded through a Vici-grant "Integrating Cognition" (277.70.006) to Rens Bod. We also thank 3 anonymous reviewers for very useful comments.

## References

Daniel M. Bikel. 2004. Intricacies of Collins' Parsing Model. *Comput. Linguist.*, 30(4):479–511.

Eugene Charniak. 1999. A Maximum-Entropy-Inspired Parser. Technical report, Providence, RI, USA.

Silvie Cinková, Josef Toman, Jan Hajič, Kristýna Čermáková, Václav Klimeš, Lucie Mladová, Jana Šindlerová, Kristýna Tomšů, and Zdeněk Žabokrtský. 2009. Tectogrammatical Annotation of the Wall Street Journal. *The Prague Bulletin of Mathematical Linguistics*, (92).

Michael J. Collins. 1999. *Head-Driven Statistical Models for Natural Language Parsing*. Ph.D. thesis, University of Pennsylvania.

Marie-Catherine de Marneffe and Christopher D. Manning. 2008. The Stanford Typed Dependencies Representation. In *Coling 2008: Proceedings of the workshop on Cross-Framework and Cross-Domain Parser Evaluation*, pages 1–8, Manchester, UK.

Yuan Ding and Martha Palmer. 2005. Machine Translation Using Probabilistic Synchronous Dependency Insertion Grammars. In *Proceedings of the 43rd Annual Meeting of the Association for Computational Linguistics (ACL'05)*, pages 541–548.

Julia Hockenmaier and Mark Steedman. 2007. CCGbank: A Corpus of CCG Derivations and Dependency Structures Extracted from the Penn Treebank. *Computational Linguistics*, 33(3):355–396.

Dekang Lin. 1995. A Dependency-based Method for Evaluating Broad-Coverage Parsers. In *In Proceedings of IJCAI-95*, pages 1420–1425.

Mitchell P. Marcus, Mary Ann Marcinkiewicz, and Beatrice Santorini. 1993. Building a Large Annotated Corpus of English: The Penn Treebank. *Computational Linguistics*, 19(2):313–330.

Domen Marinčič, Matjaž Gams, and Tomaž Šef. 2009. Intraclausal Coordination and Clause Detection as a Preprocessing Step to Dependency Parsing. In *TSD '09: Proceedings of the 12th International Conference on Text, Speech and Dialogue*, pages 147–153, Berlin, Heidelberg. Springer-Verlag.

Joakim Nivre, Johan Hall, Sandra Kübler, Ryan Mcdonald, Jens Nilsson, Sebastian Riedel, and Deniz Yuret. 2007. The CoNLL 2007 Shared Task on Dependency Parsing. In *Proceedings of the CoNLL Shared Task Session of EMNLP-CoNLL 2007*, pages 915–932, Prague, Czech Republic.

Joakim Nivre. 2005. Dependency Grammar and Dependency Parsing. Technical report, Växjö University: School of Mathematics and Systems Engineering.

Erik F. Tjong Kim Sang, Sabine Buchholz, and Kim Sang. 2000. Introduction to the CoNLL-2000 Shared Task: Chunking. In *Proceedings of CoNLL-2000 and LLL-2000, Lisbon, Portugal*.

Federico Sangati and Chiara Mazza. 2009. An English Dependency Treebank à la Tesnière. In *The 8th International Workshop on Treebanks and Linguistic Theories*, pages 173–184, Milan, Italy.

Federico Sangati, Willem Zuidema, and Rens Bod. 2009. A generative re-ranking model for dependency parsing. In *Proceedings of the 11th International Conference on Parsing Technologies (IWPT'09)*, pages 238–241, Paris, France, October.

Gerold Schneider. 2008. *Hybrid long-distance functional dependency parsing*. Ph.D. thesis, University of Zurich.

Lucien Tesnière. 1959. *Eléments de syntaxe structurale*. Editions Klincksieck, Paris.

# Sentiment Translation through Lexicon Induction

**Christian Scheible**
Institute for Natural Language Processing
University of Stuttgart
scheibcn@ims.uni-stuttgart.de

## Abstract

The translation of sentiment information is a task from which sentiment analysis systems can benefit. We present a novel, graph-based approach using SimRank, a well-established vertex similarity algorithm to transfer sentiment information between a source language and a target language graph. We evaluate this method in comparison with SO-PMI.

## 1 Introduction

Sentiment analysis is an important topic in computational linguistics that is of theoretical interest but also implies many real-world applications. Usually, two aspects are of importance in sentiment analysis. The first is the detection of subjectivity, i.e. whether a text or an expression is meant to express sentiment at all; the second is the determination of sentiment orientation, i.e. what sentiment is to be expressed in a structure that is considered subjective.

Work on sentiment analysis most often covers resources or analysis methods in a single language, usually English. However, the transfer of sentiment analysis between languages can be advantageous by making use of resources for a source language to improve the analysis of the target language.

This paper presents an approach to the transfer of sentiment information between languages. It is built around an algorithm that has been successfully applied for the acquisition of bilingual lexicons. One of the main benefits of the method is its ability of handling sparse data well.

Our experiments are carried out using English as a source language and German as a target language.

## 2 Related Work

The translation of sentiment information has been the topic of multiple publications.

Mihalcea et al. (2007) propose two methods for translating sentiment lexicons. The first method simply uses bilingual dictionaries to translate an English sentiment lexicon. A sentence-based classifier built with this list achieved high precision but low recall on a small Romanian test set. The second method is based on parallel corpora. The source language in the corpus is annotated with sentiment information, and the information is then projected to the target language. Problems arise due to mistranslations, e.g., because irony is not recognized.

Banea et al. (2008) use machine translation for multilingual sentiment analysis. Given a corpus annotated with sentiment information in one language, machine translation is used to produce an annotated corpus in the target language, by preserving the annotations. The original annotations can be produced either manually or automatically.

Wan (2009) constructs a multilingual classifier using co-training. In co-training, one classifier produces additional training data for a second classifier. In this case, an English classifier assists in training a Chinese classifier.

The induction of a sentiment lexicon is the subject of early work by (Hatzivassiloglou and McKeown, 1997). They construct graphs from coordination data from large corpora based on the intuition that adjectives with the same sentiment orientation are likely to be coordinated. For example, *fresh and delicious* is more likely than *rotten and delicious*. They then apply a graph clustering algorithm to find groups of adjectives with the same orientation. Finally, they assign the same label to all adjectives that belong to the same cluster. The authors note that some words cannot be assigned a unique label since their sentiment depends on con-



*Proceedings of the ACL 2010 Student Research Workshop*, pages 25–30,
Uppsala, Sweden, 13 July 2010. 

text.

Turney (2002) suggests a corpus-based extraction method based on his pointwise mutual information (PMI) synonymy measure He assumes that the sentiment orientation of a phrase can be determined by comparing its pointwise mutual information with a positive (*excellent*) and a negative phrase (*poor*). An introduction to SO-PMI is given in Section 5.1

## 3 Bilingual Lexicon Induction

Typical approaches to the induction of bilingual lexicons involve gathering new information from a small set of known identities between the languages which is called a *seed lexicon* and incorporating intralingual sources of information (e.g. cooccurrence counts). Two examples of such methods are a graph-based approach by Dorow et al. (2009) and a vector-space based approach by Rapp (1999). In this paper, we will employ the graph-based method.

SimRank was first introduced by Jeh and Widom (2002). It is an iterative algorithm that measures the similarity between all vertices in a graph. In SimRank, two nodes are similar if their neighbors are similar. This defines a recursive process that ends when the two nodes compared are identical. As proposed by Dorow et al. (2009), we will apply it to a graph $\mathcal{G}$ in which vertices represent words and edges represent relations between words. SimRank will then yield similarity values between vertices that indicate the degree of relatedness between them with regard to the property encoded through the edges. For two nodes $i$ and $j$ in $\mathcal{G}$, similarity according to SimRank is defined as

$$\text{sim}(i,j) = \frac{c}{|N(i)||N(j)|} \sum_{k \in N(i), l \in N(j)} \text{sim}(k,l),$$

where $N(x)$ is the neighborhood of $x$ and $c$ is a weight factor that determines the influence of neighbors that are farther away. The initial condition for the recursion is $\text{sim}(i,i) = 1$.

Dorow et al. (2009) further propose the application of the SimRank algorithm for the calculation of similarities between a source graph $\mathcal{S}$ and a target graph $\mathcal{T}$. Initially, some relations between the two graphs need to be known. When operating on word graphs, these can be taken from a bilingual lexicon. This provides us with a framework for the induction of a bilingual lexicon which can be constructed based on the obtained similarity values between the vertices of the two graphs.

One problem of SimRank observed in experiments by Laws et al. (2010) was that while words with high similarity were semantically related, they often were not exact translations of each other but instead often fell into the categories of hyponymy, hypernomy, holonymy, or meronymy. However, this makes the similarity values applicable for the translation of sentiment since it is a property that does not depend on exact synonymy.

## 4 Sentiment Transfer

Although unsupervised methods for the design of sentiment analysis systems exist, any approach can benefit from using resources that have been established in other languages. The main problem that we aim to deal with in this paper is the transfer of such information between languages. The SimRank lexicon induction method is suitable for this purpose since it can produce useful similarity values even with a small seed lexicon.

First, we build a graph for each language. The vertices of these graphs will represent adjectives while the edges are coordination relations between these adjectives. An example for such a graph is given in Figure 1.

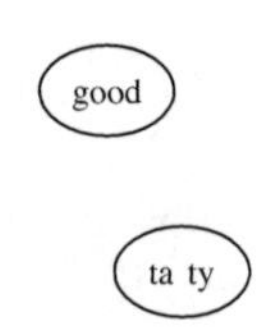

good
ta ty

| word | value |
|---|---|
| strongpos | 1.0 |
| weakpos | 0.5 |
| neutral | 0.0 |
| weakneg | −0.5 |
| strongneg | −1.0 |

Table 1: Assigned values for positivity labels

*mangelhaft* as negative seeds.

We constructed a test set by randomly selecting 200 German adjectives that occurred in a coordination in Wikipedia. We then eliminated adjectives that we deemed uncommon or too difficult to understand or that were mislabeled as adjectives. This resulted in a 150 word test set. To determine the sentiment of these adjectives, we asked 9 human judges, all native German speakers, to annotate them given the classes *neutral*, *slightly negative*, *very negative*, *slightly positive*, and *very positive*, reflecting the categories from the training data. In the annotation process, another 7 adjectives had to be discarded because one or more annotators marked them as unknown.

Since human judges tend to interpret scales differently, we examine their agreement using Kendall's coefficient of concordance ($W$) including correction for ties (Legendre, 2005) which takes ranks into account. The agreement was calculated as $W = 0.674$ with a significant confidence ($p < .001$), which is usually interpreted as substantial agreement. Manual examination of the data showed that most disagreement between the annotators occurred with adjectives that are tied to political implications, for example *nuklear* (*nuclear*).

### 5.3 Sentiment Lexicon Induction

For our experiments, we used the polarity lexicon of Wilson et al. (2005). It includes annotations of positivity in the form of the categories *neutral*, weakly positive (*weakpos*), strongly positive (*strongpos*), weakly negative (*weakneg*), and strongly positive (*strongneg*). In order to conduct arithmetic operations on these annotations, mapped them to values from the interval $[-1, 1]$ by using the assignments given in Table 1.

### 5.4 Results

To compare the two methods to the human raters, we first reproduce the evaluation by Turney (2002) and examine the correlation coefficients. Both methods will be compared to an average over the human rater values. These values are calculated on values asserted based on Table 1. The correlation coefficients between the automatic systems and the human ratings, SO-PMI yields $r = 0.551$, and SimRank yields $r = 0.587$ which are not significantly different. This shows that SO and SR have about the same performance on this broad measure.

Since many adjectives do not express sentiment at all, the correct categorization of neutral adjectives is as important as the scalar rating. Thus, we divide the adjectives into three categories – positive, neutral, and negative. Due to disagreements between the human judges there exists no clear threshold between these categories. In order to try different thresholds, we assume that sentiment is symmetrically distributed with mean 0 on the human scores. For $x \in \{\frac{i}{20} | 0 \leq i \leq 19\}$, we then assign word $w$ with human rating $score(w)$ to negative if $score(w) \leq -x$, to neutral if $-x < score(w) < x$ and to positive otherwise. This gives us a three-category gold standard for each $x$ that is then the basis for computing evaluation measures. Each category contains a certain percentile of the list of adjectives. By mapping these percentiles to the rank-ordered scores for SO-PMI and SimRank, we can create three-category partitions for them. For example if for $x = 0.35$ 21% of the adjectives are negative, then the 21% of adjectives with the lowest SO-PMI scores are deemed to have been rated negative by SO-PMI.

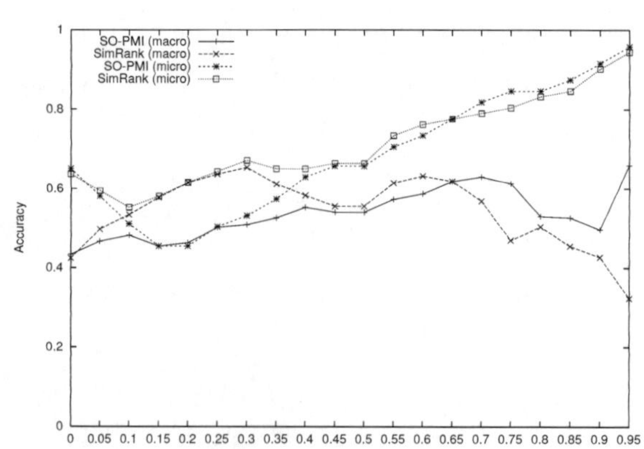


Figure 3: Macro- and micro-averaged Accuracy

First, we will look at the macro- and micro-averaged accuracies for both methods (cf. Figure 3). Overall, SimRank performs better for $x$

between 0.05 and 0.4 which is a plausible interval for the neutral threshold on the human ratings. The results diverge for very low and high values of $x$, however these values can be considered unrealistic since they implicate neutral areas that are too small or too large. When comparing the accuracies for each of the classes (cf. Figure 4), we observe that in the aforementioned interval, SimRank has higher accuracy values than SO-PMI for all of them.

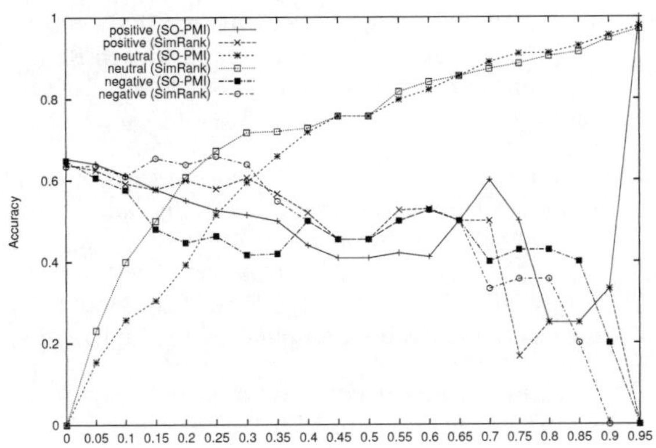


Figure 4: Accuracy for individual classes

Table 2 lists some interesting example words including their human ratings and SO-PMI and SimRank scores which illustrate advantages and possible shortcomings of the two methods. The medians of SO-PMI and SimRank scores are $-15.58$ and $-0.05$, respectively. The mean values are $-9.57$ for SO-PMI and $0.08$ for SimRank, the standard deviations are $13.75$ and $0.22$. SimRank values range between $-0.67$ and $0.41$, SO-PMI ranges between $-46.21$ and $46.59$. We will assume that the medians mark the center of the set of neutral adjectives.

*Ausdrucksvoll* receives a positive score from SO-PMI which matches the human rating, however not from SimRank, which assigns a score close to 0 and would likely be considered neutral. This error can be explained by examining the similarity distribution for *ausdrucksvoll* which reveals that there are no nodes that are similar to this node, which was most likely caused by its low degree. *Auferstanden* (resurrected) is perceived as a positive adjective by the human judges, however it is misclassified by SimRank as negative due to its occurrence with words like *gestorben* (*deceased*) and *gekreuzigt* (*crucified*) which have negative associations. This suggests that coordinations are sometimes misleading and should not be used as the only data source. *Grafisch* (*graphics-related*) is an example for a neutral word misclassified by SO-PMI due to its occurrence in positive contexts on the web. Since SimRank is not restricted to relations between an adjective and a seed word, all adjective-adjective coordinations are used for the estimation of a sentiment score. *Kriminell* is also misclassified by SO-PMI for the same reason.

| word (translation) | SR | SO | judges |
|---|---|---|---|
| ausdrucksvoll (expressive) | 0.069 | 22.93 | 0.39 |
| grafisch (graphic) | -0.050 | -4.75 | 0.00 |
| kriminell (criminal) | -0.389 | -15.98 | -0.94 |
| auferstanden (resurrected) | -0.338 | -10.97 | 0.34 |

Table 2: Example adjectives including translation, and their scores

## 6 Conclusion and Outlook

We presented a novel approach to the translation of sentiment information that outperforms SO-PMI, an established method. In particular, we could show that SimRank outperforms SO-PMI for values of the threshold $x$ in an interval that most likely leads to the correct separation of positive, neutral, and negative adjectives. We intend to compare our system to other available work in the future. In addition to our findings, we created an initial gold standard set of sentiment-annotated German adjectives that will be publicly available.

The two methods are very different in nature; while SO-PMI is suitable for languages in which very large corpora exist, this might not be the case for knowledge-sparse languages. For some German words (e.g. *schwerstkrank* (*seriously ill*)), SO-PMI lacked sufficient results on the web whereas SimRank correctly assigned negative sentiment. SimRank can leverage knowledge from neighbor words to circumvent this problem. In turn, this information can turn out to be misleading (cf. *auferstanden*). An advantage of our method is that it uses existing resources from another language and can thus be applied without much knowledge about the target language. Our future work will include a further examination of the merits of its application for knowledge-sparse languages.

The underlying graph structure provides a foundation for many conceivable extensions. In this paper, we presented a fairly simple experiment restricted to adjectives only. However, the method is suitable to include arbitrary parts of speech as well as phrases, as used by Turney (2002). Another conceivable application would be the direct combination of the SimRank-based model with a statistical model.

Currently, our input sentiment list exists only of prior sentiment values, however work by Wilson et al. (2009) has advanced the notion of contextual polarity lists. The automatic translation of this information could be beneficial for sentiment analysis in other languages.

Another important problem in sentiment analysis is the treatment of ambiguity. The sentiment expressed by a word or phrase is context-dependent and is for example related to word sense (Akkaya et al., 2009). Based on regularities in graph structure and similarity, ambiguity resolution might become possible.

## References


C. Akkaya, J. Wiebe, and R. Mihalcea. 2009. Subjectivity Word Sense Disambiguation. In *Proceedings of the 2009 Conference on Empirical Methods in Natural Language Processing*, pages 190–199.

Carmen Banea, Rada Mihalcea, Janyce Wiebe, and Samer Hassan. 2008. Multilingual subjectivity analysis using machine translation. In *Proceedings of the 2008 Conference on Empirical Methods in Natural Language Processing*, pages 127–135, Honolulu, Hawaii, October. Association for Computational Linguistics.

O. Christ, B.M. Schulze, A. Hofmann, and E. Koenig. 1999. The IMS Corpus Workbench: Corpus Query Processor (CQP): User's Manual. *University of Stuttgart, March*, 8:1999.

Beate Dorow, Florian Laws, Lukas Michelbacher, Christian Scheible, and Jason Utt. 2009. A graph-theoretic algorithm for automatic extension of translation lexicons. In *Proceedings of the Workshop on Geometrical Models of Natural Language Semantics*, pages 91–95, Athens, Greece, March. Association for Computational Linguistics.

Vasileios Hatzivassiloglou and Kathleen R. McKeown. 1997. Predicting the semantic orientation of adjectives. In *Proceedings of the 35th Annual Meeting of the Association for Computational Linguistics*, pages 174–181, Madrid, Spain, July. Association for Computational Linguistics.

Glen Jeh and Jennifer Widom. 2002. Simrank: a measure of structural-context similarity. In *KDD '02: Proceedings of the eighth ACM SIGKDD international conference on Knowledge discovery and data mining*, pages 538–543, New York, NY, USA. ACM.

F. Laws, L. Michelbacher, B. Dorow, U. Heid, and H. Schütze. 2010. Building a Cross-lingual Relatedness Thesaurus Using a Graph Similarity Measure. *Submitted on Nov 7, 2009, to the International Conference on Language Resources and Evaluation (LREC)*.

P. Legendre. 2005. Species associations: the Kendall coefficient of concordance revisited. *Journal of Agricultural Biological and Environment Statistics*, 10(2):226–245.

Rada Mihalcea, Carmen Banea, and Janyce Wiebe. 2007. Learning multilingual subjective language via cross-lingual projections. In *Proceedings of the 45th Annual Meeting of the Association of Computational Linguistics*, pages 976–983, Prague, Czech Republic, June. Association for Computational Linguistics.

Reinhard Rapp. 1999. Automatic identification of word translations from unrelated english and german corpora. In *Proceedings of the 37th Annual Meeting of the Association for Computational Linguistics*, pages 519–526, College Park, Maryland, USA, June. Association for Computational Linguistics.

Peter Turney. 2002. Thumbs up or thumbs down? semantic orientation applied to unsupervised classification of reviews. In *Proceedings of 40th Annual Meeting of the Association for Computational Linguistics*, pages 417–424, Philadelphia, Pennsylvania, USA, July. Association for Computational Linguistics.

Xiaojun Wan. 2009. Co-training for cross-lingual sentiment classification. In *Proceedings of the Joint Conference of the 47th Annual Meeting of the ACL and the 4th International Joint Conference on Natural Language Processing of the AFNLP*, pages 235–243, Suntec, Singapore, August. Association for Computational Linguistics.

Theresa Wilson, Janyce Wiebe, and Paul Hoffmann. 2005. Recognizing contextual polarity in phrase-level sentiment analysis. In *Proceedings of Human Language Technology Conference and Conference on Empirical Methods in Natural Language Processing*, pages 347–354, Vancouver, British Columbia, Canada, October. Association for Computational Linguistics.

Theresa Wilson, Janyce Wiebe, and Paul Hoffmann. 2009. Recognizing Contextual Polarity: an Exploration of Features for Phrase-level Sentiment Analysis. *Computational Linguistics*, 35(3):399–433.

# Unsupervised Search for The Optimal Segmentation for Statistical Machine Translation

**Coşkun Mermer**[1,3] and **Ahmet Afşın Akın**[2,3]
[1]Boğaziçi University, Bebek, Istanbul, Turkey
[2]Istanbul Technical University, Sarıyer, Istanbul, Turkey
[3]TÜBİTAK-UEKAE, Gebze, Kocaeli, Turkey
{coskun,ahmetaa}@uekae.tubitak.gov.tr

## Abstract

We tackle the previously unaddressed problem of unsupervised determination of the optimal morphological segmentation for statistical machine translation (SMT) and propose a segmentation metric that takes into account both sides of the SMT training corpus. We formulate the objective function as the posterior probability of the training corpus according to a generative segmentation-translation model. We describe how the IBM Model-1 translation likelihood can be computed incrementally between adjacent segmentation states for efficient computation. Submerging the proposed segmentation method in a SMT task from morphologically-rich Turkish to English does not exhibit the expected improvement in translation BLEU scores and confirms the robustness of phrase-based SMT to translation unit combinatorics. A positive outcome of this work is the described modification to the sequential search algorithm of Morfessor (Creutz and Lagus, 2007) that enables arbitrary-fold parallelization of the computation, which unexpectedly improves the translation performance as measured by BLEU.

## 1 Introduction

In statistical machine translation (SMT), words are normally considered as the building blocks of translation models. However, especially for morphologically complex languages such as Finnish, Turkish, Czech, Arabic etc., it has been shown that using sub-lexical units obtained after morphological preprocessing can improve the machine translation performance over a word-based system (Habash and Sadat, 2006; Oflazer and Durgar El-Kahlout, 2007; Bisazza and Federico, 2009). However, the effect of segmentation on translation performance is indirect and difficult to isolate (Lopez and Resnik, 2006).

The challenge in designing a sub-lexical SMT system is the decision of what segmentation to use. Linguistic morphological analysis is intuitive, but it is language-dependent and could be highly ambiguous. Furthermore, it is not necessarily optimal in that (i) manually engineered segmentation schemes can outperform a straightforward linguistic morphological segmentation, e.g., (Habash and Sadat, 2006), and (ii) it may result in even worse performance than a word-based system, e.g., (Durgar El-Kahlout and Oflazer, 2006).

A SMT system designer has to decide what segmentation is optimal for the translation task at hand. Existing solutions to this problem are predominantly heuristic, language-dependent, and as such are not easily portable to other languages. Another point to consider is that the optimal degree of segmentation might decrease as the amount of training data increases (Lee, 2004; Habash and Sadat, 2006). This brings into question: For the particular language pair and training corpus at hand, what is the optimal (level of) sub-word segmentation? Therefore, it is desirable to learn the optimal segmentation in an unsupervised manner.

In this work, we extend the method of Creutz and Lagus (2007) so as to maximize the translation posterior in unsupervised segmentation. The learning process is tailored to the particular SMT task via the same parallel corpus that is used in training the statistical translation models.

## 2 Related Work

Most works in SMT-oriented segmentation are supervised in that they consist of manual experimentation to choose the best among a set of segmentation schemes, and are language(pair)-dependent. For Arabic, Sadat and Habash (2006) present several morphological preprocessing schemes that entail varying degrees of decomposition and com-



*Proceedings of the ACL 2010 Student Research Workshop*, pages 31–36,
Uppsala, Sweden, 13 July 2010. ©2010 Association for Computational Linguistics

pare the resulting translation performances in an Arabic-to-English task. Shen et al. (2007) use a subset of the morphology and apply only a few simple rules in segmenting words. Durgar El-Kahlout and Oflazer (2006) tackle this problem when translating from English to Turkish, an agglutinative language. They use a morphological analyzer and disambiguation to arrive at morphemes as tokens. However, training the translation models with morphemes actually degrades the translation performance. They outperform the word-based baseline only after some selective morpheme grouping. Bisazza and Federico (2009) adopt an approach similar to the Arabic segmentation studies above, this time in a Turkish-to-English translation setting.

Unsupervised segmentation by itself has garnered considerable attention in the computational linguistics literature (Poon et al., 2009; Snyder and Barzilay, 2008; Dasgupta and Ng, 2007; Creutz and Lagus, 2007; Brent, 1999). However, few works report their performance in a translation task. Virpioja et al. (2007) used Morfessor (Creutz and Lagus, 2007) to segment both sides of the parallel training corpora in translation between Danish, Finnish, and Swedish, but without a consistent improvement in results.

Morfessor, which gives state of the art results in many tests (Kurimo et al., 2009), uses only monolingual information in its objective function. It is conceivable that we can achieve a better segmentation for translation by considering not one but both sides of the parallel corpus. A posssible choice is the post-segmentation alignment accuracy. However, Elming et al. (2009) show that optimizing segmentation with respect to alignment error rate (AER) does not improve and even degrades machine translation performance. Snyder and Barzilay (2008) use bilingual information but the segmentation is learned independently from translation modeling.

In Chang et al. (2008), the granularity of the Chinese word segmentation is optimized by training SMT systems for several values of a granularity bias parameter and it is found that the value that maximizes translation performance (as measured by BLEU) is different than the value that maximizes segmentation accuracy (as measured by precision and recall).

One motivation in morphological preprocessing before translation modeling is "morphology matching" as in Lee (2004) and in the scheme "EN" of Habash and Sadat (2006). In Lee (2004), the goal is to match the lexical granularities of the two languages by starting with a fine-grained segmentation of the Arabic side of the corpus and then merging or deleting Arabic morphemes using alignments with a part-of-speech tagged English corpus. But this method is not completely unsupervised since it requires external linguistic resources in initializing the segmentation with the output of a morphological analyzer and disambiguator. Talbot and Osborne (2006) tackle a special case of morphology matching by identifying redundant distinctions in the morphology of one language compared to another.

## 3 Method

Maximizing translation performance directly would require SMT training and decoding for each segmentation hypothesis considered, which is computationally infeasible. So we make some conditional independence assumptions using a generative model and decompose the posterior probability $P(M_f|e, f)$. In this notation $e$ and $f$ denote the two sides of a parallel corpus and $M_f$ denotes the segmentation model hypothesized for $f$. Our approach is an extension of Morfessor (Creutz and Lagus, 2007) so as to include the translation model probability in its cost calculation. Specifically, the segmentation model takes into account the likelihood of both sides of the parallel corpus while searching for the optimal segmentation. The joint likelihood is decomposed into a prior, a monolingual likelihood, and a translation likelihood, as shown in Eq. 1.

$$P(e, f, M_f) = P(M_f)P(f|M_f)P(e|f, M_f) \quad (1)$$

Assuming conditional independence between $e$ and $M_f$ given $f$, the maximum *a posteriori* (MAP) objective can be written as:

$$\hat{M}_f = \arg\max_{M_f} P(M_f)P(f|M_f)P(e|f) \quad (2)$$

The role of the bilingual component $P(e|f)$ in Eq. 2 can be motivated with a simple example as follows. Consider an occurrence of two phrase pairs in a Turkish-English parallel corpus and the two hypothesized sets of segmentations for the Turkish phrases as in Table 1. Without access to the English side of the corpus, a monolingual segmenter can quite possibly score Seg. #1

| | Phrase #1 | Phrase #2 |
|---|---|---|
| Turkish phrase: | anahtar | anahtarım |
| English phrase: | key | my key |
| Seg. #1: | anahtar | anahtarı +m |
| Seg. #2: | anahtar | anahtar +ım |

Table 1: Example segmentation hypotheses

higher than Seg. #2 (e.g., due to the high frequency of the observed morph "+m"). On the other hand, a bilingual segmenter is expected to assign a higher alignment probability $P(e|f)$ to Seg. #2 than Seg. #1, because of the aligned words key||anahtar, therefore ranking Seg. #2 higher.

The two monolingual components of Eq. 2 are computed as in Creutz and Lagus (2007). To summarize briefly, the prior $P(M_f)$ is assumed to only depend on the frequencies and lengths of the individual morphs, which are also assumed to be independent. The monolingual likelihood $P(f|M_f)$ is computed as the product of morph probabilities estimated from their frequencies in the corpus.

To compute the bilingual (translation) likelihood $P(e|f)$, we use IBM Model 1 (Brown et al., 1993). Let an aligned sentence pair be represented by $(s_e, s_f)$, which consists of word sequences $s_e = e_1, ..., e_l$ and $s_f = f_1, ..., f_m$. Using a purely notational switch of the corpus labels from here on to be consistent with the SMT literature, where the derivations are in the form of $P(f|e)$, the desired translation probability is given by the expression:

$$P(f|e) = \frac{P(m|e)}{(l+1)^m} \prod_{j=1}^{m} \sum_{i=0}^{l} t(f_j|e_i), \quad (3)$$

The sentence length probability distribution $P(m|e)$ is assumed to be Poisson with the expected sentence length equal to $m$.

### 3.1 Incremental computation of Model-1 likelihood

During search, the translation likelihood $P(e|f)$ needs to be calculated according to Eq. 3 for every hypothesized segmentation.

To compute Eq. 3, we need to have at hand the individual morph translation probabilities $t(f_j|e_i)$. These can be estimated using the EM algorithm given by (Brown, 1993), which is guaranteed to converge to a global maximum of the likelihood for Model 1. However, running the EM algorithm to optimization for each considered segmentation model can be computationally expensive, and can result in overtraining. Therefore, in this work we used the likelihood computed after the first EM iteration, which also has the nice property that $P(f|e)$ can be computed incrementally from one segmentation hypothesis to the next.

The incremental updates are derived from the equations for the count collection and probability estimation steps of the EM algorithm as follows. In the count collection step, in the first iteration, we need to compute the fractional counts $c(f_j|e_i)$ (Brown et al., 1993):

$$c(f_j|e_i) = \frac{1}{l+1}(\#f_j)(\#e_i), \quad (4)$$

where $(\#f_j)$ and $(\#e_i)$ denote the number of occurrences of $f_j$ in $s_f$ and $e_i$ in $s_e$, respectively.

Let $f_k$ denote the word hypothesized to be segmented. Let the resulting two sub-words be $f_p$ and $f_q$, any of which may or may not previously exist in the vocabulary. Then, according to Eq. (4), as a result of the segmentation no update is needed for $c(f_j|e_i)$ for $j = 1 \ldots N$, $j \neq p, q$, $i = 1 \ldots M$ (note that $f_k$ no longer exists); and the necessary updates $\Delta c(f_j|e_i)$ for $c(f_j|e_i)$, where $j = p, q$; $i = 1 \ldots M$ are given by:

$$\Delta c(f_j|e_i) = \frac{1}{l+1}(\#f_k)(\#e_i). \quad (5)$$

Note that Eq. (5) is nothing but the previous count value for the segmented word, $c(f_k|e_i)$. So, all needed in the count collection step is to copy the set of values $c(f_k|e_i)$ to $c(f_p|e_i)$ and $c(f_q|e_i)$, adding if they already exist.

Then in the probability estimation step, the normalization is performed including the newly added fractional counts.

### 3.2 Parallelization of search

In an iteration of the algorithm, all words are processed in random order, computing for each word the posterior probability of the generative model after each possible binary segmentation (splitting) of the word. If the highest-scoring split increases the posterior probability compared to not splitting, that split is accepted (for all occurrences of the word) and the resulting sub-words are explored recursively for further segmentations. The process is repeated until an iteration no more results in a significant increase in the posterior probability.

The search algorithm of Morfessor is a greedy algorithm where the costs of the next search points

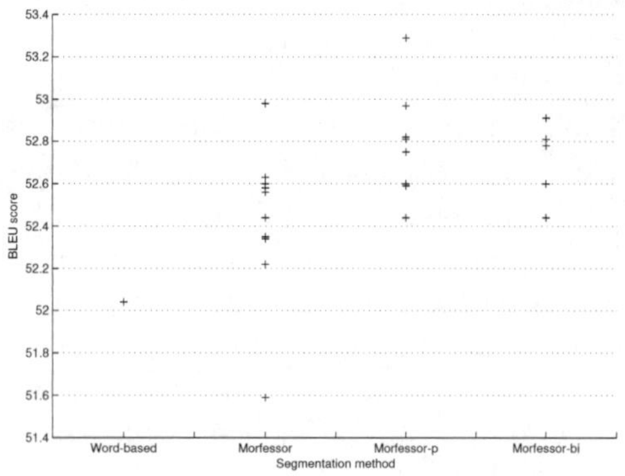


Figure 1: BLEU scores obtained with different segmentation methods. Multiple data points for a system correspond to different random orders in processing the data (Creutz and Lagus, 2007).

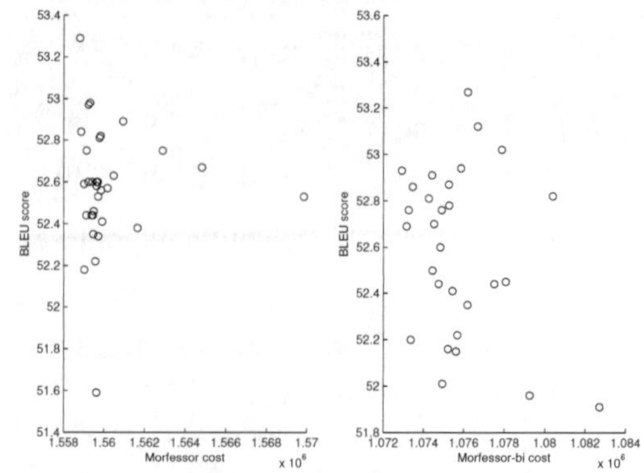


Figure 2: Cost-BLEU plots of Morfessor and Morfessor-bi. Correlation coefficients are -0.005 and -0.279, respectively.

are affected by the decision in the current step. This leads to a sequential search and does not lend itself to parallelization.

We propose a slightly modified search procedure, where the segmentation decisions are stored but not applied until the end of an iteration. In this way, the cost calculations (which is the most time-consuming component) can all be performed independently and in parallel. Since the model is not updated at every decision, the search path can differ from that in the sequential greedy search and hence result in different segmentations.

## 4 Results

We performed *in vivo* testing of the segmentation algorithm on the Turkish side of a Turkish-to-English task. We compared the segmentations produced by Morfessor, Morfessor modified for parallel search (Morfessor-p), and Morfessor with bilingual cost (Morfessor-bi) against the word-based performance. We used the ATR Basic Travel Expression Corpus (BTEC) (Kikui et al., 2006), which contains travel conversation sentences similar to those in phrase-books for tourists traveling abroad. The training corpus contained 19,972 sentences with average sentence length 5.6 and 7.7 words for Turkish and English, respectively. The test corpus consisted of 1,512 sentences with 16 reference translations. We used GIZA++ (Och and Ney, 2003) for post-segmentation token alignments and the Moses toolkit (Koehn et al., 2007) with default parameters for phrase-based translation model generation and decoding. Target language models were trained on the English side of the training corpus using the SRILM toolkit (Stolcke, 2002). The BLEU metric (Papineni et al., 2002) was used for translation evaluation.

Figure 1 compares the translation performance obtained using the described segmentation methods. All segmentation methods generally improve the translation performance (Morfessor and Morfessor-p) compared to the word-based models. However, Morfessor-bi, which utilizes both sides of the parallel corpus in segmenting, does not convincingly outperform the monolingual methods.

In order to investigate whether the proposed bilingual segmentation cost correlates any better than the monolingual segmentation cost of Morfessor, we show several cost-BLEU pairs obtained from the final and intermediate segmentations of Morfessor and Morfessor-bi in Fig. 2. The correlation coefficients show that the proposed bilingual metric is somewhat predictive of the translation performance as measured by BLEU, while the monolingual Morfessor cost metric has almost no correlation. Yet, the strong noise in the BLEU scores (vertical variation in Fig. 2) diminishes the effect of this correlation, which explains the inconsistency of the results in Fig. 1. Indeed, in our experiments even though the total cost kept decreasing at each iteration of the search algorithm, the BLEU scores obtained by those intermediate segmentations fluctuated without any consistent improvement.

Table 2 displays sample segmentations produced by both the monolingual and bilingual segmentation algorithms. We can observe that utilizing the English side of the corpus enabled

| Count | Morfessor | Morfessor-bi | English Gloss |
|---|---|---|---|
| 7 | anahtar | anahtar | (the) key |
| 6 | anahtar + ımı | anahtar + ımı | my key (*ACC.*) |
| 5 | anahtarla | anahtar + la | with (the) key |
| 4 | anahtarı | anahtar + ı | [1](the) key (*ACC.*); [2]his/her key |
| 3 | anahtarı + m | anahtar + ım | my key |
| 3 | anahtarı + n | anahtar + ın | [1]your key; [2]of (the) key |
| 1 | anahtarı + nız | anahtar + ınız | your (*pl.*) key |
| 1 | anahtarı + nı | anahtar + ını | [1]your key (*ACC.*); [2]his/her key (*ACC.*) |
| 1 | anahtar + ınızı | anahtar + ınızı | your (*pl.*) key (*ACC.*) |
| 1 | oyun + lar | oyunlar | (the) games |
| 2 | oyun + ları | oyunlar + ı | [1](the) games (*ACC.*); [2]his/her games; [3]their game(s) |
| 1 | oyun + ların | oyunlar + ı + n | [1]of (the) games; [2]your games |
| 1 | oyun + larınızı | oyunlar + ı + n + ızı | your (*pl.*) games (*ACC.*) |

Table 2: Sample segmentations produced by Morfessor and Morfessor-bi

Morfessor-bi: (i) to consistently identify the root word "anahtar" (top portion), and (ii) to match the English plural word form "games" with the Turkish plural word form "oyunlar" (bottom portion). Monolingual Morfessor is unaware of the target segmentation, and hence it is up to the subsequent translation model training to learn that "oyun" is sometimes translated as "game" and sometimes as "games" in the segmented training corpus.

## 5 Conclusion

We have presented a method for determining optimal sub-word translation units automatically from a parallel corpus. We have also showed a method of incrementally computing the first iteration parameters of IBM Model-1 between segmentation hypotheses. Being language-independent, the proposed algorithm can be added as a one-time preprocessing step prior to training in a SMT system without requiring any additional data/linguistic resources. The initial experiments presented here show that the translation units learned by the proposed algorithm improves on the word-based baseline in both translation directions.

One avenue for future work is to relax some of the several independence assumptions made in the generative model. For example, independence of consecutive morphs could be relaxed by an HMM model for transitions between morphs (Creutz and Lagus, 2007). Other future work includes optimizing the segmentation of both sides of the corpus and experimenting with other language pairs.

It is also possible that the probability distributions are not discriminative enough to outweigh the model prior tendencies since the translation probabilities are estimated only crudely (single iteration of Model-1 EM algorithm). A possible candidate solution would be to weigh the translation likelihood more in calculating the overall cost. In fact, this idea could be generalized into a log-linear modeling (e.g., (Poon et al., 2009)) of the various components of the joint corpus likelihood and possibly other features.

Finally, integration of sub-word segmentation with the phrasal lexicon learning process in SMT is desireable (e.g., translation-driven segmentation in Wu (1997)). Hierarchical models (Chiang, 2007) could cover this gap and provide a means to seamlessly integrate sub-word segmentation with statistical machine translation.

## Acknowledgements

The authors would like to thank Murat Saraçlar for valuable discussions and guidance in this work, and the anonymous reviewers for very useful comments and suggestions. Murat Saraçlar is supported by the TÜBA-GEBİP award.

## References

Arianna Bisazza and Marcello Federico. 2009. Morphological Pre-Processing for Turkish to English Statistical Machine Translation. In *Proc. of the International Workshop on Spoken Language Translation*, pages 129–135, Tokyo, Japan.

M.R. Brent. 1999. An efficient, probabilistically sound algorithm for segmentation and word discovery. *Machine Learning*, 34(1):71–105.

P.F. Brown, V.J. Della Pietra, S.A. Della Pietra, and R.L. Mercer. 1993. The mathematics of statistical machine translation: Parameter estimation. *Computational Linguistics*, 19(2):263–311.

Pi-Chuan Chang, Michel Galley, and Christopher D. Manning. 2008. Optimizing Chinese word segmentation for machine translation performance. In *Proceedings of the Third Workshop on Statistical Machine Translation*, pages 224–232, Columbus, Ohio.

David Chiang. 2007. Hierarchical phrase-based translation. *Computational Linguistics*, 33(2):201–228.

M. Creutz and K. Lagus. 2007. Unsupervised models for morpheme segmentation and morphology learning. *ACM Transactions on Speech and Language Processing*, 4(1):1–34.

Sajib Dasgupta and Vincent Ng. 2007. High-performance, language-independent morphological segmentation. In *Proceedings of HLT-NAACL*, pages 155–163, Rochester, New York.

İlknur Durgar El-Kahlout and Kemal Oflazer. 2006. Initial explorations in English to Turkish statistical machine translation. In *Proceedings of the Workshop on Statistical Machine Translation*, pages 7–14, New York City, New York, USA.

Jakob Elming, Nizar Habash, and Josep M. Crego. 2009. Combination of statistical word alignments based on multiple preprocessing schemes. In Cyrill Goutte, Nicola Cancedda, Marc Dymetman, and George Foster, editors, *Learning Machine Translation*, chapter 5, pages 93–110. MIT Press.

Nizar Habash and Fatiha Sadat. 2006. Arabic preprocessing schemes for statistical machine translation. In *Proc. of the HLT-NAACL, Companion Volume: Short Papers*, pages 49–52, New York City, USA.

G. Kikui, S. Yamamoto, T. Takezawa, and E. Sumita. 2006. Comparative study on corpora for speech translation. *IEEE Transactions on Audio, Speech and Language Processing*, 14(5):1674–1682.

Philipp Koehn, Hieu Hoang, Alexandra Birch, Chris Callison-Burch, Marcello Federico, Nicola Bertoldi, Brooke Cowan, Wade Shen, Christine Moran, Richard Zens, Chris Dyer, Ondrej Bojar, Alexandra Constantin, and Evan Herbst. 2007. Moses: Open source toolkit for statistical machine translation. In *Proceedings of the 45th Annual Meeting of the Association for Computational Linguistics, Companion Volume: Proceedings of the Demo and Poster Sessions*, pages 177–180, Prague, Czech Republic.

M. Kurimo, S. Virpioja, V.T. Turunen, G.W. Blackwood, and W. Byrne. 2009. Overview and Results of Morpho Challenge 2009. In *Working notes of the CLEF workshop*.

Young-Suk Lee. 2004. Morphological analysis for statistical machine translation. In *Proceedings of HLT-NAACL, Companion Volume: Short Papers*, pages 57–60, Boston, Massachusetts, USA.

Adam Lopez and Philip Resnik. 2006. Word-based alignment, phrase-based translation: What's the link? In *Proceedings of the 7th Conference of the Association for Machine Translation in the Americas (AMTA-06)*, pages 90–99.

Franz Josef Och and Hermann Ney. 2003. A systematic comparison of various statistical alignment models. *Computational Linguistics*, 29(1):19–51.

Kemal Oflazer and İlknur Durgar El-Kahlout. 2007. Exploring different representational units in English-to-Turkish statistical machine translation. In *Proceedings of the Second Workshop on Statistical Machine Translation*, pages 25–32, Prague, Czech Republic.

Kishore Papineni, Salim Roukos, Todd Ward, and Wei-Jing Zhu. 2002. BLEU: a method for automatic evaluation of machine translation. In *Proceedings of 40th Annual Meeting of the Association for Computational Linguistics*, pages 311–318, Philadelphia, Pennsylvania, USA.

Hoifung Poon, Colin Cherry, and Kristina Toutanova. 2009. Unsupervised morphological segmentation with log-linear models. In *Proceedings of HLT-NAACL*, pages 209–217, Boulder, Colorado.

Fatiha Sadat and Nizar Habash. 2006. Combination of Arabic preprocessing schemes for statistical machine translation. In *Proc. of the 21st International Conference on Computational Linguistics and 44th Annual Meeting of the Association for Computational Linguistics*, pages 1–8, Sydney, Australia.

Wade Shen, Brian Delaney, and Tim Anderson. 2007. The MIT-LL/AFRL IWSLT-2007 MT system. In *Proc. of the International Workshop on Spoken Language Translation*, Trento, Italy.

Benjamin Snyder and Regina Barzilay. 2008. Unsupervised multilingual learning for morphological segmentation. In *Proceedings of the 46th Annual Meeting of the Association for Computational Linguistics: HLT*, pages 737–745, Columbus, Ohio.

A. Stolcke. 2002. SRILM-an extensible language modeling toolkit. In *Seventh International Conference on Spoken Language Processing*, volume 3.

David Talbot and Miles Osborne. 2006. Modelling lexical redundancy for machine translation. In *Proceedings of the 21st International Conference on Computational Linguistics and 44th Annual Meeting of the Association for Computational Linguistics*, pages 969–976, Sydney, Australia.

S. Virpioja, J.J. Väyrynen, M. Creutz, and M. Sadeniemi. 2007. Morphology-aware statistical machine translation based on morphs induced in an unsupervised manner. In *Machine Translation Summit XI*, pages 491–498, Copenhagen, Denmark.

D. Wu. 1997. Stochastic inversion transduction grammars and bilingual parsing of parallel corpora. *Computational Linguistics*, 23(3):377–403.

# How spoken language corpora can refine current speech motor training methodologies

**Daniil Umanski, Niels O. Schiller**
Leiden Institute for Brain and Cognition
Leiden University, The Netherlands
daniil.umanski@gmail.com
N.O.Schiller@hum.leidenuniv.nl

**Federico Sangati**
Institute for Logic,
Language and Computation
University of Amsterdam, the Netherlands
f.sangati@uva.nl

**Abstract**

The growing availability of spoken language corpora presents new opportunities for enriching the methodologies of speech and language therapy. In this paper, we present a novel approach for constructing speech motor exercises, based on linguistic knowledge extracted from spoken language corpora. In our study with the Dutch Spoken Corpus, syllabic inventories were obtained by means of automatic syllabification of the spoken language data. Our experimental syllabification method exhibited a reliable performance, and allowed for the acquisition of syllabic tokens from the corpus. Consequently, the syllabic tokens were integrated in a tool for clinicians, a result which holds the potential of contributing to the current state of speech motor training methodologies.

## 1 Introduction

Spoken language corpora are often accessed by linguists, who need to manipulate specifically defined speech stimuli in their experiments. However, this valuable resource of linguistic information has not yet been systematically applied for the benefit of speech therapy methodologies. This is not surprising, considering the fact that spoken language corpora have only appeared relatively recently, and are still not easily accessible outside the NLP community. Existing applications for selecting linguistic stimuli, although undoubtedly useful, are not based on spoken language data, and are generally not designed for utilization by speech therapists per se (Aichert et al., 2005). As a first attempt to bridge this gap, a mechanism is proposed for utilizing the relevant linguistic information to the service of clinicians. In coordination with speech pathologists, the domain of speech motor training was identified as an appropriate area of application. The traditional speech motor programs are based on a rather static inventory of speech items, and clinicians do not have access to a modular way of selecting speech targets for training.

Therefore, in this project, we deal with developing an interactive interface to assist speech therapists with constructing individualized speech motor practice programs for their patients. The principal innovation of the proposed system in regard to existing stimuli selection applications is twofold: first, the syllabic inventories are derived from spoken word forms, and second, the selection interface is integrated within a broader platform for conducting speech motor practice.

## 2 Principles of speech motor practice

### 2.1 Speech Motor Disorders

Speech motor disorders (SMD) arise from neurological impairments in the motor systems involved in speech production. SMD include acquired and developmental forms of dysarthria and apraxia of speech. Dysarthria refers to the group of disorders associated with weakness, slowness and inability to coordinate the muscles used to produce speech (Duffy, 2005). Apraxia of speech (AOS) is referred to the impaired planning and programming of speech (Ziegler , 2008). Fluency disorders, namely stuttering and cluttering, although not always classified as SMD, have been extensively studied from the speech motor skill perspective (Van Lieshout et al., 2001).

### 2.2 Speech Motor Training

The goal of speech therapy with SMD patients is establishing and maintaining correct speech motor routines by means of practice. The process of learning and maintaining productive speech motor skills is referred to as speech motor training.



*Proceedings of the ACL 2010 Student Research Workshop*, pages 37–42,
Uppsala, Sweden, 13 July 2010. 

An insightful design of speech motor training exercises is crucial in order to achieve an optimal learning process, in terms of efficiency, retention, and transfer levels (Namasivayam, 2008).

Maas et al. (2008) make the attempt to relate findings from research on non-speech motor learning principles to the case of speech motor training. They outline a number of critical factors in the design of speech motor exercises. These factors include the training program structure, selection of speech items, and the nature of the provided feedback.

It is now generally agreed that speech motor exercises should involve simplified speech tasks. The use of non-sense syllable combinations is a generally accepted method for minimizing the effects of higher-order linguistic processing levels, with the idea of tapping as directly as possible to the motor component of speech production (Smits-Bandstra et al., 2006) .

### 2.3 Selection of speech items

The main considerations in selecting speech items for a specific patient are functional relevance and motor complexity. Functional relevance refers to the specific motor, articulatory or phonetic deficits, and consequently to the treatment goals of the patient. For example, producing correct stress patterns might be a special difficulty for one patient, while producing consonant clusters might be challenging for another. Relative motor complexity of speech segments is much less defined in linguistic terms than, for example, syntactic complexity (Kleinow et al., 2000). Although the part-whole relationship, which works well for syntactic constructions, can be applied to syllabic structures as well (e.g., 'flake' and 'lake'), it may not be the most suitable strategy.

However, in an original recent work, Ziegler presented a non-linear probabilistic model of the phonetic code, which involves units from a sub-segmental level up to the level of metrical feet (Ziegler , 2009). The model is verified on the basis of accuracy data from a large sample of apraxic speakers, and thus provides a quantitive index of a speech segment's motor complexity.

Taken together, it is evident that the task of selecting sets of speech items for an individualized, optimal learning process is far from obvious, and much can be done to assist the clinicians with going through this step.

## 3 The role of the syllable

The syllable is the primary speech unit used in studies on speech motor control (Namasivayam, 2008). It is also the basic unit used for constructing speech items in current methodologies of speech motor training (Kent, 2000). Since the choice of syllabic tokens is assumed to affect speech motor learning, it would be beneficial to have access to the syllabic inventory of the spoken language. Besides the inventory of spoken syllables, we are interested in the distribution of syllables across the language.

### 3.1 Syllable frequency effects

The observation that syllables exhibit an exponential distribution in English, Dutch and German has led researchers to infer the existence of a 'mental syllabary' component in the speech production model (Schiller et al., 1996). Since this hypothesis assumes that production of high frequency syllables relies on highly automated motor gestures, it bears direct consequences on the utility of speech motor exercises. In other words, manipulating syllable sets in terms of their relative frequency is expected to have an effect on the learning process of new motor gestures. This argument is supported by a number of empirical findings. In a recent study, Staiger et al. report that syllable frequency and syllable structure play a decisive role with respect to articulatory accuracy in the spontaneous speech production of patients with AOS (Staiger et al., 2008). Similarly, (Laganaro, 2008) confirms a significant effect of syllable frequency on production accuracy in experiments with speakers with AOS and speakers with conduction aphasia.

### 3.2 Implications on motor learning

In that view, practicing with high-frequency syllables could promote a faster transfer of skills to everyday language, as the most 'required' motor gestures are being strengthened. On the other hand, practicing with low-frequency syllables could potentially promote plasticity (or 'stretching' ) of the speech motor system, as the learner is required to assemble motor plans from scratch, similar to the process of learning to pronounce words in a foreign language. In the next section, we describe our study with the Spoken Dutch Corpus, and illustrate the performed data extraction strategies.

## 4 A study with the Spoken Dutch Corpus

The Corpus Gesproken Nederlands (CGN) is a large corpus of spoken Dutch[1]. The CGN contains manually verified phonetic transcriptions of 53,583 spoken forms, sampled from a wide variety of communication situations. A spoken form reports the phoneme sequence as it was actually uttered by the speaker as opposed to the canonical form, which represents how the same word would be uttered in principle.

### 4.1 Motivation for accessing spoken forms

In contrast to written language corpora, such as CELEX (Baayenet al., 1996), or even a corpus like TIMIT (Zue et al., 1996), in which speakers read prepared written material, spontaneous speech corpora offer an access to an informal, unscripted speech on a variety of topics, including speakers from a range of regional dialects, age and educational backgrounds.

Spoken language is a dynamic, adaptive, and generative process. Speakers most often deviate from the canonical pronunciation, producing segment reductions, deletions, insertions and assimilations in spontaneous speech (Mitterer, 2008). The work of Greenberg provides an in-depth account on the pronunciation variation in spoken English. A detailed phonetic transcription of the Switchboard corpus revealed that the spectral properties of many phonetic elements deviate significantly from their canonical form (Greenberg, 1999).

In the light of the apparent discrepancy between the canonical forms and the actual spoken language, it becomes apparent that deriving syllabic inventories from spoken word forms will approximate the reality of spontaneous speech production better than relying on canonical representations. Consequently, it can be argued that clinical applications will benefit from incorporating speech items which optimally converge with the 'live' realization of speech.

### 4.2 Syllabification of spoken forms

The syllabification information available in the CGN applies only to the canonical forms of words, and no syllabification of spoken word forms exists. The methods of automatic syllabification have been applied and tested exclusively on canonical word forms (Bartlett, 2007). In order to obtain the syllabic inventory of spoken language per se, a preliminary study on automatic syllabification of spoken word forms has been carried out. Two methods for dealing with the syllabification task were proposed, the first based on an n-gram model defined over sequences of phonemes, and the second based on statistics over syllable units. Both algorithms accept as input a list of possible segmentations of a given phonetic sequence, and return the one which maximizes the score of the specific function they implement. The list of possible segmentations is obtained by exhaustively generating all possible divisions of the sequence, satisfying the condition of keeping exactly one vowel per segment.

[1](see http://lands.let.kun.nl/cgn/)

### 4.3 Syllabification Methods

The first method is a reimplementation of the work of (Schmid et al., 2007). The authors describe the syllabification task as a tagging problem, in which each phonetic symbol of a word is tagged as either a syllable boundary ('B') or as a non-syllable boundary ('N'). Given a set of possible segmentations of a given word, the aim is to select the one, viz. the tag sequence $\hat{b}_1^n$, which is more probable for the given phoneme sequence $p_1^n$, as shown in equation (1). This probability in equations (3) is reduced to the joint probability of the two sequences: the denominator of equation (2) is in fact constant for the given list of possible syllabifications, since they all share the same sequence of phonemes. Equation (4) is obtained by introducing a Markovian assumption of order 3 in the way the phonemes and tags are jointly generated

$$\hat{b}_1^n = \arg\max_{b_1^n} P(b_1^n | p_1^n) \quad (1)$$

$$= \arg\max_{b_1^n} P(b_1^n, p_1^n)/P(p_1^n) \quad (2)$$

$$= \arg\max_{b_1^n} P(b_1^n, p_1^n) \quad (3)$$

$$= \arg\max_{b_1^n} \prod_{i=1}^{n+1} P(b_i, p_i | b_{i-3}^{i-1}, p_{i-3}^{i-1}) \quad (4)$$

The second syllabification method relies on statistics over the set of syllables unit and bigram (bisegments) present in the training corpus. Broadly speaking, given a set of possible segmentations of a given phoneme sequence, the algorithm, selects the one which maximizes the presence and frequency of its segments.

| Corpus | Phonemes | | Syllables | |
|---|---|---|---|---|
| | Boundaries | Words | Boundaries | Words |
| CGN_Dutch | 98.62 | 97.15 | 97.58 | 94.99 |
| CELEX_Dutch | 99.12 | 97.76 | 99.09 | 97.70 |
| CELEX_German | 99.77 | 99.41 | 99.51 | 98.73 |
| CELEX_English | 98.86 | 97.96 | 96.37 | 93.50 |

Table 1: Summary of syllabification results on canonical word forms.

### 4.4 Results

The first step involved the evaluation of the two algorithms on syllabification of canonical word forms. Four corpora comprising three different languages (English, German, and Dutch) were evaluated: the CELEX2 corpora (Baayenet al., 1996) for the three languages, and the Spoken Dutch Corpus (CGN). All the resources included manually verified syllabification transcriptions. A 10-fold cross validation on each of the corpora was performed to evaluate the accuracy of our methods. The evaluation is presented in terms of percentage of correct syllable boundaries[2], and percentage of correctly syllabified words.
Table 1 summarizes the obtained results. For the CELEX corpora, both methods produce almost equally high scores, which are comparable to the state of the art results reported in (Bartlett, 2007). For the Spoken Dutch Corpus, both methods demonstrate quite high scores, with the phoneme-level method showing an advantage, especially with respect to correctly syllabified words.

### 4.5 Data extraction

The process of evaluating syllabification of spoken word forms is compromised by the fact that there exists no gold annotation for the pronunciation data in the corpus. Therefore, the next step involved applying both methods on the data set and comparing the two solutions. The results revealed that the two algorithms agree on 94.29% of syllable boundaries and on 90.22% of whole word syllabification. Based on the high scores reported for lexical word forms syllabification, an agreement between both methods most probably implies a correct solution. The 'disagreement' set can be assumed to represent the class of ambiguous cases, which are the most problematic for automatic syllabification. As an example, consider the following pair of possible syllabification, on which the two methods disagree: 'bEl-kOm-pjut' vs 'bEl-kOmp-jut'[3].
Motivated by the high agreement score, we have applied the phoneme-based method on the spoken word forms in the CGN, and compiled a syllabic inventory. In total, 832,236 syllable tokens were encountered in the corpus, of them 11,054 unique syllables were extracted and listed. The frequencies distribution of the extracted syllabary, as can be seen in Figure 1, exhibits an exponential curve, a result consistent with earlier findings reported in (Schiller et al., 1996). According to our statistics, 4% of unique syllable tokens account for 80% of all extracted tokens, and 10% of unique syllables account for 90% respectively. For each extracted syllable, we have recorded its structure, frequency rank, and the articulatory characteristics of its consonants. Next, we describe the speech items selection tool for clinicians.

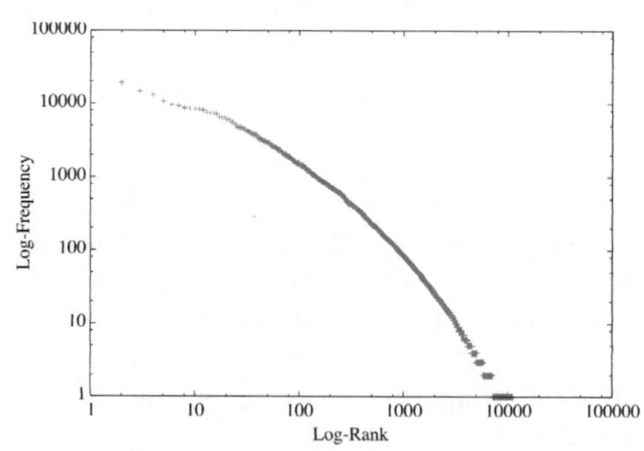


Figure 1: Syllable frequency distribution over the spoken forms in the Dutch Spoken Corpus.
The x-axis represents 625 ranked frequency bins. The y-axis plots the total number of syllable tokens extracted for each frequency bin.

[2]Note that recall and precision coincide since the number of boundaries (one less than the number of vowels) is constant for different segmentations of the same word.

[3]A manual evaluation of the disagreement set revealed a clear advantage for the phoneme-based method

## 5 An interface for clinicians

In order to make the collected linguistic information available for clinicians, an interface has been built which enables clinicians to compose individual training programs. A training program consists of several training sessions, which in turn consists of a number of exercises. For each exercise, a number of syllable sets are selected, according to the specific needs of the patient. The main function of the interface, thus, deals with selection of customized syllable sets, and is described next. The rest of the interface deals with the different ways in which the syllable sets can be grouped into exercises, and how exercises are scheduled between treatment sessions.

### 5.1 User-defined syllable sets

The process starts with selecting the number of syllables in the current set, a number between one and four. Consequently, the selected number of 'syllable boxes' appear on the screen. Each box allows for a separate configuration of one syllable group. As can be seen in Figure 2, a syllable box contains a number of menus, and a text grid at the bottom of the box.

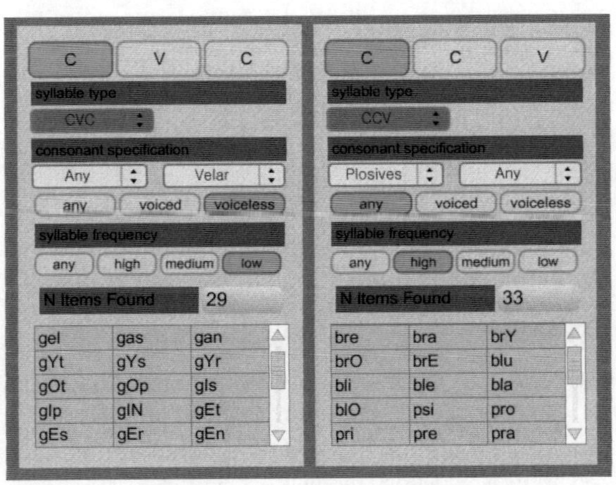


Figure 2: A snapshot of the part of the interface allowing configuration of syllable sets

Here follows the list of the parameters which the user can manipulate, and their possible values:

- Syllable Type[4]
- Syllable Frequency[5]
- Voiced - Unvoiced consonant [6]
- Manner of articulation[7]
- Place of articulation[8]

Once the user selects a syllable type, he/she can further specify each consonant within that syllable type in terms of voiced/unvoiced segment choice and manner and place of articulation. For the sake of simplicity, syllable frequency ranks have been divided in three rank groups. Alternatively, the user can bypass this criterion by selecting 'any'. As the user selects the parameters which define the desired syllable type, the text grid is continuously filled with the list of syllables satisfying these criteria, and a counter shows the number of syllables currently in the grid.
Once the configuration process is accomplished, the syllables which 'survived' the selection will constitute the speech items of the current exercise, and the user proceeds to select how the syllable sets should be grouped, scheduled and so on.

## 6 Final remarks

### 6.1 Future directions

A formal usability study is needed in order to establish the degree of utility and satisfaction with the interface. One question which demands investigation is the degrees of choice that the selection tool should provide. With too many variables and hinges of choice, the configuration process for each patient might become complicated and time consuming. Therefore, a usability study should provide guidelines for an optimal design of the interface, so that its utility for clinicians is maximized.
Furthermore, we plan to integrate the proposed interface within an computer-based interactive platform for speech therapy. A seamless integration of a speech items selection module within biofeedback games for performing exercises with these items seems straight forward, as the selected items can be directly embedded (e.g., as text symbols or more abstract shapes) in the graphical environment where the exercises take place.

[4]CV, CVC, CCV, CCVC, etc.

[5]Syllables are divided in three rank groups - high, medium, and low frequency.

[6]when applicable

[7]for a specific consonant. Plosives, Fricatives, Sonorants

[8]for a specific consonant. Bilabial, Labio-Dental, Alveolar, Post-Alveolar, Palatal, Velar, Uvular, Glottal

**Acknowledgments**

This research is supported with the 'Mosaic' grant from The Netherlands Organisation for Scientific Research (NWO). The authors are grateful for the anonymous reviewers for their constructive feedback.

## References

Aichert, I., Ziegler, W. 2004. *Syllable frequency and syllable structure in apraxia of speech.* Brain and Language, 88, 148-159.

Aichert, I., Marquardt, C., Ziegler, W. 2005. *Frequenzen sublexikalischer Einheiten des Deutschen: CELEX-basierte Datenbanken.* Neurolinguistik, 19, 55-81

Baayen R.H., Piepenbrock R. and Gulikers L. 1996. *CELEX2. Linguistic Data Consortium, Philadelphia.*

Bartlett, S. 2007. *Discriminative approach to automatic syllabication.* Masters thesis, Departmentof-Computing Science, University of Alberta.

Duffy, J.R 2005. *Motor speech disorder: Substrates, Differential Diagnosis, and Management.* (2nd Ed.) 507-524. St. Louis, MO: Elsevier Mosby

Greenberg, S. 1999. *Speaking in shorthanda syllable-centric perspective for understanding pronunciation variation.* Speech Comm., 29(2-4):159-176

Kent, R. 2000. *Research on speech motor control and its disorders, a review and prospectives.* Speech Comm., 29(2-4):159-176 J.

Kleinow, J., Smith, A. 2000. *Inuences of length and syntactic complexity on the speech motor stability of the uent speech of adults who stutter.* Journal of Speech, Language, and Hearing Research, 43, 548559.

Laganaro, M. 2008. *Is there a syllable frequency effect in aphasia or in apraxia of speech or both?* Aphasiology, Volume 22, Number 11, November 2008 , pp. 1191-1200(10)

Maas, E., Robin, D.A., Austermann Hula, S.N., Freedman, S.E., Wulf, G., Ballard, K.J., Schmidt, R.A. 2008. *Principles of Motor Learning in Treatment of Motor Speech Disorders* American Journal of Speech-Language Pathology, 17, 277-298.

Mitterer, H. 2008. *How are words reduced in spontaneous speech?* In A. Botinis (Ed.), Proceedings of the ISCA Tutorial and Research Workshop on Experimental Linguistics (pages 165-168). University of Athens.

Namasivayam, A.K., van Lieshout, P. 2008. *Investigating speech motor practice and learning in people who stutter* Journal of Fluency Disorders 33 (2008) 3251

Schiller, N. O., Meyer, A. S., Baayen, R. H., Levelt, W. J. M. 1996. *A Comparison of Lexeme and Speech Syllables in Dutch.* Journal of Quantitative Linguistics, 3, 8-28.

Schmid H., Möbius B. and Weidenkaff J. 2007. *Tagging Syllable Boundaries With Joint N-Gram Models.* Proceedings of Interspeech-2007 (Antwerpen), pages 2857-2860.

Smits-Bandstra, S., DeNil, L. F., Saint-Cyr, J. 2006. *Speech and non-speech sequence skill learning in adults who stutter.* Journal of Fluency Disorders, 31,116136.

Staiger, A., Ziegler, W. 2008. *Syllable frequency and syllable structure in the spontaneous speech production of patients with apraxia of speech.* Aphasiology, Volume 22, Number 11, November 2008 , pp. 1201-1215(15)

Tjaden, K. 2000. *Exploration of a treatment technique for prosodic disturbance following stroke training.* Clinical Linguistics and Phonetics 2000, Vol. 14, No. 8, Pages 619-641

Riley, J., Riley, G. 1995. *Speech motor improvement program for children who stutter.* In C.W. Starkweather, H.F.M. Peters (Eds.), Stuttering (pp.269-272) New York: Elsevier

Van Lieshout, P. H. H. M. 2001. *Recent developments in studies of speech motor control in stuttering.* In B. Maassen, W. Hulstijn, R. D. Kent, H. F. M. Peters, P. H. H. M. Van Lieshout (Eds.), Speech motor control in normal and disordered speech(pp. 286290). Nijmegen, The Netherlands:Vantilt.

Ziegler W. 2009. *Modelling the architecture of phonetic plans: Evidence from apraxia of speech.* Language and Cognitive Processes 24, 631 - 661

Ziegler W. 2008. *Apraxia of speech.* In: Goldenberg G, Miller B (Eds.), Handbook of Clinical Neurology, Vol. 88 (3rd series), pp. 269 - 285. Elsevier. London

Zue, V.W. and Seneff, S. 1996. *"Transcription and alignment of the TIMIT database.* In Recent Research Towards Advanced Man-Machine Interface Through Spoken Language. H. Fujisaki (ed.), Amsterdam: Elsevier, 1996, pp. 515-525.

# Mood Patterns and Affective Lexicon Access in Weblogs

**Thin Nguyen**
Curtin University of Technology
Bentley, WA 6102, Australia
thin.nguyen@postgrad.curtin.edu.au

## Abstract

The emergence of social media brings chances, but also challenges, to linguistic analysis. In this paper we investigate a novel problem of discovering patterns based on emotion and the association of moods and affective lexicon usage in blogosphere, a representative for social media. We propose the use of normative emotional scores for English words in combination with a psychological model of emotion measurement and a nonparametric clustering process for inferring meaningful emotion patterns automatically from data. Our results on a dataset consisting of more than 17 million mood-groundtruthed blogposts have shown interesting evidence of the emotion patterns automatically discovered that match well with the core-affect emotion model theorized by psychologists. We then present a method based on information theory to discover the association of moods and affective lexicon usage in the new media.

## 1 Introduction

Social media provides communication and interaction channels where users can freely participate in, express their opinions, make their own content, and interact with other users. Users in this new media are more comfortable in expressing their feelings, opinions, and ideas. Thus, the resulting user-generated content tends to be more subjective than other written genres, and thus, is more appealing to be investigated in terms of subjectivity and sentiment analysis. Research in sentiment analysis has recently attracted much attention (Pang and Lee, 2008), but modeling emotion patterns and studying the affective lexicon used in social media have received little attention.

Work in sentiment analysis in social media is often limited to finding the sentiment sign in the dipole pattern (negative/positive) for given text. Extensions to this task include the three-class classification (adding neutral to the polarity) and locating the value of emotion the text carries across a spectrum of valence scores. On the other hand, it is well appreciated by psychologists that sentiment has much richer structures than the aforementioned simplified polarity. For example, emotion – a form of expressive sentiment – was suggested by psychologists to be measured in terms of *valence* and *arousal* (Russell, 2009). Thus, we are motivated to analyze the sentiment in blogosphere in a more fine-grained fashion. In this paper we study the grouping behaviors of the emotion, or emotion patterns, expressed in the blogposts. We are inspired to get insights into the question of whether these structures can be discovered directly from data without the cost of involving human participants as in traditional psychological studies. Next, we aim to study the relationship between the data-driven emotion structures discovered and those proposed by psychologists.

Work on the analysis of effects of sentiment on lexical access is great in a psychology perspective. However, to our knowledge, limited work exists to examine the same tasks in social media context.

The contribution in this paper is twofold. To our understanding, we study a novel problem of emotion-based pattern discovery in blogosphere. We provide an initial solution for the matter using a combination of psychological models, affective norm scores for English words, a novel feature representation scheme, and a nonparametric clustering to automatically group moods into meaningful emotion patterns. We believe that we are the first to consider the matter of data-driven emotion pattern discovery at the scale presented in this



*Proceedings of the ACL 2010 Student Research Workshop*, pages 43–48,
Uppsala, Sweden, 13 July 2010. 

paper. Secondly, we explore a novel problem of detecting the mood – affective lexicon usage correlation in the new media, and propose a novel use of a term-goodness criterion to discover this sentiment – linguistic association.

## 2 Related Work

Much work in sentiment analysis measures the value of emotion the text convey in a continuum range of valence (Pang and Lee, 2008). Emotion patterns have often been used in sentiment analysis limited to this one-dimensional formulation. On the other hand, in psychology, emotions have often been represented in dimensional and discrete perspectives. In the former, emotion states are conceptualized as combinations of some factors like valence and arousal. In contrast, the latter style argues that each emotion has a unique coincidence of experience, psychology and behavior (Mauss and Robinson, 2009). Our work utilizes the dimensional representation, and in particular, the core-affect model (Russell, 2009), which encodes emotion states along the valence and arousal dimensions. The sentiment scoring for emotion bearing words is available in a lexicon known as Affective Norms for English Words (ANEW) (Bradley and Lang, 1999). Related work making use of ANEW includes (Dodds and Danforth, 2009) for estimating happiness levels in three types of data: song lyrics, blogs, and the State of the Union addresses.

From a psychological perspective, for estimating mood effects in lexicon decisions, (Chastain et al., 1995) investigates the influence of moods on the access of affective words. For learning affect in blogosphere, (Leshed and Kaye, 2006) utilizes Support Vector Machines (SVM) to predict moods for coming blog posts and detect mood synonymy.

## 3 Moods and Affective Lexicon Access

### 3.1 Mood Pattern Detection

Livejournal provides a comprehensive set of 132 moods for users to tag their moods when blogging. The provided moods range diversely in the emotion spectrum but typically are observed to fall into soft clusters such as happiness (*cheerful* or *grateful*) or sadness (*discontent* or *uncomfortable*). We call each cluster of these moods an *emotion pattern* and aim to detect them in this paper.

We observe that the blogposts tagged with moods in the same emotion pattern have similar

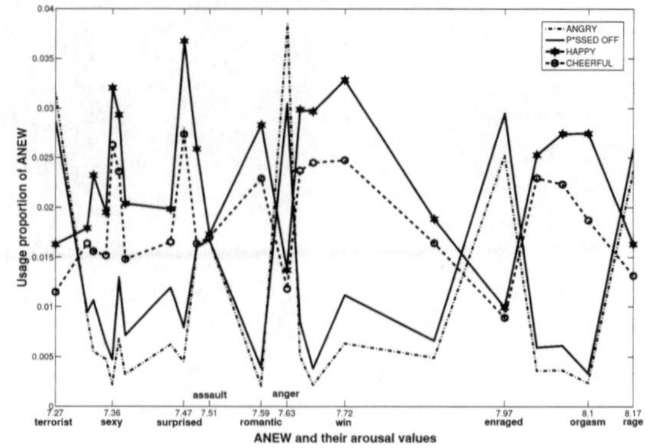


Figure 1: ANEW usage proportion in the posts tagged with *happy/cheerful* and *angry/p*ssed off*

proportions in the usage of ANEW. For example, in Figure 1 – a plot of the usage of ANEW having arousal in the range of 7.2 – 8.2 in the blogposts – we could see that the ANEW usage patterns of *happy/cheerful* and *angry/p*ssed off* are well separated. *Anger*, *enraged*, and *rage* will be most likely found in the *angry/p*ssed off* tagged posts and least likely found in the *happy/cheerful* ones. In contrast, the ANEW as *romantic* or *surprised* are not commonly used in the posts tagged with *angry/p*ssed off* but most popularly used in the *happy/cheerful* ones; suggesting that, the similarity between ANEW usage patterns can be used as a basis to study the structure of mood space.

Let us denote by $\mathcal{B}$ the corpus of all blogposts and by $\mathcal{M}$= {*sad, happy, ...*} the predefined set of moods ($|\mathcal{M}| = 132$). Each blogpost $b \in \mathcal{B}$ in the corpus is labeled with a mood $l_b \in \mathcal{M}$. Denote by $n$ the number of ANEW ($n = 1034$). Let $\boldsymbol{x}^m = [\boldsymbol{x}_1^m, ..., \boldsymbol{x}_i^m, ..., \boldsymbol{x}_n^m]$ be the vector representing the usage of ANEW by the mood $m$. Thus, $\boldsymbol{x}_i^m = \sum_{b \in \mathcal{B}, l_b = m} c_{ib}$, where $c_{ib}$ is the counting of the ANEW $i$-th occurrence in the blogpost $b$ tagged with the mood $m$. The usage vector is normalized so that $\sum_{i=1}^n \boldsymbol{x}_i^m = 1$ for all $m \in \mathcal{M}$. To discover the grouping of the moods based on the usage vectors we use a nonparametric clustering algorithm known as Affinity Propagation (AP) (Frey and Dueck, 2007). AP is desirable here because it automatically discovers the number of clusters as well as the cluster exemplars. The algorithm only requires the pairwise similarities between moods, which we compute based on the Euclidean distances for simplicity.

To map the emotion patterns detected to their psychological meaning, we proceed to measure the sentiment scores of those $|\mathcal{M}|$ mood words. In particular, we use ANEW (Bradley and Lang, 1999), which is a set of 1034 sentiment conveying English words. The valence and arousal of moods are assigned by those of the same words in the ANEW lexicon. For those moods which are not in ANEW, their values are assigned by those of the nearest father words in the mood hierarchical tree[1], where those moods conveying the same meaning, to some extent, are in the same level of the tree. Thus, each member of the mood clusters can be placed onto the a 2D representation along the valence and arousal dimensions, making it feasible to compare with the *core-affect* model (Russell, 2009) theorized by psychologists.

### 3.2 Mood and ANEW Usage Association

To study the statistical strength of an ANEW word with respect to a particular mood, the information gain measure (Mitchell, 1997) is adopted. Given a collection of blog posts $\mathcal{B}$ consisting of those tagged or not tagged with a target class attribute mood $m$. The entropy of $\mathcal{B}$ relative to this binary classification is

$$\mathcal{H}(\mathcal{B}) = -p_{\oplus} \log_2(p_{\oplus}) - p_{\ominus} \log_2 p_{\ominus}$$

where $p_{\oplus}$ and $p_{\ominus}$ are the proportions of the posts tagged and not tagged with $m$ respectively.

The entropy of $\mathcal{B}$ relative to the binary classification given a binary attribute $A$ (e.g. if the word $A$ present or not) observed is computed as

$$\mathcal{H}(\mathcal{B}|A) = \frac{|\mathcal{B}_{\oplus}|}{|\mathcal{B}|}\mathcal{H}(\mathcal{B}_{\oplus}) + \frac{|\mathcal{B}_{\ominus}|}{|\mathcal{B}|}\mathcal{H}(\mathcal{B}_{\ominus})$$

where $\mathcal{B}_{\oplus}$ is the subset of $\mathcal{B}$ for which attribute $A$ is present in the corpus and $\mathcal{B}_{\ominus}$ is the subset of $\mathcal{B}$ for which attribute $A$ is absent in the corpus.

The information gain of an attribute ANEW $A$ in classifying the collection with respect to the target class attribute mood $m$, $IG(m, A)$, is the reduction in entropy caused by partitioning the examples according to the attribute $A$. Thus,

$$IG(m, A) = \mathcal{H}(\mathcal{B}) - \mathcal{H}(\mathcal{B}|A)$$

With respect to a given mood $m$, those ANEW having high information gain are considered likely to be associated with the mood. This measure, also often considered a term-goodness criterion, outperforms others in feature selection in text categorization (Yang and Pedersen, 1997).

[1] http://www.livejournal.com/moodlist.bml

## 4 Experimental Results

### 4.1 Mood Patterns

We use a large Livejournal blogpost dataset, which contains more than 17 million blogposts tagged with the predefined moods. These journals were posted from May 1, 2001 to April 23, 2005. The ANEW usage vectors of all moods are subjected to a clustering to learn emotion patterns. After running the Affinity Propagation algorithm, 16 patterns of moods are clustered as below (the moods in upper case are the exemplars).

---

1. CHEERFUL, ecstatic, jubilant, giddy, happy, excited, energetic, bouncy, chipper
2. PENSIVE, determined, contemplative, thoughtful
3. REJUVENATED, optimistic, relieved, refreshed, hopeful, peaceful
4. QUIXOTIC, surprised, enthralled, devious, geeky, creative, recumbent, artistic, impressed, amused, complacent, curious, weird
5. CRAZY, horny, giggly, high, flirty, hyper, drunk, naughty, dorky, ditzy, silly
6. MELLOW, pleased, satisfied, relaxed, content, anxious, good, full, calm, okay
7. GRATEFUL, loved, thankful, touched
8. AGGRAVATED, irritated, bitchy, annoyed, frustrated, cynical
9. ANGRY, p*ssed off, infuriated, irate, enraged
10. GLOOMY, jealous, envious, rejected, confused, worried, lonely, guilty, scared, pessimistic, discontent, distressed, indescribable, crushed, depressed, melancholy, numb, morose, sad, sympathetic
11. PRODUCTIVE, accomplished, working, nervous, busy, rushed
12. TIRED, sore, lazy, sleepy, awake, groggy, exhausted, lethargic, drained
13. NAUSEATED, sick
14. MOODY, disappointed, grumpy, cranky, stressed, uncomfortable, crappy
15. THIRSTY, nerdy, mischievous, hungry, dirty, hot, cold, bored, blah
16. EXANIMATE, intimidated, predatory, embarrassed, restless, nostalgic, indifferent, listless, apathetic, blank, shocked

---

Generally, the patterns 1–7 contain moods in high valence (pleasure) and the patterns 8–16 include mood in low valence (displeasure). To examine whether members in these emotion patterns

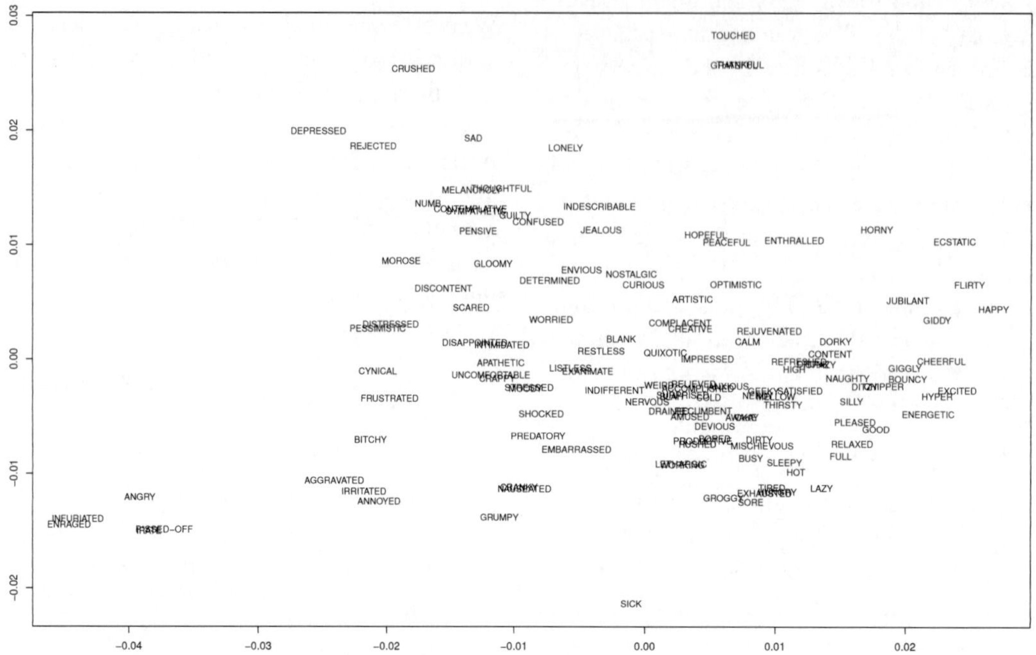


Figure 2: Projection of moods onto a 2D mesh using classical multidimensional scaling

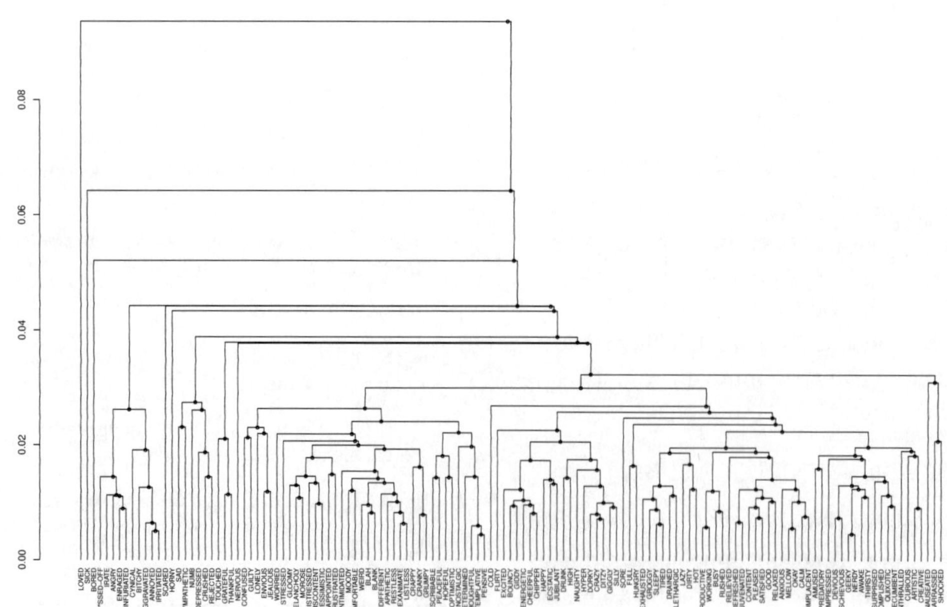


Figure 3: The clustered patterns in a dendrogram using hierarchical clustering

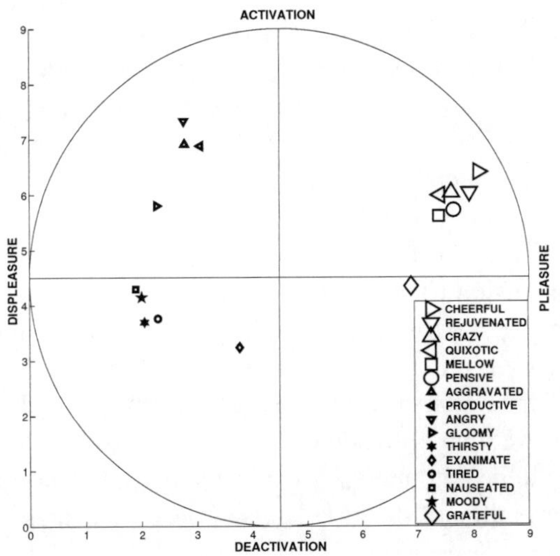


Figure 4: Discovered emotion patterns in the affect circle

follow an affect concept, we place them on the affect circle (Russell, 2009). We learn that nearly all members in the same patterns express a common affect concept. Those moods in the patterns with *cheerful*, *pensive*, and *rejuvenated* as the exemplars are mostly located in the first quarter of the affect circle ($0^0$ – $90^0$), which should contain moods being high in both pleasure and activation measures. Meanwhile, many members of the *angry* and *aggravated* patterns are found in the second quarter ($90^0$ – $180^0$), which roughly means that those moods express the feeling of sadness in the high of activation. The patterns with the exemplars *nauseated* and *tired* contain a majority of moods found in the third quarter ($180^0$ – $270^0$), which could be representatives for the mood fashion of sadness and deactivation. In addition, the *grateful* group could be a representative for moods which are both low in pleasure and in the degree of activation ($270^0$ – $360^0$ of the affect circle). Thus, the clustering process based on the ANEW usage could separate moods having similar affect scores into corresponding segments in the circle proposed in (Russell, 2009).

To visualize mood patterns that have been detected, we plot these emotion modes on the affect circle plane in Figure 4. For each pattern, the valence and arousal are computed by averaging of the values of those moods in the quarter where most of the members in the pattern are.

To further visualize the similarity of moods, the ANEW usage vectors are subject to a classical multidimensional scaling (Borg and Groenen,

| Mood | Top ANEW words associated |
|---|---|
| Cheerful | fun, happy, hate, good, christmas, merry, birthday, cute, sick, love |
| Happy | happy, hate, fun, good, birthday, sick, love, mind, alone, bored |
| Angry | angry, hate, fun, mad, love, anger, good, stupid, pretty, movie |
| P*ssed off | hate, stupid, mad, love, hell, fun, good, god, pretty, movie |
| Gloomy | sad, depressed, hate, wish, life, alone, lonely, upset, pain, heart |
| Sad | sad, fun, heart, upset, wish, funeral, hurt, pretty, loved, cancer |

(a) Moods and the most associated ANEW words

| ANEW | Most likely moods | Least likely moods |
|---|---|---|
| Desire | contemplative, thoughtful | enraged, drained |
| Anger | angry, p*ssed off | nauseated, grateful |
| Accident | sore, bored | exanimate, indifferent |
| Terrorist | angry, cynical | rejuvenated, touched |
| Wine | drunk, p*ssed off | ditzy, okay |

(b) ANEW words and the most associated moods

Table 1: Mood and ANEW correlation

2005) (MDS) and a hierarchical clustering. Figure 2 and Figure 3 show views of the distance between moods, based on the Euclidean measure of their corresponding ANEW usage, using MDS and hierarchical clustering respectively.

### 4.2 Mood and ANEW Association

Based on the IG values between moods and ANEW, we learn the correlation of moods and the affective lexicon. With respect to a given mood, those ANEW having high information gain are most likely to be found in the blogposts tagged with the mood. The ANEW most likely happened in the blogposts tagged with a given mood are shown in Table 1a; the most likely moods for the blog posts containing a given ANEW are shown in Table 1b.

The ANEW used in the blog posts tagged with moods in the same pattern are more similar than those in the posts tagged with moods in different patterns. In Table 1a, the most associated ANEW

Figure 5: Top 100 ANEW words used in the dataset

in the blogposts tagged with *cheerful* are more similar to those in *happy* ones than those in *angry* or *p*ssed off* ones.

For a given mood, a majority of the ANEW used in the blog posts tagged with the mood is similar in the valence with the mood. The occurrence of some ANEW having valence much different with the tagging mood, e.g. the ANEW *hate* in the posts tagged with *cheerful* or *happy* moods, might be the result of a negation construction used in the text or of other context.

For a given ANEW, the most likely moods tagged to the blog posts containing the word are similar with the word in the affective scores. In addition, the least likely moods are much different with the ANEW in the affect measure. A plot of top ANEWs used in the blogposts is shown in Figure 5.

Other than the ANEW conveying abstract concept, e.g. *desire* or *anger*, those ANEW expressing more concrete existence, e.g. *terrorist* or *accident*, might be a good source for learning opinions from social network towards the things. In the corpus, the posts containing the ANEW *terrorist* are most likely tagged with *angry* or *cynical* moods. Also, the posts containing the ANEW *accident* are most likely tagged with *bored* and *sore* moods.

## 5 Conclusion and Future Work

We have investigated the problems of emotion-based pattern discovery and mood – affective lexicon usage correlation detection in blogosphere. We presented a method for feature representation based on the affective norms of English scores usage. We then presented an unsupervised approach using Affinity Propagation, a nonparametric clustering algorithm that does not require the number of clusters a priori, for detecting emotion patterns in blogosphere. The results are showing that those automatically discovered patterns match well with the core-affect model for emotion, which is independently formulated in the psychology literature. In addition, we proposed a novel use of a term-goodness criterion to discover mood–lexicon correlation in blogosphere, giving hints on predicting moods based on the affective lexicon usage and vice versa in the social media. Our results could also have potential uses in sentiment-aware social media applications.

Future work will take into account the temporal dimension to trace changes in mood patterns over time in blogosphere. Another direction is to integrate negation information to learn more cohesive association in affect scores between moods and affective words. In addition, a new affective lexicon could be automatically detected based on learning correlation of the blog text and the moods tagged.

## References

I. Borg and P.J.F. Groenen. 2005. *Modern multidimensional scaling: Theory and applications*. Springer Verlag.

M.M. Bradley and P.J. Lang. 1999. Affective norms for English words (ANEW): Stimuli, instruction manual and affective ratings. Technical report, University of Florida.

G. Chastain, P.S. Seibert, and F.R. Ferraro. 1995. Mood and lexical access of positive, negative, and neutral words. *Journal of General Psychology*, 122(2):137–157.

P.S. Dodds and C.M. Danforth. 2009. Measuring the happiness of large-scale written expression: Songs, blogs, and presidents. *Journal of Happiness Studies*, pages 1–16.

B.J. Frey and D. Dueck. 2007. Clustering by passing messages between data points. *Science*, 315(5814):972.

G. Leshed and J.J. Kaye. 2006. Understanding how bloggers feel: recognizing affect in blog posts. In *Proc. of ACM Conf. on Human Factors in Computing Systems (CHI)*.

I.B. Mauss and M.D. Robinson. 2009. Measures of emotion: A review. *Cognition & emotion*, 23:2(2):209–237.

T. Mitchell. 1997. *Machine Learning*. McGraw Hill.

B. Pang and L. Lee. 2008. Opinion mining and sentiment analysis. *Foundations and Trends in Information Retrieval*, 2(1-2):1–135.

J.A. Russell. 2009. Emotion, core affect, and psychological construction. *Cognition & Emotion*, 23:7(1):1259–1283.

Y. Yang and J.O. Pedersen. 1997. A comparative study on feature selection in text categorization. In *Proc. of Intl. Conf. on Machine Learning (ICML)*, pages 412–420.

# Growing Related Words from Seed via User Behaviors: A Re-ranking Based Approach

**Yabin Zheng** **Zhiyuan Liu** **Lixing Xie**
State Key Laboratory on Intelligent Technology and Systems
Tsinghua National Laboratory for Information Science and Technology
Department of Computer Science and Technology, Tsinghua University, Beijing 100084,China
{yabin.zheng, lzy.thu, lavender087}@gmail.com

## Abstract

Motivated by Google Sets, we study the problem of growing related words from a single seed word by leveraging user behaviors hiding in user records of Chinese input method. Our proposed method is motivated by the observation that the more frequently two words co-occur in user records, the more related they are. First, we utilize user behaviors to generate candidate words. Then, we utilize search engine to enrich candidate words with adequate semantic features. Finally, we reorder candidate words according to their semantic relatedness to the seed word. Experimental results on a Chinese input method dataset show that our method gains better performance.

## 1 Introduction

What is the relationship between "自然语言处理" (Natural Language Processing) and "人工智能" (Artificial Intelligence)? We may regard NLP as a research branch of AI. Problems arise when we want to find more words related to the input query/seed word. For example, if seed word "自然语言处理" (Natural Language Processing) is entered into Google Sets (Google, 2010), Google Sets returns an ordered list of related words such as "人工智能" (Artificial Intelligence) and "计算机" (Computer). Generally speaking, it performs a large-scale clustering algorithm that can gather related words.

In this paper, we want to investigate the advantage of user behaviors and re-ranking framework in related words retrieval task using Chinese input method user records. We construct a User-Word bipartite graph to represent the information hiding in user records. The bipartite graph keeps users on one side and words on the other side. The underlying idea is that the more frequently two words co-occur in user records, the more related they are. For example, "机器翻译" (Machine Translation) is quite related to "中文分词" (Chinese Word Segmentation) because the two words are usually used together by researchers in natural language processing community. As a result, user behaviors offer a new perspective for measuring relatedness between words. On the other hand, we can also recommend related words to users in order to enhance user experiences. Researchers are always willing to accept related terminologies in their research fields.

However, the method is purely statistics based if we only consider co-occurrence aspect. We want to add semantic features. Sahami and Helman (2006) utilize search engine to supply web queries with more semantic context and gains better results for query suggestion task. We borrow their idea in this paper. User behaviors provide statistic information to generate candidate words. Then, we can enrich candidate words with additional semantic features using search engine to retrieve more relevant candidates earlier. Statistical and semantic features can complement each other. Therefore, we can gain better performance if we consider them together.

The contributions of this paper are threefold. First, we introduce user behaviors in related word retrieval task and construct a User-Word bipartite graph from user behaviors. Words are used by users, and it is reasonable to measure relatedness between words by analyzing user behaviors. Second, we take the advantage of semantic features using search engine to reorder candidate words. We aim to return more relevant candidates earlier. Finally, our method is unsupervised and language independent, which means that we do not require any training set or manual labeling efforts.

The rest of the paper is organized as follows. Some related works are discussed in Section 2. Then we introduce our method for related words retrieval in Section 3. Experiment results and discussions are showed in Section 4. Finally, Section 5 concludes the whole paper and gives some future works.



*Proceedings of the ACL 2010 Student Research Workshop*, pages 49–54,
Uppsala, Sweden, 13 July 2010. ©2010 Association for Computational Linguistics

## 2 Related Work

For related words retrieval task, Google Sets (Google, 2010) provides a remarkably interesting tool for finding words related to an input word. As stated in (Zheng et al., 2009), Google Sets performs poor results for input words in Chinese language. Bayesian Sets (Ghahramani and Heller, 2006) offers an alternative method for related words retrieval under the framework of Bayesian inference. It computes a score for each candidate word by comparing the posterior probability of that word given the input, to the prior probability of that candidate word. Then, it returns a ranked list of candidate words according to their computed scores.

Recently, Zheng et al. (2009) introduce user behaviors in new word detection task via a collaborative filtering manner. They extend their method to related word retrieval task. Moreover, they prove that user behaviors provide a new point for new word detection and related word retrieval tasks. However, their method is purely statistical method without considering semantic features.

We can regard related word retrieval task as problem of measuring the semantic relatedness between pairs of very short texts. Sahami and Helman (2006) introduce a web kernel function for measuring semantic similarities using snippets of search results. This work is followed by Metzler et al., (2007), Yih and Meek, (2007). They combine the web kernel with other metrics of similarity between word vectors, such as Jaccard Coefficient and KL Divergence to enhance the result.

In this paper, we follow the similar idea of using search engine to enrich semantic features of a query word. We regard the returned snippets as the context of a query word. And then we reorder candidate words and expect more relevant candidate words can be retrieved earlier. More details are given in Section 3.

## 3 Related Words Retrieval

In this section, we will introduce how to find related words from a single seed word via user behaviors and re-ranking framework.

First, we introduce the dataset utilized in this paper. All the resource used in this paper comes from Sogou Chinese pinyin input method (Sogou, 2006). We use Sogou for abbreviation hereafter. Users can install Sogou on their computers and the word lists they have used are kept in their user records. Volunteers are encouraged to upload their anonymous user records to the server side. In order to preserve user privacy, usernames are hidden using MD5 hash algorithm.

Then we demonstrate how to build a User-Word bipartite graph based on the dataset. The construction can be accomplished while traversing the dataset with linear time cost. We will give more details in Section 3.1.

Second, we adopt conditional probability (Deshpande and Karypis, 2004) to measure the relatedness of two words. Intuitively, two words are supposed to be related if there are a lot of users who have used both of them. In other words, the two words always co-occur in user records. Starting from a single seed word, we can generate a set of candidate words. This is the candidate generation step.

Third, in order to take the advantage of semantic features, we carry out feature extraction techniques to represent generated candidate words with enriched semantic context. In this paper, we generally make use of search engine to conduct the feature extraction step. After this step, input seed word and candidate words are represented as feature vectors in the vector space.

Finally, we can reorder generated candidate words according to their semantic relatedness of the input seed word. We expect to retrieve more relevant candidate words earlier. We will make further explanations about the mentioned steps in the next subsections.

### 3.1 Bipartite Graph Construction

As stated before, we first construct a User-Word bipartite graph from the dataset. The bipartite graph has two layers, with users on one side and the words on the other side. We traverse the user records, and add a link between user $u$ and word $w$ if $w$ appears in the user record of $u$. Thus this procedure can be accomplished in linear time.

In order to give better explanations of bipartite graph construction step, we show some user records in Figure 1 and the corresponding bipartite graph in Figure 2.

Fig. 1. User Records Sample

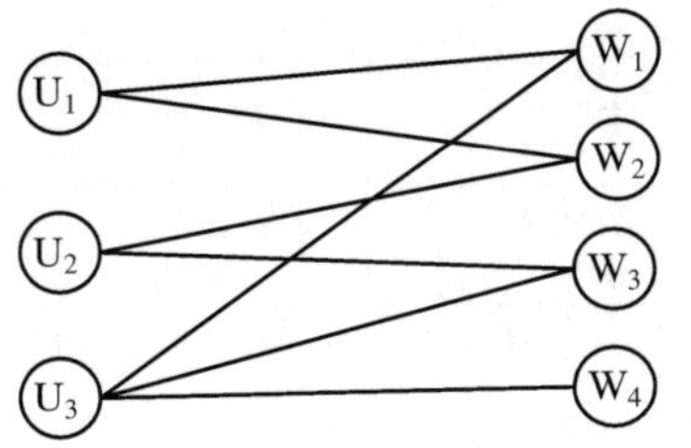


Fig. 2. Corresponding Bipartite Graph

From Figure 1, we can see that $Word_1$ and $Word_2$ appear in $User_1$'s record, which indicates that $User_1$ has used $Word_1$ and $Word_2$. As a result, in Figure 2, node $User_1$ is linked with node $Word_1$ and $Word_2$. The rest can be done in the same manner.

### 3.2 Candidates Generation

After the construction of bipartite graph, we can measure the relatedness of words from the bipartite graph. Intuitively, if two words always co-occur in user records, they are related to each other. Inspired by (Deshpande and Karypis, 2004), we adopt conditional probability to measure the relatedness of two words.

In particular, the conditional probability of word *j* occurs given that word *i* has already appeared is the number of users that used both word *i* and word *j* divided by the total number of users that used word *i*.

$$P(j \mid i) = \frac{Freq(ij)}{Freq(i)} \quad (1)$$

In formula 1, *Freq(X)* is the number of users that have used words in the set *X*. We can clearly see that $P(j|i) \neq P(i|j)$, which means that conditional probability leads to asymmetric relations. The disadvantage is that each word *i* tends to have a close relationship with stop words that are used quite frequently in user records, such as "的" (of) and "一个" (a).

In order to alleviate this problem, we consider the conditional probabilities $P(j|i)$ and $P(i|j)$ together. Word *i* and word *j* is said to be quite related if conditional probabilities $P(j|i)$ and $P(i|j)$ are both relatively high. We borrow the idea proposed in (Li and Sun, 2007). In their paper, a *weighted harmonic averaging* is used to define the relatedness score between word *i* and word *j* because either $P(j|i)$ or $P(i|j)$ being too small is a severe detriment.

$$Score(i,j) = \left( \frac{\lambda}{P(i \mid j)} + \frac{1-\lambda}{P(j \mid i)} \right)^{-1} \quad (2)$$

In formula 2, parameter $\lambda \in [0,1]$ is the weight for $P(i|j)$, which denotes how much $P(i|j)$ should be emphasized. We carry out some comparative experiments when parameter $\lambda$ varies from 0 to 1 stepped by 0.1. We also tried other co-occurrence based measures like mutual information, Euclidean and Jaccard distance, and found that weight harmonic averaging gives relatively better results. Due to space limitation, we are not able to report detailed results.

So far, we have introduced how to calculate the relatedness *Score(i, j)* between word *i* and word *j*. When a user enters an input seed word *w*, we can compute *Score(w,c)* between seed word *w* and each candidate word *c*, and then sort candidate words in a descending order. Top *N* candidate words are kept for re-ranking, we aim to reorder top *N* candidate words and return the more related candidate words earlier. Alternatively, we can also set a threshold for *Score(w,c)*, which keeps the candidate word *c* with *Score(w,c)* larger than the threshold. We argue that this threshold is difficult to set because different seed words have different score thresholds.

Note that this candidate generation step is completely statistical method as we only consider the co-occurrence of words. We argue that semantic features can be a complement of statistical method.

### 3.3 Semantic Feature Representation and Re-ranking

As stated before, we utilize search engine to enrich semantic features of the input seed word and top *N* candidate words. To be more specific, we issue a word to a search engine (Sogou, 2004) and get top 20 returned snippets. We regard snippets as the context and the semantic representation of this word.

For an input seed word *w*, we can generate top *N* candidate words using formula (2). We issue each word to search engine and get returned snippets. Then, each word is represented as a feature vector using bag-of-words model. Following the conventional approach, we calculate the relatedness between the input seed word *w* and a candidate word *c* as the cosine similarity between their feature vectors. Intuitively, if we introduce more candidate words, we are more likely to find related words in the candidate sets. However, noisy words are inevitably included. We will show how to tune parameter *N* in the experiment part.

As a result, candidate words with higher semantic similarities can be returned earlier with enriched semantic features. Re-ranking can be regarded as a complementary step after candidate generation. We can improve the performance of related word retrieval task if we consider user behaviors and re-ranking together.

# 4 Experiment

In this section, we demonstrate our experiment results. First, we introduce the dataset used in this paper and some statistics of the dataset. Then, we build our ground truth for related word retrieval task using Baidu encyclopedia. Third, we give some example of related word retrieval task. We show that more related words can be returned earlier if we consider semantic features. Finally, we make further analysis of the parameter tuning mentioned before.

## 4.1 Experiment Settings

We carry out our experiment on Sogou Chinese input method dataset. The dataset contains 10,000 users and 183,870 words, and the number of edges in the constructed bipartite graph is 42,250,718. As we can see, the dataset is quite sparse, because most of the users tend to use only a small number of words.

For related word retrieval task, we need to judge whether a candidate word is related to the input seed word. We can ask domain experts to answer this question. However, it needs a lot of manual efforts. To alleviate this problem, we adopt Baidu encyclopedia (Baidu, 2006) as our ground truth. In Baidu encyclopedia, volunteers give a set of words that are related to the particular seed word. As related words are provided by human, we are confident enough to use them as our ground truth.

We randomly select 2,000 seed words as our validation set. However, whether two words are related is quite subjective. In this paper, Baidu encyclopedia is only used as a relatively accurate standard for evaluation. We just want to investigate whether user behaviors and re-ranking framework is helpful in the related word retrieval task under various evaluation metrics.

We give a simple example of our method in Table 1. The input seed word is "机器学习" (Machine Learning). Generally speaking, all these returned candidate words are relevant to the seed word to certain degree, which indicates the effectiveness of our method.

| | |
|---|---|
| 特征向量(feature vector) | 核函数(kernel function) |
| 训练集(training set) | 决策树(decision tree) |
| 分类器(classifier) | 测试集(test set) |
| 降维(dimension reduction) | 特征提取(feature extraction) |

Table 1. Words Related to "Machine Learning"

## 4.2 Evaluation Metrics

In this paper, we use three evaluation metrics to validate the performance of our method:

1. Precision@N (**P@N**). P@N measures how much percent of the topmost results returned are correct. We consider P@5 and P@10.
2. Binary preference measure (**Bpref**) (Buckley and Voorhees, 2004). As we cannot list all the related words of an input seed word, we use Bpref to evaluate our method. For an input seed word with $R$ judged candidate words where $r$ is a related word and $n$ is a nonrelated word. Bpref is defined as follow:

$$Bpref = \frac{1}{R}\sum_{r} 1 - \frac{|n \text{ ranked higher than } r|}{R} \qquad (3)$$

3. Mean reciprocal rank of the first retrieved result (**MRR**). For a sample of input seed words $W$, $rank_i$ is the rank of the first related candidate word for the input seed word $w_i$, MRR is the average of the reciprocal ranks of results, which is defined as follow:

$$MRR = \frac{1}{|W|}\sum_{i} \frac{1}{rank_i} \qquad (4)$$

## 4.3 Candidate Re-ranking

In order to show the effectiveness of semantic features and re-ranking framework, we give an example in Table 2. The input seed word is "爱立信" (Ericsson), and if we only take user behaviors into consideration, top 5 words returned are shown on the left side. After using search engine and semantic representation, we reorder the candidate words as shown on the right side.

| Input Seed Word: 爱立信 (Ericsson) | |
|---|---|
| Top 5 Candidates | After Re-ranking |
| 北电 (Nortel) | 索尼爱立信 (Sony Ericsson) |
| 中兴 (ZTE Corporation) | 索爱 (Sony Ericsson) |
| 基站 (Base Station) | 阿尔卡特 (Alcatel) |
| 阿尔卡特 (Alcatel) | 索尼 (Sony) |
| 核心网 (Core Network) | 华为 (Huawei) |

Table 2. Candidate Re-ranking

As shown in Table 2, we can clearly see that we return the most related candidate words such as "索尼爱立信" (Sony Ericsson) and "索爱" (the abbreviation of Sony Ericsson in Chinese) in the first two places. Moreover, after re-ranking, top candidate words are some famous brands that are quite related to query word "爱立信" (Ericsson). Some words like "核心网" (Core Network) that are not quite related to the query word are removed from the top list. From this observation, we can see that semantic features and re-ranking framework can improve the performance.

### 4.4 Parameter Tuning

As discussed in Section 3, we have introduced two parameters in this paper. The first is the parameter λ in the candidate generation step, and the other is the parameter *N* in the re-ranking step. We show how these two parameters affect the performance. In addition, we should emphasize that the ground truth is not a complete answer, so all the results are only useful for comparisons. The absolute value is not very meaningful.

As we have shown in Section 3.2, parameter λ adjusts the weight of conditional probability between two word *i*, *j*. The parameter λ is varied from 0 to 1 stepped by 0.1. We record the corresponding values of P@5, P@10, Bpref and MRR. The results are shown in Figure 3.

We can clearly see that all the values increase when λ increases first. And then all the values decrease dramatically when λ is close to 1. This indicates that either $P(j|i)$ or $P(i|j)$ being too small is a severe detriment. The result reaches peak value when λ=0.5, i.e. we should treat $P(j|i)$ and $P(i|j)$equally to get the best result. Therefore, we use λ=0.5 to generate candidate words, those candidates are used for re-ranking.

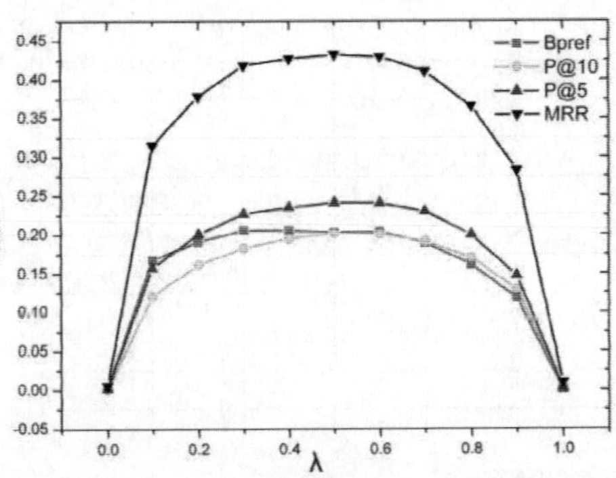


Fig. 3. Parameter λ for Candidate Generation

We also carry out the comparisons with Bayesian Sets, which is shown in Table 3. It is clear that our method gains better results than Bayesian Sets with different values of parameter λ. Results of Google Sets are omitted here because Zheng et al. (2009) have already showed that Google Sets performs worse than Bayesian Sets with query words in Chinese.

| | Bpref | MRR | P@5 | P@10 |
|---|---|---|---|---|
| λ = 0.4 | **0.2057** | 0.4267 | 0.2352 | 0.195 |
| λ = 0.5 | 0.2035 | **0.4322** | **0.2414** | **0.2019** |
| λ = 0.6 | 0.2038 | 0.4292 | 0.2408 | 0.2009 |
| Bayesian Sets | 0.2033 | 0.3291 | 0.1842 | 0.1512 |

Table 3. Comparisons with Bayesian Sets

To investigate the effectiveness of re-ranking framework, we also conduct experiments on the parameter *N* that is used for re-ranking. The experimental results are shown in Figure 4.

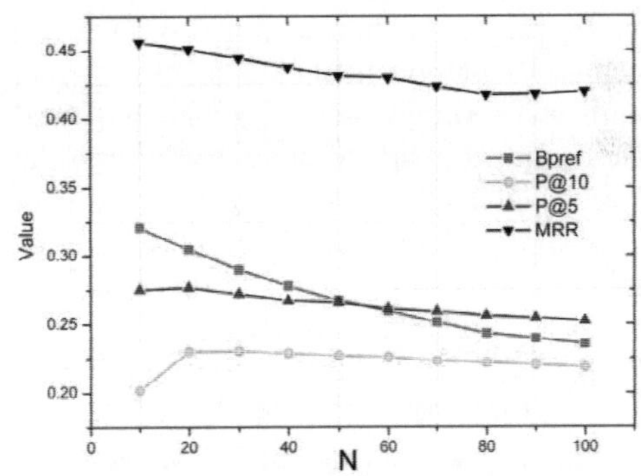


Fig. 4. Top *N* Candidates for Re-ranking

We can observe that more candidates tend to harm the performance as noisy words are introduced inevitably. For example, Bpref drops to less than 0.25 when N = 100. More comparative results are shown in Table 4. We can see that N = 20 gives relatively best results, which indicates that we should select Top 20 candidate words for re-ranking.

| | Bpref | MRR | P@5 | P@10 |
|---|---|---|---|---|
| Non Re-ranking | 0.2035 | 0.4322 | 0.2414 | 0.2019 |
| N = 10 | **0.3208** | **0.456** | 0.2752 | 0.2019 |
| N = 20 | 0.3047 | 0.4511 | **0.2769** | 0.2301 |
| N = 30 | 0.2899 | 0.4444 | 0.272 | **0.2305** |

Table 4. Comparisons with Re-ranking Method

## 5 Conclusions and Future Work

In this paper, we have proposed a novel method for related word retrieval task. Different from other method, we consider user behaviors, semantic features and re-ranking framework together. We make a reasonable assumption that if two words always co-occur in user records, then they tend to have a close relationship with each other. Based on this assumption, we first generate a set of candidate words that are related to an input seed word via user behaviors. Second, we utilize search engine to enrich candidates with semantic features. Finally, we can reorder the candidate words to return more related candidates earlier. Experiment results show that our method is effective and gains better results.

However, we also observed some noisy words in the returned results. As our dataset is generated from Chinese input method, users can type whatever they want, which will bring some noise in the dataset. We plan to remove noisy words in the future. Furthermore, we want to take the advantage of learning to rank literature (Liu, 2009) to further improve the performance of related word retrieval task. We may need to extract more features to represent the word pairs and build a labeled training set. Then various machine learning techniques can be used in this task.

Another important issue is how to build a complete and accurate ground truth for related word retrieval task. People may have different opinions about whether two words are related or not, which makes this problem complicate.

Thirdly, our method can only process a single seed word, so we aim to extend our method to process multiple seed words. In addition, we want to build a network of Chinese word association. We can discover how words are organized and connected within this network. And this word association network will be quite useful for foreigners to learn Chinese.

Fourthly, how to deal with ambiguous query word is also left as our future work. For example, query word "apple" can refer to a kind of fruit or an IT company. As a result, we are expected to return two groups of related words instead of mixing them together.

Finally, our dataset provides a new perspective for many interesting research tasks like new word detection, social network analysis, user behavior analysis, and so on. We are trying to release our dataset for research use in the future.

## Acknowledgement

We thank Xiance Si and Wufeng Ke for providing the Baidu encyclopedia corpus for evaluation. We also thank the anonymous reviewers for their helpful comments and suggestions. This work is supported by a Tsinghua-Sogou joint research project.

## References

Baidu. 2006. Baidu Encyclopedia. Available at http://baike.baidu.com

Chris Buckley and Ellen M. Voorhees. 2004. Retrieval Evaluation with Incomplete Information. In *Proceedings of the 27th annual international ACM SIGIR conference on Research and development in information retrieval*, pp 25-32

Mukund Deshpande and George Karypis. 2004. Item-Based Top-N Recommendation Algorithms, *ACM Trans. Information Systems*, 22(1): 143-177

Zoubin Ghahramani and Katherine A. Heller. 2005. Bayesian Sets. In *Advances in Neural Information Processing Systems*

Google. Google Sets. Accessed on Feb. 9th, 2010, available at: http://labs.google.com/sets

Jingyang Li and Maosong Sun. 2007. Scalable term selection for text categorization, In *Proceedings of the 2007 Joint Conference on Empirical Methods in Natural Language Processing and Computational Natural Language Learning*, pp. 774-782

Tie-Yan Liu. 2009. Learning to Rank for Information Retrieval, *Foundation and Trends on Information Retrieval*, Now Publishers

Donald Metzler, Susan T. Dumais, and Christopher Meek. 2007. Similarity measures for short segments of text. In *Proceeding of the 29th European Conference on Information Retrieval*, pp 16-27

Mehran Sahami and Timothy D. Heilman. 2006. A web-based kernel function for measuring the similarity of short text snippets. In *Proceedings of the 15th International Conference on World Wide Web*, pp 377-386

Sogou. 2006. Sogou Chinese Pinyin Input Method. Available at http://pinyin.sogou.com/

Sogou. 2004. Sogou Search Engine. Available at http://www.sogou.com

Wen-Tau Yih and Christopher Meek. 2007. Improving similarity measures for short segments of text. In *Proceedings of AAAI 2007*, pp 1489-1494

Yabin Zheng, Zhiyuan Liu, Maosong Sun, Liyun Ru, and Yang Zhang. 2009. Incorporating User Behaviors in New Word Detection. In *Proceedings of the Twenty-First International Joint Conference on Artificial Intelligence*, pp 2101-2106

# Transition-based parsing with Confidence-Weighted Classification

**Martin Haulrich**
Dept. of International Language Studies and Computational Linguistics
Copenhagen Business School
mwh.isv@cbs.dk

## Abstract

We show that using confidence-weighted classification in transition-based parsing gives results comparable to using SVMs with faster training and parsing time. We also compare with other online learning algorithms and investigate the effect of pruning features when using confidence-weighted classification.

## 1 Introduction

There has been a lot of work on data-driven dependency parsing. The two dominating approaches have been graph-based parsing, e.g. MST-parsing (McDonald et al., 2005b) and transition-based parsing, e.g. the MaltParser (Nivre et al., 2006a). These two approaches differ radically but have in common that the best results have been obtained using margin-based machine learning approaches. For the MST-parsing MIRA (McDonald et al., 2005a; McDonald and Pereira, 2006) and for transition-based parsing Support-Vector Machines (Hall et al., 2006; Nivre et al., 2006b).

Dredze et al. (2008) introduce a new approach to margin-based online learning called *confidence-weighted classification* (CW) and show that the performance of this approach is comparable to that of Support-Vector Machines. In this work we use confidence-weighted classification with transition-based parsing and show that this leads to results comparable to the state-of-the-art results obtained using SVMs.

We also compare training time and the effect of pruning when using confidence-weighted learning.

## 2 Transition-based parsing

Transition-based parsing builds on the idea that parsing can be viewed as a sequence of transitions between states. A transition-based parser (deterministic classifier-based parser) consists of three essential components (Nivre, 2008):

1. A parsing algorithm
2. A feature model
3. A classifier

The focus here is on the classifier but we will briefly describe the parsing algorithm in order to understand the classification task better.

The parsing algorithm consists of two components, a *transition system* and an *oracle*. Nivre (2008) defines a transition system $S = (C, T, c_s, C_t)$ in the following way:

1. $C$ is a set of configurations, each of which contains a buffer $\beta$ of (remaining) nodes and a set $A$ of dependency arcs,
2. $T$ is a set of transitions, each of which is a partial function $t : C \rightarrow C$,
3. $c_s$ is a initialization function mapping a sentence $x = (w_0, w_1, \ldots, w_n)$ to a configuration with $\beta = [1, \ldots, n]$,
4. $C_t$ is a set of terminal configurations.

A *transition sequence* for a sentence $x$ in $S$ is a sequence $C_{0,m} = (c_0, c_1 \ldots, c_m)$ of configurations, such that

1. $c_0 = c_s(x)$,
2. $c_m \in C_t$,
3. for every i $(1 \leq i \leq m) c_i = t(c_{i-1})$ for some $t \in T$

The oracle is used during training to determine a transition sequence that leads to the correct parse. The job of the classifier is to 'imitate' the oracle, i.e. to try to always pick the transitions that



*Proceedings of the ACL 2010 Student Research Workshop*, pages 55–60,
Uppsala, Sweden, 13 July 2010. 

lead to the correct parse. The information given to the classifier is the current configuration. Therefore the training data for the classifier consists of a number of configurations and the transitions the oracle chose with these configurations.

Here we focus on stack-based parsing algorithms. A stack-based configuration for a sentence $x = (w_0, w_1, \ldots, w_n)$ is a triple $c = (\sigma, \beta, A)$, where

1. $\sigma$ is a stack of tokens $i \leq k$ (for some $k \leq n$),
2. $\beta$ is a buffer of tokens $j > k$ ,
3. $A$ is a set of dependency arcs such that $G = (0, 1, \ldots, n, A)$ is a dependency graph for $x$. (Nivre, 2008)

In the work presented here we use the NivreEager algorithm which has four transitions:

**Shift** Push the token at the head of the buffer onto the stack.

**Reduce** Pop the token on the top of the stack.

**Left-Arc$_l$** Add to the analysis an arc with label $l$ from the token at the head of the buffer to the token on the top of the stack, and push the buffer-token onto the stack.

**Right-Arc$_l$** Add to the analysis an arc with label $l$ from the token on the top of the stack to the token at the head of the buffer, and pop the stack.

### 2.1 Classification

Transition-based dependency parsing reduces parsing to consecutive multiclass classification. From each configuration one amongst some predefined number of transitions has to be chosen. This means that any classifier can be plugged into the system. The training instances are created by the oracle so the training is offline. So even though we use online learners in the experiments these are used in a batch setting.

The best results have been achieved using Support-Vector Machines placing the MaltParser very high in both the CoNNL shared tasks on dependency parsing in 2006 and 2007 (Buchholz and Marsi, 2006; Nivre et al., 2007) and it has been shown that SVMs are better for the task than Memory-based learning (Hall et al., 2006). The standard setting in the MaltParser is to use a 2nd-degree polynomial kernel with the SVM.

## 3 Confidence-weighted classification

Dredze et al. (2008) introduce confidence-weighted linear classifiers which are online-classifiers that maintain a confidence parameter for each weight and uses this to control how to change the weights in each update. A problem with online algorithms is that because they have no memory of previously seen examples they do not know if a given weight has been updated many times or few times. If a weight has been updated many times the current estimation of the weight is probably relatively good and therefore should not be changed too much. On the other hand if it has never been updated before the estimation is probably very bad. CW classification deals with this by having a confidence-parameter for each weight, modeled by a Gaussian distribution, and this parameter is used to make more aggressive updates on weights with lower confidence (Dredze et al., 2008). The classifiers also use Passive-Aggressive updates (Crammer et al., 2006) to try to maximize the margin between positive and negative training instances.

CW classifiers are online-algorithms and are therefore fast to train, and it is not necessary to keep all training examples in memory. Despite this they perform as well or better than SVMs (Dredze et al., 2008). Crammer et al. (2009) extend the approach to multiclass classification and show that also in this setting the classifiers often outperform SVMs. They show that updating only the weights of the best of the wrongly classified classes yields the best results. We also use this approach, called top-1, here.

Crammer et al. (2008) present different update-rules for CW classification and show that the ones based on standard deviation rather than variance yield the best results. Our experiments have confirmed this, so in all experiments the update-rule from equation 10 (Crammer et al., 2008) is used.

## 4 Experiments

### 4.1 Software

We use the open-source parser MaltParser[1] for all experiments. We have integrated confidence-weighted, perceptron and MIRA classifiers into the code. The code for the online classifiers has

[1]We have used version 1.3.1, available at `maltparser.org`

been made available by the authors of the CW-papers.

### 4.2 Data

We have used the 10 smallest data sets from CoNNL-X (Buchholz and Marsi, 2006) in our experiments. Evaluation has been done with the official evaluation script and evaluation data from this task.

### 4.3 Features

The standard setting for the MaltParser is to use SVMs with polynomial kernels, and because of this it uses a relatively small number of features. In most of our experiments the default feature set of MaltParser consisting of 14 features has been used.

When using a linear-classifier without a kernel we need to extend the feature set in order to achieve good results. We have done this very uncritically by adding all pair wise combinations of all features. This leads to 91 additional features when using the standard 14 features.

## 5 Results and discussion

We will now discuss various results of our experiments with using CW-classifiers in transition-based parsing.

### 5.1 Online classifiers

We compare CW-classifiers with other online algorithms for linear classification. We compare with perceptron (Rosenblatt, 1958) and MIRA (Crammer et al., 2006). With both these classifiers we use the same top-1 approach as with the CW-classifers and also averaging which has been shown to alleviate overfitting (Collins, 2002). Table 2 shows Labeled Attachment Score obtained with the three online classifiers. All classifiers were trained with 10 iterations.

These results confirm those by Crammer et al. (2009) and show that confidence-weighted classifiers are better than both perceptron and MIRA.

### 5.2 Training and parsing time

The training time of the CW-classifiers depends on the number of iterations used, and this of course affects the accuracy of the parser. Figure 1 shows Labeled Attachment Score as a function of the number of iterations used in training. The horizontal line shows the LAS obtained with SVM.

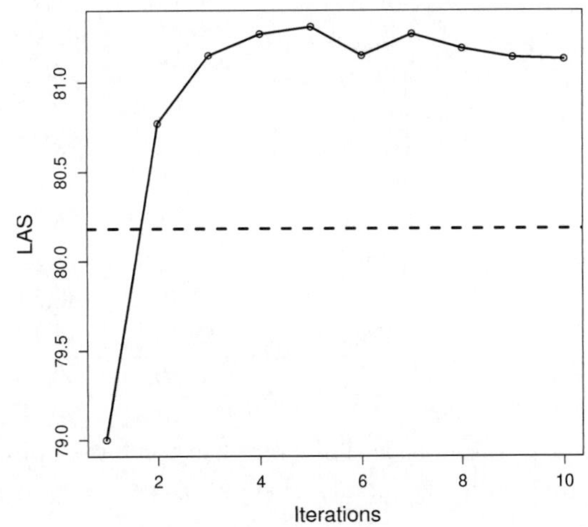


Figure 1: LAS as a function of number of training iterations on Danish data. The dotted horizontal line shows the performance of the parser trained with SVM.

We see that after 4 iterations the CW-classifier has the best performance for the data set (Danish) used in this experiment. In most experiments we have used 10 iterations. Table 1 compares training time (10 iterations) and parsing time of a parser using a CW-classifiers and a parser using SVM on the same data set. We see that training of the CW-classifier is faster, which is to be expected given their online-nature. We also see that parsing is much faster.

| | SVM | CW |
|---|---|---|
| Training | 75 min | 8 min |
| Parsing | 29 min | 1.5 min |

Table 1: Training and parsing time on Danish data.

### 5.3 Pruning features

Because we explicitly represent pair wise combinations of all of the original features we get an extremely high number of binary features. For some of the larger data sets, the number of features is so big that we cannot hold the weight-vector in memory. For instance the Czech data-set has 16 million binary features, and almost 800 classes - which means that in practice there are 12 billion binary features[2].

[2]Which is also why we only have used the 10 smallest data sets from CoNNL-X.

| | Perceptron | MIRA | CW, manual fs | CW | SVM |
|---|---|---|---|---|---|
| Arabic | 58.03 | 59.19 | 60.55 | †**60.57** | 59.93 |
| Bulgarian | 80.46 | 81.09 | 82.57 | †**82.76** | 82.12 |
| Danish | 79.42 | 79.90 | 81.06 | †**81.13** | 80.18 |
| Dutch | 75.75 | 77.47 | 77.65 | †**78.65** | 77.76 |
| Japanese | 87.74 | 88.06 | 88.14 | 88.19 | †**89.47** |
| Portuguese | 85.69 | 85.95 | 86.11 | 86.20 | **86.25** |
| Slovene | 64.35 | 65.38 | 66.09 | †**66.28** | 65.45 |
| Spanish | 74.06 | 74.86 | 75.58 | **75.90** | 75.46 |
| Swedish | 79.79 | 80.31 | 81.03 | †**81.24** | 80.56 |
| Turkish | 46.48 | 47.13 | 46.98 | 47.09 | **47.49** |
| All | 78.26 | 79.00 | 79.68 | †**79.86** | 79.59 |

Table 2: LAS on development data for three online classifers, CW-classifiers with manual feature selection and SVM. Statistical significance is measuered between CW-classifiers without feature selection and SVMs.

To solve this problem we have tried to use pruning to remove the features occurring fewest times in the training data. If a feature occurs fewer times than a given cutoff limit the feature is not included. This goes against the idea of CW classifiers which are exactly developed so that rare features can be used. Experiments also show that this pruning hurts accuracy. Figure 2 shows the labeled attachment score as a function of the cutoff limit on the Danish data.

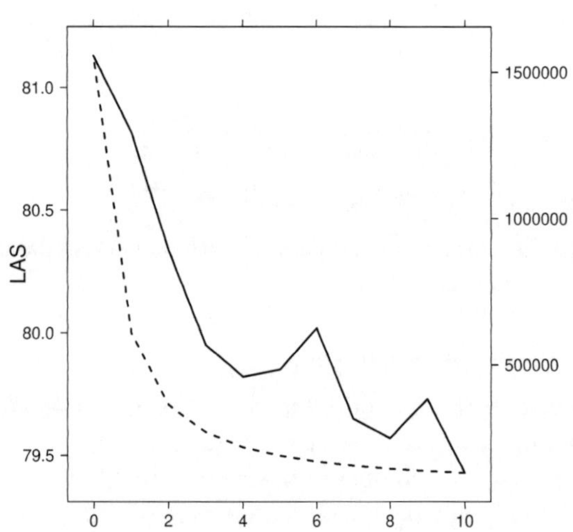


Figure 2: LAS as a function of the cutoff limit when pruning rare features. The dotted line shows the number of features left after pruning.

### 5.4 Manual feature selection

Instead of pruning the features we tried manually removing some of the pair wise feature combinations. We removed some of the combinations that lead to the most extra features, which is especially the case with combinations of lexical features. In the extended default feature set for instance we removed all combinations of lexical features except the combination of the word form of the token at the top of the stack and of the word form of the token at the head of the buffer.

Table 2 shows that this consistently leads to a small decreases in LAS.

### 5.5 Results without optimization

Table 2 shows the results for the 10 CoNNL-X data sets used. For comparison we have included the results from using the standard classifier in the MaltParser, i.e. SVM with a polynomial kernel. The hyper-parameters for the SVM have not been optimized, and neither has the number of iterations for the CW-classifiers, which is always 10. We see that in many cases the CW-classifier does significantly [3] better than the SVM, but that the opposite is also the case.

### 5.6 Results with optimization

The results presented above are suboptimal for the SVMs because default parameters have been used for these, and optimizing these can improve ac-

[3] In all tables statistical significance is marked with †. Significance is calculated using McNemar's test ($p = 0.05$). These tests were made with MaltEval (Nilsson and Nivre, 2008)

| | SVM | | | CW | | |
|---|---|---|---|---|---|---|
| | LAS | UAS | LA | LAS | UAS | LA |
| Arabic | 66.71 | 77.52 | 80.34 | **67.03** | 77.52 | †**81.20** |
| Bulgarian* | **87.41** | **91.72** | **90.44** | 87.25 | 91.56 | 89.77 |
| Danish | †**84.77** | †**89.80** | **89.16** | 84.15 | 88.98 | 88.74 |
| Dutch* | †**78.59** | †**81.35** | †**83.69** | 77.21 | 80.21 | 82.63 |
| Japanese | †**91.65** | †**93.10** | †**94.34** | 90.41 | 91.96 | 93.34 |
| Portuguese* | †**87.60** | †**91.22** | †**91.54** | 86.66 | 90.58 | 90.34 |
| Slovene | **70.30** | 78.72 | **80.54** | 69.84 | †**79.62** | 79.42 |
| Spanish | 81.29 | 84.67 | 90.06 | **82.09** | †**85.55** | **90.52** |
| Swedish* | †**84.58** | **89.50** | **87.39** | 83.69 | 89.11 | 87.01 |
| Turkish | †**65.68** | †**75.82** | †**78.49** | 62.00 | 73.15 | 76.12 |
| All | †**79.86** | †**85.35** | †**86.60** | 79.04 | 84.83 | 85.91 |

Table 3: Results on the CoNNL-X evaluation data. Manuel feature selection has been used for languages marked with an *.

curacy a lot. In this section we will compare results obtained with CW-classifiers with the results for the MaltParser from CoNNL-X. In CoNNL-X both the hyper parameters for the SVMs and the features have been optimized. Here we do not do feature selection but use the features used by the MaltParser in CoNNL-X[4].

The only hyper parameter for CW classification is the number of iterations. We optimize this by doing 5-fold cross-validation on the training data. Although the manual feature selection has been shown to decrease accuracy this has been used for some languages to reduce the size of the model. The results are presented in table 3.

We see that even though the feature set used are optimized for the SVMs there are not big differences between the parses that use SVMs and the parsers that use CW classification. In general though the parsers with SVMs does better than the parsers with CW classifiers and the difference seems to be biggest on the languages where we did manual feature selection.

## 6 Conclusion

We have shown that using confidence-weighted classifiers with transition-based dependency parsing yields results comparable with the state-of-the-art results achieved with Support Vector Machines - with faster training and parsing times. Currently we need a very high number of features to achieve these results, and we have shown that pruning this big feature set uncritically hurts performance of the confidence-weighted classifiers.

## 7 Future work

Currently the biggest challenge in the approach outlined here is the very high number of features needed to achieve good results. A possible solution is to use kernels with confidence-weighted classification in the same way they are used with the SVMs.

Another possibility is to extend the feature set in a more critical way than what is done now. For instance the combination of a POS-tag and CPOS-tag for a given word is now included. This feature does not convey any information that the POS-tag-feature itself does not. The same is the case for some word-form and word-lemma features. All in all a lot of non-informative features are added as things are now. We have not yet tried to use automatic features selection to select only the combinations that increase accuracy.

We will also try to do feature selection on a more general level as this can boost accuracy a lot. The results in table 3 are obtained with the features optimized for the SVMs. These are not necessarily the optimal features for the CW-classifiers.

Another comparison we would like to do is with linear SVMs. Unlike the polynomial kernel SVMs used as default in the MaltParser linear SVMs can be trained in linear time (Joachims, 2006). Trying to use the same extended feature set we use with the CW-classifiers with a linear SVM would provide an interesting comparison.

[4]Available at `http://maltparser.org/conll/conllx/`

## 8 Acknowledgements

The author thanks three anonymous reviewers and Anders Søgaard for their helpful comments and the authors of the CW-papers for making their code available.

## References

Sabine Buchholz and Erwin Marsi. 2006. Conll-x shared task on multilingual dependency parsing. In *Proceedings of the Tenth Conference on Computational Natural Language Learning (CoNLL-X)*, pages 149–164, New York City, June. Association for Computational Linguistics.

Michael Collins. 2002. Discriminative training methods for hidden markov models: theory and experiments with perceptron algorithms. In *EMNLP '02: Proceedings of the ACL-02 conference on Empirical methods in natural language processing*, pages 1–8, Morristown, NJ, USA. Association for Computational Linguistics.

Koby Crammer, Ofer Dekel, Joseph Keshet, Shai Shalev-Shwartz, and Yoram Singer. 2006. Online passive-aggressive algorithms. *J. Mach. Learn. Res.*, 7:551–585.

Koby Crammer, Mark Dredze, and Fernando Pereira. 2008. Exact convex confidence-weighted learning. In Daphne Koller, Dale Schuurmans, Yoshua Bengio, and Léon Bottou, editors, *NIPS*, pages 345–352. MIT Press.

Koby Crammer, Mark Dredze, and Alex Kulesza. 2009. Multi-class confidence weighted algorithms. In *Proceedings of the 2009 Conference on Empirical Methods in Natural Language Processing*, pages 496–504, Singapore, August. Association for Computational Linguistics.

Mark Dredze, Koby Crammer, and Fernando Pereira. 2008. Confidence-weighted linear classification. In *ICML '08: Proceedings of the 25th international conference on Machine learning*, pages 264–271, New York, NY, USA. ACM.

Johan Hall, Joakim Nivre, and Jens Nilsson. 2006. Discriminative classifiers for deterministic dependency parsing. In *Proceedings of the COLING/ACL 2006 Main Conference Poster Sessions*, pages 316–323, Sydney, Australia, July. Association for Computational Linguistics.

Thorsten Joachims. 2006. Training linear svms in linear time. In *KDD '06: Proceedings of the 12th ACM SIGKDD international conference on Knowledge discovery and data mining*, pages 217–226, New York, NY, USA. ACM.

Ryan T. McDonald and Fernando C. N. Pereira. 2006. Online learning of approximate dependency parsing algorithms. In *EACL*. The Association for Computer Linguistics.

Ryan T. McDonald, Koby Crammer, and Fernando C. N. Pereira. 2005a. Online large-margin training of dependency parsers. In *ACL*. The Association for Computer Linguistics.

Ryan T. McDonald, Fernando Pereira, Kiril Ribarov, and Jan Hajic. 2005b. Non-projective dependency parsing using spanning tree algorithms. In *HLT/EMNLP*. The Association for Computational Linguistics.

Jens Nilsson and Joakim Nivre. 2008. Malteval: An evaluation and visualization tool for dependency parsing. In *Proceedings of the Sixth International Language Resources and Evaluation*, Marrakech, Morocco, May. LREC.

Joakim Nivre, Johan Hall, and Jens Nilsson. 2006a. Maltparser: A data-driven parser-generator for dependency parsing. In *Proceedings of the fifth international conference on Language Resources and Evaluation (LREC2006)*, pages 2216–2219, May.

Joakim Nivre, Johan Hall, Jens Nilsson, Gülşen Eryiğit, and Svetoslav Marinov. 2006b. Labeled pseudo-projective dependency parsing with support vector machines. In *Proceedings of the Tenth Conference on Computational Natural Language Learning (CoNLL-X)*, pages 221–225, New York City, June. Association for Computational Linguistics.

Joakim Nivre, Johan Hall, Sandra Kübler, Ryan McDonald, Jens Nilsson, Sebastian Riedel, and Deniz Yuret. 2007. The CoNLL 2007 shared task on dependency parsing. In *Proceedings of the CoNLL Shared Task Session of EMNLP-CoNLL 2007*, pages 915–932.

Joakim Nivre. 2008. Algorithms for deterministic incremental dependency parsing. *Computational Linguistics*, 34(4):513–553.

Frank Rosenblatt. 1958. The perceptron: A probabilistic model for information storage and organization in the brain. *Psychological Review*, 65(6):386–408.

# Expanding Verb Coverage in Cyc With VerbNet

**Clifton J. McFate**
Northwestern University
Evanston, Il. USA.
c-mcfate@northwestern.edu

## Abstract

A robust dictionary of semantic frames is an essential element of natural language understanding systems that use ontologies. However, creating lexical resources that accurately capture semantic representations en masse is a persistent problem. Where the sheer amount of content makes hand creation inefficient, computerized approaches often suffer from over generality and difficulty with sense disambiguation. This paper describes a semi-automatic method to create verb semantic frames in the Cyc ontology by converting the information contained in VerbNet into a Cyc usable format. This method captures the differences in meaning between types of verbs, and uses existing connections between WordNet, VerbNet, and Cyc to specify distinctions between individual verbs when available. This method provides 27,909 frames to OpenCyc which currently has none and can be used to extend ResearchCyc as well. We show that these frames lead to a 20% increase in sample sentences parsed over the Research Cyc verb lexicon.

## 1 Introduction

The Cyc[1] knowledge base represents general purpose knowledge across a vast array of domains. Low level event and individual facts are contained in larger definitional hierarchical representations and contextualized through microtheories (Matuszek *et al*, 2006). Higher order predicates built into Cyc's formal language, CycL, allow efficient inferencing about context and meta-language reasoning above and beyond first-order logic rules (Ramachandran *et al*, 2005).

Because of the expressiveness and size of the ontology, Cyc has been used in NL applications including word sense disambiguation and rule acquisition by reading (Curtis, Cabral, & Baxter, 2006; Curtis *et al*, 2009). Such applications use NL-to-Cycl parsers which use Cyc semantic frames to convert natural language into Cyc representations. These frames represent sentence content through a set of propositional logic assertions that first reify the sentence in terms of a real world event and then define the semantic relationships between the elements of the sentence, as described later. Because these parsers require semantic frames to represent sentence content, existing parsers are limited due to Cyc's limited coverage (Curtis *et al*, 2009). The goal is to increase this coverage by automatically translating the class frames in VerbNet into individual verb templates.

## 2 Previous Work

The Cyc knowledge base is continuously expanding and much work has been done on automatic fact acquisition as well as merging ontologies. However, the semantic frames remain mostly hand-made in ResearchCyc[2] and non-existent in the open-license OpenCyc[3]. Translating VerbNet frames into Cyc will expand the natural language capabilities of both.

There has been previous research on mapping existing Cyc templates to VerbNet, but thus far these approaches have not created new templates to address Cyc's lapses in coverage. One such attempt, King and Crouch's (2005) unified lexicon, compiled many lexical resources into a unified representation. While this research created a valuable resource, it did not extend the existing Cyc coverage. Of the 45, 704 entries in the UL only 3,544 have Cyc entries (King & Crouch, 2005).

Correspondences between a few VerbNet frames and ResearchCyc templates have also been mapped out through the VxC VerbNet Cyc

[1] http://www.opencyc.org/cyc

[2] http://research.cyc.com
[3] http://opencyc.org



*Proceedings of the ACL 2010 Student Research Workshop*, pages 61–66,
Uppsala, Sweden, 13 July 2010. 

Mapper (Trumbo 2006). These mappings became a standard that we later used to evaluate the quality of our created frames.

A notable exception to the hand-made paradigm is Curtis *et al*'s (2009) TextLearner which uses rules and existing semantic frames to handle novel sentence structures. Given an existing template that fits some of the syntactic constraints of the sentence, TextLearner will attempt to create a new frame by suggesting a predicate that fits the missing part. Often these are general underspecified predicates, but TextLearner is able to use common sense reasoning and existing facts to find better matches (Curtis *et al*, 2009).

While TextLearner improves its performance with time, it is not an attempt to create new frames on a large scale. Creating generalized frames based on verb classes will increase the depth of the Cyc Lexicon quickly. Furthermore, automatic processes like those in TextLearner could be used to make individual verb semantic frames more specific.

## 3 VerbNet

VerbNet is an extension of Levin's (1993) verb classes that uses the class structure to apply general syntactic frames to member verbs that have those syntactic uses and similar semantic meanings (Kipper *et al*, 2000). The current version has been expanded to include class distinctions not included in Levin's original proposal (Kipper *et al*, 2006).

VerbNet is an appealing lexical resource for this task because it represents semantic meaning as the union of both syntactic structure and semantic predicates. VerbNet uses Lexicalized Tree Adjoining Grammar to generate the syntactic frames. The syntactic roles in the frame are appended with general thematic roles that fill arguments of semantic predicates. Each event is broken down into a tripartite structure as described by Moens & Steedman (1988) and uses a time modifier for each predicate to indicate when specific predicates occur in the event. This allows for a dynamic representation of change over an event. (Kipper *et* al, 2000).

This approach is transferable to Cyc's semantic templates in which syntactic slots fill predicate arguments in the context of a specific syntactic frame. Both also have extensive connections to WordNet2.0, an electronic edition of Miller's (1985) WordNet (Fellbaum, 1998).

## 4 Method

The general method for creating semantic templates in Cyc requires creating Verb Class Frames and then using Cyc predicates and heuristic rules to create individual frames for each member verb.

### 4.1 OpenCyc

The existing semantic templates are accessible through the ResearchCyc KB. However, for the purposes of this study the OpenCyc KB was used. The OpenCyc KB is an open source version of ResearchCyc that contains much of the definitional information and higher order predicates, but has had much of the lower level specific facts and the entire word lexicon removed (Matuszek *et al*, 2006). However, the assertions generated by this method are fully usable in ResearchCyc. OpenCyc was used so as to minimize the effect of existing semantic frames on new frame creation. Since OpenCyc and VerbNet are open-licensed, our translation provides an open-license extension to OpenCyc to support its use in natural language research.

### 4.2 Knowledge Representation

The primary difficulty with integrating VerbNet frames into Cyc was overcoming differences in knowledge representation. Cyc semantic templates reify events as an instance of a collection of events. The arguments correspond to syntactic roles. The following is a semantic template for a ditransitive use of the word *give* from ResearchCyc.

```
(verbSemTrans Give-TheWord 0
(PPCompFrameFn
 DitransitivePPFrameType To-TheWord)
(and
(isa ACTION GivingSomething)

(objectGiven ACTION OBJECT)
(giver ACTION SUBJECT)
(givee ACTION OBLIQUE-OBJECT)))
```

However, VerbNet uses semantic predicates that describe relationships between two thematic roles. The following is a frame for the VerbNet class *Give* as presented in the Unified Verb Index[4].

```
NP V NP PP.recipient
example
```

[4] http://verbs.colorado.edu/verb-index/

```
 "They lent a bicycle to me."
syntax
 Agent V Theme {to} Recipient
semantics
 -has_possession(start(E), Agent,
 Theme)
 -has_possession(end(E), Recipient,
 Theme)
 -transfer(during(E), Theme)
 -cause(Agent, E)
```

The predicate `has_possession` occurs twice, at the beginning and end of the event. In one case the `Agent` has possession and in the second the `Recipient` does. Both refer to the `Theme` which is being transferred.

In Cyc the `hasPossession` relationship to `Agent` and `Recipient` is represented with the predicates `giver` and `givee`. The subject and oblique-object of the sentence fill those arguments, and the actual change of possession is represented by the collection of events `GivingSomething`. The VerbNet `Theme` is the object in `objectGiven`. Thus an individual VerbNet semantic predicate often has a many-to-one mapping with Cyc predicates.

### 4.3 Predicates

To account for representation differences, a single Cyc predicate was mapped to a unique combination of Verbnet predicate and thematic role (ie. `Has_Possession Agent at start(E) => givee`). 56 of these mappings were done by hand. Though far from exhaustive, these hand mappings represent many frequently used predicates in VerbNet. The hand mapping was done by looking at the uses of the predicate across different classes.

Because the mappings were not exhaustive, a safety net automatically catches predicates that haven't been mapped. The VerbNet predicates `Cause` and `InReactionTo` corresponded to the Cyc predicates `performedBy`, `doneBy`, and `causes-Underspecified`. These predicates were selected whenever the VerbNet predicates occurred with a theme role that was the subject of the sentence. The more specific `performedBy` was selected in cases where the frame's temporal structure suggested a result. The predicate `doneBy` was selected in other cases. The `causes-Underspecified` predicate was used in frames whose time modifiers suggested that they were continuous states. The predicates `patientGeneric` and `patientGeneric-Direct` were used when a predicate was not found for a required object or oblique object.

Some Cyc templates don't have predicates that reference the event. For example, the verb *touch* can be efficiently represented with the relation `(objectsInContact :SUBJECT :OBJECT)`. Situations like this were hand assigned.

### 4.4 Collections

In Cyc, concepts are represented by collections. Inheritance between collections is specified by the `genls` relationship, which can be viewed as subset. Most verb frames have an associated collection of events of which each use is an instance. The associated collection of the class frame templates was automatically selected using the common link that both resources share with WordNet (Fellbaum, 1998). To do this, the WordNet synsets of the member verbs for a class were matched with their Cyc-WordNet `synonymousExternalConcept` assertion. The Cyc representation became a denoted collection. The most general collection out of the list of viable collections was chosen as the general class frame collection. The number of `genls` links to a collection was used as a proxy for generality. In the case of a tie the first was chosen.

While the most general collection was used for the class semantic frame, at the level of individual verb frames the specific synset denoted collection was substituted for the more general one when applicable. Verbs with multiple meanings across classes were given a unique index number for each sense. However, within a given class each word only received one denotation. The general class level collection was used in cases where no Cyc-WordNet-VerbNet link existed. If no verb had a synset in Cyc, the general collection `Situation` was used.

### 4.5 Subcategorization Frames

Each syntactic frame is a subcategorization frame or a subset of one. In this case, the naming conventions were different between VerbNet and Cyc. Frames with prepositions kept Cyc's notation for prepositional phrases. However, since VerbNet had a much broader coverage the VerbNet subcat names were kept.

### 4.6 Assertions

The process above was used to create general class frames, for example,

```
(verbClassSemTrans give-13.1
(TransitiveNPFrame)
```

```
(and
(isa :ACTION
MakingSomethingAvailable)
(patient-GenericDirect :ACTION
:OBJECT)
(performedBy :ACTION :SUBJECT)
(fromPossessor :ACTION :SUBJECT)
(objectOfPossessionTransfer :ACTION
:OBJECT)))
```

These frames use more generic collections and apply to a VerbNet class rather than a specific verb.

Specific verb semantic templates were created by inferring that each member verb of a VerbNet class participated in every template in a class. Again, collections were taken from existing WordNet connections if possible. The output was assertions in the Cyc semantic template format:

```
(verbSemTrans Loan-TheWord 0
(PPCompFrameFn NP-PP (WordFn to))
(and
(isa :ACTION Lending)
(patient-GenericDirect :ACTION
:OBJECT)
(performedBy :ACTION :SUBJECT)
(fromPossessor :ACTION :SUBJECT)
(toPossessor :ACTION :OBLIQUE-
OBJECT)
(objectOfPossessionTransfer :ACTION
:OBJECT)))
```

This method for giving class templates to each verb in a class was written as a Horn clause for the FIRE reasoning engine. FIRE is a reasoning engine that incorporates both logical inference based on axioms and analogy-based reasoning over a Cyc-derived knowledge base (Forbus, Mostek, & Ferguson, 2002). FIRE could then be queried for implied verb templates which became the final list of verb templates.

### 4.7 Subclasses

VerbNet has an extensive classification system involving subclasses. Subclasses contain verbs that take all of the syntactic formats of the main class plus additional frames that verbs in the main class cannot.

Verbs in a subclass inherit frames from their superordinate classes. FIRE was used again to create the verb semantic templates.

Each subclass template's collection was selected using the same process as the main class. If no subclass member had a Cyc denotation, then the main class collection was used.

## 5 Results

The end result of this process was the creation of 27,909 verb semantic template assertions for 5,050 different verbs. This substantially increases the number of frames for ResearchCyc and creates frames for OpenCyc.

To test the accuracy of the results and their contribution to the knowledge base we ran two tests. The first was to compare our frames with the 139 hand-checked VxC matches by hand. Of the 139 frames from VxC, 81 were qualified as "good" matches, and 58 as "maybe" (Trumbo, 2006). Since these frames already existed in Cyc and were hand matched we used them as the current gold standard for what a VerbNet frame translated into Cyc should look like.

Matches between frames were evaluated along several criteria. First was whether the frame had as good a syntactic parse as the manual version. This was defined as having predicates that addressed all syntactic roles in the sentence or, if not enough, as many as the VxC match. Secondly we asked if the collection was similar to the manual version. Frames with collections that were too specific, unrelated, or just `Situation` were discarded. Because frame-specific predicates were not created on a large scale, a frame was not rejected for using general predicates.

It is important to note a difference in matching methodology between the VxC matches and our frames. First, the VxC mappings included frames in Cyc that only partially matched more syntactically robust VerbNet frames. Our frames were only included if they matched the intended VerbNet syntactic frame. Because of this some of our frames beat the VxC gold standard for syntactic completeness. The VxC frames also included multiple similar senses for an individual verb. Our verbs had one denotation per class or subclass. Thus in some cases our frames failed not from over generalizing but because they were only meant to represent one meaning per class. Since the strength of our approach lies in generating a near exhaustive list of syntactic frames and not multiple word senses, these kinds of failures are not necessarily representative of the success of the frames as a whole.

A total of 55 frames (39.5%) were correct with seventeen (30.9%) of the correct frames having a more complete syntactic parse than the manually mapped frame. 48 frames (34.5%) were rejected only for having too general or specific a collection; however ten (20.8%) of the collection rejected frames had a more complete parse than their manual counterparts. Thus 103 frames (74.1%) were as syntactically correct or better than the existing Cyc frame mapped to that VerbNet frame. Nine (6.47%) frames failed syntactically, with four (44.4%) of the syntax failures also having the wrong collection. Thirteen frames ( 9.3%) were not matched.

Fifteen frames (10.8%) from the *Hold* class, were separated out for a formatting error that resulted in a duplicate, though not syntactically incorrect, predicate. The predicate repeated was `(objectsInContact :ACTION :OBJECT)`. 12 of 15 frames (80%) had accurate collections.

The second test compared the results of a natural language understanding system using either ResearchCyc alone or a version of ResearchCyc with our frames substituted for theirs. The test corpus was 50 randomly selected example sentences from the VerbNet frame examples. We used the EA NLU parser, which uses a bottom-up chart parser and compositional semantics to convert the semantic content of a sentence in CycL (Tomai & Forbus 2009). Possible frames are returned in choice sets. A parse was judged correct if it returned a verb frame for the central verb of the example sentence that either wholly or in combination with preposition frames addressed the syntactic constituents of the sentence with an acceptable collection and acceptable predicates. Again general predicates were acceptable.

ResearchCyc got sixteen out of 50 frames correct (32%). Eleven frames (22%) did not return a template but did return a denotation to a Cyc collection. Twelve verbs (24%) retuned nothing, while eleven (22%) returned frames that were either not the correct syntactic frame or were a different sense of the verb.

EA NLU running the VerbNet generated frames got 26 out of 50 (52%) frames correct. Twelve frames (24%) returned nothing. Eight frames, (16%) failed because of a too specific or too general collection. Four generated frames (8%) were either not the correct syntactic frame or were for a different sense of the verb. This was an overall 20% improvement in accuracy.

Five (10%) parses using the VerbNet generated correct frames that were labeled as noisy. Noisy frames had duplicate predicates or more general predicates in addition to the specific ones. The *Hold* frames separated out in the VxC test are an example of noisy frames. None of these frames were syntactically incorrect or contradictory. The redundant predicates arise because the predicate safety net had to be greedy. This was in the interest of capturing more complex frames that may have multiple relations for the same thematic role in a sentence.

This evaluation is based on parser recall and frame semantic accuracy only. As would be expected, adding more frames to the knowledge base did result in more parser retrievals and possible interpretations. The implications for this on word sense disambiguation is evaluated further in the discussion. To improve predicate specificity, the next phase of research with these frames will be to implement predicate strengthening methods that move down the hierarchy to find more specific predicates to replace the generalized ones. Thus in the future precision both in terms of frame retrieval and predicate specificity will be a vital metric for evaluating success.

## 6 Discussion

As has been demonstrated in this approach and in previous research like Curtis *et al*'s (2009) TextLearner, Cyc provides powerful reasoning capabilities that can be used to successfully infer more specific information from general existing facts. We hope that future research is able to use this feature to provide more specific individual frames. Because Cyc is consistently changing and growing, an approach that uses Cyc relationships will be able to improve as the knowledge base improves its coverage.

While many of the frames are general, they provide a solid foundation for further research. As they are now, the added 27,909 frames increase the language capabilities of OpenCyc which previously had none. For ResearchCyc the contribution is less clear-cut. The 27,909 VerbNet frames have approximately 7.93 times the coverage of the existing 3,517 ResearchCyc frames[5] and they improved ResearchCyc parser performance by 20%. However, with 35% of frames in the VxC comparison and 16% in the parse test failing because of collections, and 10.8% of the VxC comparison set and 10% of correct parses classified as noisy, these frames are not as precise as the existing frames. The goal of these frames is not necessarily to replace the existing frames, but rather to extend coverage and provide a platform for further development whether by hand or through automatic methods. Precision can be improved upon in future

[5] D. Lenat briefing, March 15, 2006

research and is facilitated by the expressiveness of Cyc. Predicate strengthening, using existing relationships to infer more specific predicates, is the next step in creating robust frames.

Additionally, there is a tradeoff between the number of frames covered and efficiency of disambiguation. More frame choices make it harder for parsers to choose the correct frame, but it will hopefully improve their handling of more complex sentence structures.

One possible solution to competition and over-generality is to add verbs incrementally by class. The class based approach makes it easy to separate verbs by types, such as verbs that relate to mechanical processes or emotion verbs. One could use classes of frames to strengthen specific areas of parsing while choosing not to take verbs from a class covering a domain that the parser already performs strongly in. This approach can reduce interference with existing domains that have been hand built and extended beyond the standard Cyc KB for individual research.

Furthermore, semi-automatic approaches like this generate information more quickly than one could do by hand. Thus an approach to computational verb semantic representation that is rooted in classes can take advantage of modern reasoning sources like Cyc to efficiently create semantic knowledge.

## Acknowledgments

This research was supported by the Air Force Office of Scientific Research and Northwestern University. A special thanks to Kenneth Forbus and the members of QRG for their continued invaluable guidance.

## References

Crouch, Dick, and Tracy Holloway King. 2005. Unifying Lexical Resources. In *Proceedings of the Interdisciplinary Workshop on the Identification and Representation of Verb Features and Verb Classes*, Saarbruecken, Germany

Curtis, John, David Baxter, Peter Wagner, John Cabral, Dave Schneider, and Michael Witbrock. 2009. Methods of Rule Acquisition in the TextLearner Systerm. In *Proceedings of the 2009 AAAI Spring Symposium on Learning by Reading and Learning to Read*, pages 22-28, Palo Alto, CA. AAAI Press.

Curtis, John, John Cabral, and David Baxter. 2006. On the Application of the Cyc Ontology to Word Sense Disambiguation. In *Proceedings of the Nineteenth International FLAIRS Conference*, pages 652-657, Melbourne Beach, FL.

Fellbaum, Christiane. Ed. 1998. *WordNet: An Electronic Database*. MIT Press, Cambridge, MA.

Forbus, Kenneth, Thomas Mostek , and Ron Ferguson. 2002. An Analogy Ontology for Integrating Analogical Processing and First-principle Reasoning. In *Proceedings of the Thirteenth Conference on Innovative Applications of Artificial Intelligence*. Menlo Park, CA. AAAI Press.

Kipper, Karin, Hoa Trang Dang, and Martha Palmer. 2000. Class-Based Construction of a Verb Lexicon. In *AAAI-2000 Seventeenth National Conference on Artificial Intelligence*, Austin, TX.

Kipper, Karin, Anna Korhonen, Neville Ryant, and Martha Palmer. 2006. Extending VerbNet with Novel Verb Classes. In *Fifth International Conference on Language Resources and Evaluation (LREC 2006)*. Genoa, Italy.

Levin, Beth. 1993. *English Verb Classes and Alternation: A Preliminary Investigation*. The University of Chicago Press, Chicago.

Matuszek, Cynthia, John Cabral, Michael Witbrock, and John DeOliveira. 2006. An Introduction to the Syntax and Content of Cyc. In *Proceedings of the 2006 AAAI Spring Symposium on Formalizing and Compiling Background Knowledge and Its Applications to Knowledge Representation and Question Answering*, Stanford, CA.

Moens, Marc, and Mark Steedman. 1988. Temporal Ontology and Temporal Reference. *Computational Linguistics*. 14(2):15-28.

Miller, G. 1985. WORDNET: A Dictionary Browser. In *Proceedings of the First International Conference on Information in Data*.

Ramachandran, Deepak, Pace Reagan, and Keith Goolsbey. 2005. First-Orderized Research Cyc: Expressivity and Efficiency in a Common-Sense Ontology. In *Papers from the AAAI Workshop on Contexts and Ontologies: Theory, Practice and Applications*. Pittsburgh, PA.

Tomai, Emmet, and Kenneth Forbus. 2009. EA NLU: Practical Language Understanding for Cognitive Modeling. In *Proceedings of the 22nd International Florida Artificial Intelligence Research Society Conference*, Sanibel Island, FL.

Trumbo, Derek. 2006. VxC: A VerbNet-Cyc Mapper. http://verbs.colorado.edu/verb-index/vxc/

# A Framework for Figurative Language Detection Based on Sense Differentiation

**Daria Bogdanova**
University of Saint Petersburg
Saint Petersburg
dasha.bogdanova@gmail.com

## Abstract

Various text mining algorithms require the process of feature selection. High-level semantically rich features, such as figurative language uses, speech errors etc., are very promising for such problems as e.g. writing style detection, but automatic extraction of such features is a big challenge. In this paper, we propose a framework for figurative language use detection. This framework is based on the idea of sense differentiation. We describe two algorithms illustrating the mentioned idea. We show then how these algorithms work by applying them to Russian language data.

## 1 Introduction

Various text mining algorithms require the process of feature selection. For example, authorship attribution algorithms need to determine features to quantify the writing style. Previous work on authorship attribution among computer scientists is mostly based on low-level features such as word frequencies, sentence length counts, n-grams etc. A significant advantage of such features is that they can be easily extracted from any corpus. But the study by Batov and Sorokin (1975) shows that such features do not always provide accurate measures for authorship attribution. The linguistic approach to the problem involves such high-level characteristics as the use of figurative language, irony, sound devices and so on. Such characteristics are very promising for the mentioned above tasks, but the extraction of these features is extremely hard to automate. As a result, very few attempts have been made to exploit high-level features for stylometric purposes (Stamatatos, 2009). Therefore, our long-term objective is the extraction of high-level semantically rich features.

Since the mentioned topic is very broad, we focus our attention only on some particular problems and approaches. In this paper, we examine one of such problems, the problem of automatic figurative language use detection. We propose a framework for figurative language detection based on the idea of sense differentiation. Then, we describe two algorithms illustrating the mentioned idea. One of them is intended to decide whether a usage is literal by comparing the texts related to the target expression and the set of texts related to the context itself. The other is aimed at grouping instances into literal and non-literal uses and is based on DBSCAN clustering (Ester et al, 1996). We illustrate then how these algorithms work by applying them to Russian language data. Finally, we propose some ideas on modifications which can significantly improve the accuracy of the algorithms.

## 2 Related Work

Sporleder and Li (April 2009) proposed an unsupervised method for recognition of literal and non-literal use of idiomatic expressions. Given an idiom the method detects the presence or absence of cohesive links between the words the idiom consists of and the surrounding text. When such links exist, the occurence is considered as a literal usage and as a non-literal when there are no such links. For most idioms the experiments showed an accuracy above 50% (it varies between 11% and 98% for different idioms). The authors then proposed an improvement of the algorithm (Li and Sporleder, August 2009) by adding the Support Vector Machine classifier as a second stage. They use the mentioned above unsupervised algorithm to label the training data for the supervised classifier. The average accuracy of the improved algorithm is about 90%. Our approach is also based on the idea of the relatedness between the expression and the surrounding context. Unlike the mentioned study, we do not focus our attention only on idioms. So far we have mostly dealt with ex-



*Proceedings of the ACL 2010 Student Research Workshop*, pages 67–72,
Uppsala, Sweden, 13 July 2010. 

pressions, which are not necessarily idiomatic by themselves, but become metaphors in a particular context (e.g. "she is the *sunshine*", "life is a *journey*") and expressions that are invented by an author (e.g. "*my heart's in the Highlands*"). Moreover, the improved algorithm (Li and Sporleder, August 2009) is supervised, and our approach is unsupervised.

The study by Katz and Giesbrecht (2006) is also supervised, unlike ours. It also considers multiword expressions that have idiomatic meanings. They propose an algorithm, which computes the vectors for literal and non-literal usages and then use the nearest neighbor classifier to label an unseen occurence of the given idiom.

The approach proposed by Birke and Sarkar (2006) is nearly unsupervised. They constructed two seed sets: one consists of literal usages of different expressions and the other consists of non-literal usages. They calculate the distance between an occurence in question and these two sets and assign to the occurence the label of the closest set. This work, as well as ours, refers to the ideas from Word Sense Disambiguation area. Unlike our approach, the authors focus their attention only on the detection of figuratevely used verbs and, whereas we only refer to the concepts and ideas of WSD, they adapt a particular existing one-word disambiguation method.

As we have already said, we deal with different types of figurative language (metaphors, metonymies etc.). However, there are some works aimed at extracting particular types of figurative language. For example, Nissim and Markert (2003) proposed a machine learning algorithm for metonymy resolution. They state the problem of metonymy resolution as a classification task between literal use of a word and a number of predefined metonymy types.

## 3 Sense Differentiation

We could treat a figurative meaning of a word as an additional, not common meaning of this word. Actually, some metaphors are quite common (e.g. *eye of a needle*, *leg of a table*, etc.) and are called catachretic metaphors. They appear in a language to remedy the gap in vocabulary (Black, 1954). These metaphors do not indicate an author's writing style: an author uses such metaphor for an object because the language has no other name for that object. Therefore the algorithms we are developing do not work with this type of metaphors.

Our approach to figurative language detection is based on the following idea: the fact that the sense of a word significantly differs from the sense of the surrounding text usually indicates that the word is used figuratively. Two questions arise immediately:

1. How do we represent the sense of both the word and the surrounding context?

2. How do we find out that these senses differ significantly?

To answer the first question, we refer to the ideas popular in the Word Sense Disambiguation community: sense is a group of contextually similar occurrences of a word (Schütze, 1996). Hence, we represent the senses of both a word and its context as sets of documents related to the word and the context respectively. These sets can be obtained e.g. by searching Wikipedia, Google or another web search engine. For a word the query can be the word itself. As for a text, this query can be formulated as the whole text or as a set of some words contained in this text. It seems to us that querying the lexical chains (Halliday and Hasan, 1976) extracted from the text should provide better results than querying the whole text.

As soon as we have a sense representation for such objects as a word and a text, we should find a way to measure the difference between these sense representations and find out what difference is strong enough for the considered occurence to be classified as a non-literal usage. One way to do this is representing sets of documents as sets of vectors and measuring the distance between the centers of the obtained vector sets. Another way is to apply clustering techniques to the sets and to measure the accuracy of the produced clustering. The higher the accuracy is, the more different the sets are.

Besides, this can be done by calculating text-to-text semantic similarity using for example the measure proposed by Mihalcea et al (2006). This is rather difficult in case of the Russian language because at the moment there is no WordNet-like taxonomies for Russian.

In the next section, we propose two algorithms based on the mentioned above idea. We state the algorithms generally and try to find out experimentally what combination of the described techniques provides the best results.

## 4 Finding the Distance to the Typical Context Set

The algorithm is intended to determine whether a word (or an expression) in a given context is used literaly or not.

As it was mentioned above, we decided to represent senses of both an expression and a context as sets of documents. Our hypothesis is that these document sets differ significantly if and only if an expression is used figuratevely. Thus, the algorithm decides whether the occurence is literal by comparing two sets of documents: the *typical context set*, which represents a sense of the expression, and the *related context set*, which represents a sense of the context. A naive way to construct the *typical context set* is searching some searching engine (e.g. Google) for the expression. Given a context with a target expression, the *related context set* can be constructed as follows:

1. Remove the target expression from the context;
2. Extract the longest lexical chains from the resulting context;
3. For every chain put to the set the first N articles retrieved by searching a searching engine for the chain;

After constructing the sets the algorithm should estimate the similarity between these two sets. This, for example, can be done by applying any clustering algorithm to the data and measuring the accuracy. Evidently, the higher the accuracy of the obtained clustering is, the more separated the sets are. It means that, when the usage is literal, the accuracy should be lower because we try to make two clusters out of data that should appear as the only cluster.

We hypothesize that in case of non-literal usages these two sets should be significantly separated.

Our experiments include two stages. During the first one we test our idea and estimate the parameters of the algorithms. During the second stage we test the more precise algorithm obtained during the first stage.

For the first stage, we found literal and non-literal occurences of the following Russian words and expressions:

вьюга (snowstorm), дыхание (breath), кинжальный (dagger), плясать (dance), стебель гибкий (flexible (flower) stalk), утонуть (be drowned), хрустальный (crystal), шотландская волынка (bagpipes), мед (honey), лекарство (medicine).

For every expression, the *typical context set* consists of the first 10 articles retrieved by searching Google for the expression. In order to construct the second set we removed the target expression from the context and manually extracted lexical chains from the texts, although, the process of lexical chains extraction can be done automatically. However the algorithms on lexical chains extraction usually use WordNet to calculate the relatedness, but as it was already mentioned WordNet for the Russian language does not exist yet. Another way to calculate semantic relatedness is using Wikipedia (Mihalcea, 2007; Turdakov and Velikhov, 2008), but it takes much effort. The second set for each occurence consists of the first 10 articles retrieved by searching Google for the extracted chains. Then we applied k-means clustering algorithm ($k = 2$) to these sets. To evaluate the clustering we used measures from the clustering literature. We denote our sets by $G = g_1, g_2$ and the clusters obtained by k-means as $C = c_1, c_2$. We define a mapping $f$ from the elements of $G$ to the elements of $C$, such that each set $g_i$ is mapped to a cluster $c_j = f(g_i)$ that has the highest percentage of common elements with $g_i$. Precision and recall for a cluster $g_i, i = 1, 2$ are defined as follows:

$$Pr_i = \frac{| f(g_i) \cap g_i |}{| f(g_i) |} \text{ and } Re_i = \frac{| f(g_i) \cap g_i |}{| g_i |}$$

Precision, $Pr$, and recall, $Re$, of the clustering are defined as the weighted averages of the precision and recall values over the sets:

$$Pr = \frac{1}{2}(Pr_1 + Pr_2) \text{ and } Re = \frac{1}{2}(Re_1 + Re_2)$$

$F_1$-measure is defined as the harmonic mean of precision and recall, i.e.,

$$F_1 = \frac{2 \times Pr \times Re}{Pr + Re}.$$

Table 1 shows the results of the clustering. For 9 expressions out of 10, the clustering accuracy is higher in case of a metaphorical usage than in case of a literal one. Moreover, for 9 out of 10

| | Figurative usage | | | Literal usage | | |
|---|---|---|---|---|---|---|
| | *Pr* | *Re* | *F* | *Pr* | *Re* | *F* |
| вьюга | 0,85 | 0,85 | 0,85 | 0,50 | 0,50 | 0,50 |
| дыхание | 0,83 | 0,75 | 0,79 | 0,65 | 0,60 | 0,63 |
| кинжальный | 0,85 | 0,85 | 0,85 | 0,70 | 0,65 | 0,67 |
| плясать | 0,95 | 0,95 | 0,95 | 0,66 | 0,65 | 0,66 |
| стебель гибкий | 0,85 | 0,85 | 0,85 | 0,88 | 0,85 | 0,86 |
| утонул | 0,85 | 0,85 | 0,85 | 0,81 | 0,70 | 0,75 |
| хрустальный | 0,95 | 0,95 | 0,95 | 0,83 | 0,75 | 0,78 |
| шотландская волынка | 0,88 | 0,85 | 0,86 | 0,70 | 0,70 | 0,70 |
| мед | 0,90 | 0,90 | 0,90 | 0,88 | 0,85 | 0,87 |
| лекарство | 0,90 | 0,90 | 0,90 | 0,81 | 0,70 | 0,75 |

Table 1: Results provided by k-means clustering

metaphorical usages, F-measure is 0,85 or higher. And for 7 out of 10 literal usages, F-measure is 0,75 or less.

The first stage of the experiments illustrates the idea of sense differentiation. Based on the obtained results, we have concluded, that F-measure value equal to 0,85 or higher indicates a figurative usage, and the value equal to 0,75 or less indicates a literal usage.

At the second stage, we applied the algorithm to several Russian language expressions used literally or figuratively. The accuracy of the k-means clustering is shown in Table 2.

| Figurative usages | | | |
|---|---|---|---|
| живой костер из снега и вина | 0,76 | 0,55 | 0,64 |
| лев | 1,00 | 1,00 | 1,00 |
| иней | 0,90 | 0,90 | 0,90 |
| ключ | 0,95 | 0,93 | 0,94 |
| лютый зверь | 0,88 | 0,85 | 0,87 |
| рогатый | 0,92 | 0,90 | 0,91 |
| терлась о локоть | 0,88 | 0,85 | 0,86 |
| иглою снежного огня | 0,95 | 0,95 | 0,95 |
| клавишей стая | 0,76 | 0,55 | 0,64 |
| горели глаза | 0,95 | 0,95 | 0,95 |
| цветок | 0,80 | 0,80 | 0,80 |
| загорелся | 0,91 | 0,90 | 0,90 |
| **Literal usages** | | | |
| ловил рыбу | 0,71 | 0,70 | 0,70 |
| играл в футбол | 0,74 | 0,70 | 0,71 |
| детство | 0,66 | 0,65 | 0,66 |
| кухня | 0,88 | 0,85 | 0,87 |
| снег | 0,95 | 0,95 | 0,95 |
| весна | 0,50 | 0,50 | 0,50 |
| пить кофе | 0,85 | 0,85 | 0,85 |
| танцы | 0,90 | 0,90 | 0,90 |
| платье | 0,65 | 0,65 | 0,65 |
| человек | 0,81 | 0,70 | 0,75 |
| ветер | 0,85 | 0,85 | 0,85 |
| дождь | 0,91 | 0,90 | 0,90 |

Table 2: Testing the algorithm. Accuracy of the k-means clustering

For 75% of metaphorical usages F-measure is 0,85 or more as was expected and for 50% of literal usages F-measure is 0,75 or less.

## 5 Figurative Language Uses as Outliers

The described above approach is to decide whether a word in a context is used literally or not. Unlike the first one, the second approach we propose, deals with a set of occurences of a word as to label every occurence as 'literal' or 'non-literal'. We formulate this task as a clustering problem and apply DBSCAN (Ester et al, 1996) clustering algorithm to the data. Miller and Charles (1991) hypothesized that words with similar meanings are often used in similar contexts. As it was mentioned, we can treat a meaning of a metaphoric usage of an expression as an additional, not common for the expression. That's why we expect metaphorical usages to be ouliers, while clustering together with common (i.e. literal) usages. Theoretically, the algorithm should also distinguish between all literal senses so that the contexts of the same meaning appear in the same cluster and the contexts of different meanings - in different clusters. Therefore, ideally, the algorithm should solve word sense discrimination and non-literal usages detection tasks simultaneously.

For each Russian word shown in Table 3, we extracted from the Russian National Corpora (`http://ruscorpora.ru/`) several literal and non-literal occurences. Some of these words have more than one meaning in Russian, e.g. ключ can be translated as a *key* or *water spring* and the word коса as a *plait*, *scythe* or *spit*.

| word | literal | non-literal |
|---|---|---|
| бабочка (butterfly, bow-tie) | 12 | 2 |
| иней (frost) | 14 | 2 |
| ключ (key, spring(water)) | 14 | 2 |
| коса (plait, scythe, spit) | 21 | 2 |
| лев (lion, Bulgarian lev) | 17 | 5 |
| лук (onion, bow) | 17 | 1 |
| мука (flour, pain) | 21 | 2 |
| пыль (dust) | 14 | 4 |

Table 3: Data used in the first experiment

All the documents are stemmed and all stopwords are removed with the SnowBall Stemmer (`http://snowball.tartarus.org/`) for the Russian language.

As it was mentioned above, this algorithm is aimed at providing word sense discrimination and non-literal usages detection simultaneously. So far we have paid attention only to the non-literal usages detection aspects. DBSCAN algorithm is a density-based clustering algorithm designed to discover clusters of arbitrary shape. This algorithm requires two parameters: $\varepsilon$ (eps) and the minimum number of points in a cluster (minPts).

We set minPts to 3 and run the algorithm for different eps between 1.45 and 1.55.

As was mentioned, so far we have considered only figurative language detection issues: The algorithm marks an instance as a figurative usage iff the instance is labeled as an outlier. Thus, we measure the accuracy of the algorithm as follows:

$$precision = \frac{|\ figurative\ uses\ | \bigcap |\ outliers\ |}{|\ outliers\ |},$$

$$recall = \frac{|\ figurative\ uses\ | \bigcap |\ outliers\ |}{|\ figurative\ uses\ |}.$$

Figures 1 and 2 show the dependency between the eps parameter and the algorithm's accuracy for different words.

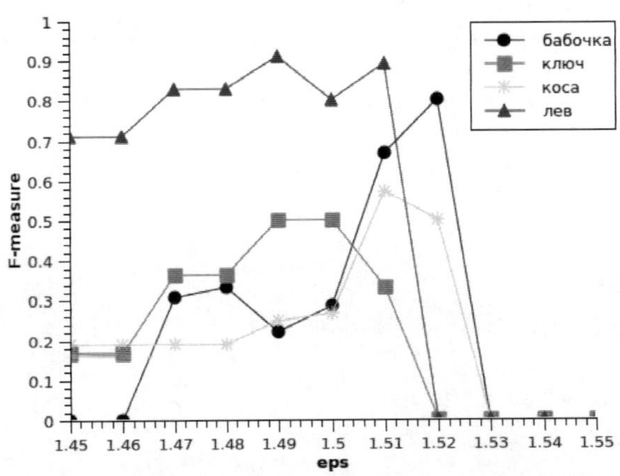


Figure 1: Dependency between eps and F-measure

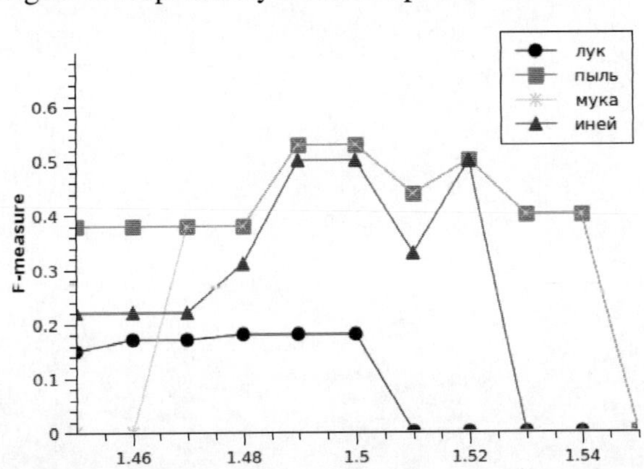


Figure 2: Dependency between eps and F-measure

Table 4 shows "the best" eps for each word and the corresponding accuracies of metaphor detection

| word | eps | precision | recall |
|---|---|---|---|
| бабочка | 1.520 | 0.66 | 1.00 |
| иней | 1.520 | 0.50 | 0.50 |
| ключ | 1.500 | 0.33 | 1.00 |
| коса | 1.510 | 0.40 | 1.00 |
| лев | 1.490 | 1.00 | 0.83 |
| лук | 1.505 | 0.17 | 1.00 |
| мука | 1.525 | 0.67 | 0.50 |
| пыль | 1.505 | 0.50 | 0.60 |

Table 4: The best eps parameters and corresponding accuracies of the algorithm

## 6 Future Work

So far we have worked only with tf-idf and word frequency model for both algorithms. The next step in our study is utilizing different text representation models, e.g. second order context vectors. We are also going to develop an efficient parameter estimation procedure for the algorithm based on DBSCAN clustering.

As for the other algorithm, we are going to distinguish between different figurative language expressions:

- one word expressions
  - monosemous word
  - polysemous word
- multiword expressions

We expect the basic algorithm to provide different accuracy in case of different types of expressions. Dealing with multiword expressions and monosemous words should be easier than with polysemous words: i.e., for monosemous word we expect the second set to appear as one cluster, whereas this set for a polysemous word is expected to have the number of clusters equal to the number of senses it has.

Another direction of the future work is developing an algorithm for figurative language uses *extraction*. The algorithm has to *find* figuratively used expressions in a text.

## 7 Conclusion

In this paper, we have proposed a framework for figurative language detection based on the idea of sense differentiation. We have illustrated how this idea works by presenting two clustering-based algorithms. The first algorithm deals with only one context. It is based on comparing two context sets: one is related to the expression and the other is semantically related to the given context. The second algorithm groups the given contexts in literal and non-literal usages. This algorithm should also distinguish between different senses of a word, but we have not yet paid enough attention to this aspect. By applying these algorithms to small data sets we have illustrated how the idea of sense differentiation works. These algorithms show quite good results and are worth further work.

## Acknowledgments

This work was partially supported by Russian Foundation for Basic Research RFBR, grant 10-07-00156.

## References

Vitaly I. Batov and Yury A. Sorokin. 1975. Text attribution based on objective characteristics. *Seriya yazyka i literatury*, 34, 1.

Julia Birke and Anoop Sarkar. 2006. A Clustering Approach for the Nearly Unsupervised Recognition of Nonliteral Language. *Proceedings of EACL-06*

Max Black. 1954. Metaphor. *Proceedings of the Aristotelian Society*, 55, pp. 273-294.

Martin Ester, Hans-Peter Kriegel, Jörg Sander and Xiaowei Xu. 1996. A density-based algorithm for discovering clusters in large spatial databases with noise. *Proceedings of the Second International Conference on Knowledge Discovery and Data Mining (KDD-96)*, AAAI Press, pp. 226231

Michael Halliday and Ruqaiya Hasan. 1976. Cohesion in English. *Longman, London*

Graham Katz and Eugenie Giesbrecht. 2006. Automatic identification of non-compositional multiword expressions using latent semantic analysis. *Proceedings of the ACL/COLING-06 Workshop on Multiword Expressions: Identifying and Exploiting Underlying Properties*

Linlin Li and Caroline Sporleder. August 2009. Classifier combination for contextual idiom detection without labeled data. *Proceedings of the 2009 Conference on Empirical Methods in Natural Language Processing*, pp. 315-323.

Rada Mihalcea, Courtney Corley and Carlo Strapparava. 2006. Corpus-based and Knowledge-based Measures of Text Semantic Similarity. *Proceedings of AAAI-06*

Rada Mihalcea. 2007. Using Wikipedia for Automatic Word Sense Disambiguation. *Proceedings of the North American Chapter of the Association for Computational Linguistics (NAACL 2007)*

George A. Miller and Walter G. Charles. 1991. Contextual correlates of semantic similarity. *Language and Cognitive Processes*, 6(1):128.

Malvina Nissim and Katja Markert. 2003. Syntactic features and word similarity for supervised metonymy resolution. *Proceedings of the 41st Annual Meeting of the Association for Computational Linguistics* (ACL-03) (Sapporo, Japan, 2003). 56-63.

Hinrich Schütze. 1998. Automatic word sense discrimination. *Computational Linguistics*, 24(1), pp. 97-123

Caroline Sporleder and Linlin Li. April 2009. Unsupervised recognition of literal and non-literal use of idiomatic expressions. *Proceedings of EACL-09*

Efstathios Stamatatos. 2009. A survey of modern authorship attribution methods. *Journal of the American Society for information Science and Technology*, 60(3): 538-556.

Denis Turdakov and Pavel Velikhov. 2008. Semantic Relatedness Metric for Wikipedia Concepts Based on Link Analysis and its Application to Word Sense Disambiguation *SYRCoDIS 2008*

# Automatic Selectional Preference Acquisition for Latin verbs

**Barbara McGillivray**
University of Pisa
Italy
b.mcgillivray@ling.unipi.it

## Abstract

We present a system that automatically induces Selectional Preferences (SPs) for Latin verbs from two treebanks by using Latin WordNet. Our method overcomes some of the problems connected with data sparseness and the small size of the input corpora. We also suggest a way to evaluate the acquired SPs on unseen events extracted from other Latin corpora.

## 1 Introduction

Automatic acquisition of semantic information from corpora is a challenge for research on low-resourced languages, especially when semantically annotated corpora are not available. Latin is definitely a high-resourced language for what concerns the number of available texts and traditional lexical resources such as dictionaries. Nevertheless, it is a low-resourced language from a computational point of view (McGillivray et al., 2009).

As far as NLP tools for Latin are concerned, parsing experiments with machine learning techniques are ongoing (Bamman and Crane, 2008; Passarotti and Ruffolo, forthcoming), although more work is still needed in this direction, especially given the small size of the training data. As a matter of fact, only three syntactically annotated Latin corpora are available (and still in progress): the Latin Dependency Treebank (LDT, 53,000 tokens) for classical Latin (Bamman and Crane, 2006), the *Index Thomisticus* Treebank (IT-TB, 54,000 tokens) for Thomas Aquinas's works (Passarotti, 2007), and the PROIEL treebank (approximately 100,000 tokens) for the Bible (Haug and Jøndal, 2008). In addition, a Latin version of WordNet – Latin WordNet (LWN; Minozzi, (2009) – is being compiled, consisting of around 10,000 lemmas inserted in the multilingual structure of MultiWordNet (Bentivogli et al., 2004). The number and the size of these resources are small when compared with the corpora and the lexicons for modern languages, e. g. English.

Concerning semantic processing, no semantically annotated Latin corpus is available yet; building such a corpus manually would take considerable time and energy. Hence, research in computational semantics for Latin would benefit from exploiting the existing resources and tools through automatic lexical acquisition methods.

In this paper we deal with automatic acquisition of verbal selectional preferences (SPs) for Latin, i. e. the semantic preferences of verbs on their arguments: e. g. we expect the object position of the verb *edo* 'eat' to be mostly filled by nouns from the food domain. For this task, we propose a method inspired by Alishahi (2008) and outlined in an earlier version on the IT-TB in McGillivray (2009). SPs are defined as probability distributions over semantic features extracted as sets of LWN nodes. The input data are two subcategorization lexicons automatically extracted from the LDT and the IT-TB (McGillivray and Passarotti, 2009).

Our main contribution is to create a new tool for semantic processing of Latin by adapting computational techniques developed for extant languages to the special case of Latin. A successful adaptation is contingent on overcoming corpus size differences. The way our model combines the syntactic information contained in the treebanks with the lexical semantic knowledge from LWN allows us to overcome some of the difficulties related to the small size of the input corpora. This is the main difference from corpora for modern languages, together with the absence of semantic annotation. Moreover, we face the problem of evaluating our system's ability to generalize over unseen cases by using text occurrences, as access to human linguistic judgements is denied for Latin.

In the rest of the paper we will briefly summarize previous work on SP acquisition and motivate



*Proceedings of the ACL 2010 Student Research Workshop*, pages 73–78,
Uppsala, Sweden, 13 July 2010. 

our approach (section 2); we will then describe our system (section 3), report on first results and evaluation (section 4), and finally conclude by suggesting future directions of research (section 5).

## 2 Background and motivation

The state-of-the-art systems for automatic acquisition of verbal SPs collect argument headwords from a corpus (for example, *apple*, *meat*, *salad* as objects of *eat*) and then generalize the observed behaviour over unseen cases, either in the form of words (how likely is it to find *sausage* in the object position of *eat*?) or word classes (how likely is it to find VEGETABLE, FOOD, etc?).

WN-based approaches translate the generalization problem into estimating preference probabilities over a noun hierarchy and solve it by means of different statistical tools that use the input data as a training set: cf. inter al. Resnik (1993), Li and Abe (1998), Clark and Weir (1999). Agirre and Martinez (2001) acquire SPs for verb classes instead of single verb lemmas by using a semantically annotated corpus and WN.

Distributional methods aim at automatically inducing semantic classes from distributional data in corpora by means of various similarity measures and unsupervised clustering algorithms: cf. e. g. Rooth et al. (1999) and Erk (2007). Bamman and Crane (2008) is the only distributional approach dealing with Latin. They use an automatically parsed corpus of 3.5 million words, then calculate SPs with the log-likelihood test, and obtain an association score for each (verb, noun) pair.

The main difference between these previous systems and our case is the size of the input corpus. In fact, our dataset consists of subcategorization frames extracted from two relatively small treebanks, amounting to a little over 100,000 word tokens overall. This results in a large number of low-frequency (verb, noun) associations, which may not reflect the actual distributions of Latin verbs. This state improves if we group the observations into clusters. Such a method, proposed by Alishahi (2008), proved effective in our case.

The originality of this approach is an incremental clustering algorithm for verb occurrences called *frames* which are identified by specific syntactic and semantic features, such as the number of verbal arguments, the syntactic pattern, and the semantic properties of each argument, i. e. the WN hypernyms of the argument's fillers. Based on a probabilistic measure of similarity between the frames' features, the clustering produces larger sets called *constructions*. The constructions for a verb contribute to the next step, which acquires the verb's SPs as *semantic profiles*, i. e. probability distributions over the semantic properties. The model exploits the structure of WN so that predictions over unseen cases are possible.

## 3 The model

The input data are two corpus-driven subcategorization lexicons which record the subcategorization frames of each verbal token occurring in the corpora: these frames contain morpho-syntactic information on the verb's arguments, as well as their lexical fillers. For example, 'eo + A_(in)Obj[acc]{exsilium}' represents an active occurrence of the verb *eo* 'go' with a prepositional phrase introduced by the preposition *in* 'to, into' and composed by an accusative noun phrase filled by the lemma *exsilium* 'exile', as in the sentence[1]

(1) eat in exsilium
go:SBJV.PRS.3SG to exile:ACC.N.SG
'he goes into exile'.

We illustrate how we adapted Alishahi's definitions of frame features and formulae to our case. Alishahi uses a semantically annotated English corpus, so she defines the verb's semantic primitives, the arguments' participant roles and their semantic categories; since we do not have such annotation, we used the WN semantic information.

The syntactic feature of a frame ($ft_1$) is the set of syntactic slots of its verb's subcategorization pattern, extracted from the lexicons. In the above example, 'A_(in)Obj[acc]'. In addition, the first type of semantic features of a frame ($ft_2$) collects the semantic properties of the verb's arguments as the set of LWN synonyms and hypernyms of their fillers. In the previous example this is {*exsilium* 'exile', *proscriptio* 'proscription', *rejection*, *actio*, *actus* 'act'}.[2] The second type of semantic features of a frame ($ft_3$) collects the semantic properties of the verb in the form of the verb's synsets. In the above example, these are all synsets of *eo* 'go', among which '{*eo*, *gradior*, *grassor*, *ingredior*, *procedo*, *prodeo*,

[1] Cicero, *In Catilinam*, II, 7.

[2] We listed the LWN node of the lemma *exsilium*, followed by its hypernyms; each node – apart from *rejection*, which is English and is not filled by a Latin lemma in LWN – is translated by the corresponding node in the English WN.

*vado}*' ('{*progress, come_on, come_along, advance, get_on, get_along, shape_up*}' in the English WN).

### 3.1 Clustering of frames

The constructions are incrementally built as new frames are included in them; a new frame $F$ is assigned to a construction $K$ if $F$ probabilistically shares some features with the frames in $K$ so that

$$K = \arg\max_k P(k|F) = \arg\max_k P(k)P(F|k),$$

where $k$ ranges over the set of all constructions, including the baseline $k_0 = \{F\}$. The prior probability $P(k)$ is calculated from the number of frames contained in $k$ divided by the total number of frames. Assuming that the frame features are independent, the posterior probability $P(F|k)$ is the product of three probabilities, each one corresponding to the probability that a feature displays in $k$ the same value it displays in $F$: $P_i(ft_i(F)|k)$ for $i = 1, 2, 3$:

$$P(F|k) = \prod_{i=1,2,3} P_i(ft_i(F)|k)$$

We estimated the probability of a match between the value of $ft_1$ in $k$ and the value of $ft_1$ in $F$ as the sum of the *syntactic scores* between $F$ and each frame $h$ contained in $k$, divided the number $n_k$ of frames in $k$:

$$P(ft_1(F)|k) = \frac{\sum_{h\in k} synt\_score(h, F)}{n_k}$$

where the syntactic score $synt\_score(h, F) = \frac{|SCS(h)\cap SCS(F)|}{|SCS(F)|}$ calculates the number of syntactic slots shared by $h$ and $F$ over the number of slots in $F$. $P(ft_1(F)|k)$ is 1 when all the frames in $k$ contain all the syntactic slots of $F$.

For each argument position $a$, we estimated the probability $P(ft_2(F)|k)$ as the sum of the *semantic scores* between $F$ and each $h$ in $k$:

$$P(ft_2(F)|k) = \frac{\sum_{h\in k} sem\_score(h, F)}{n_k}$$

where the semantic score $sem\_score(h, F) = \frac{|S(h)\cap S(F)|}{|S(F)|}$ counts the overlap between the semantic properties $S(h)$ of $h$ (i. e. the LWN hypernyms of the fillers in $h$) and the semantic properties $S(F)$ of $F$ (for argument $a$), over $|S(F)|$.

$$P(ft_3(F)|k) = \frac{\sum_{h\in k} syns\_score(h, F)}{n_k}$$

where the synset score $syns\_score(h, F) = \frac{|Synsets(verb(h))\cap Synsets(verb(F))|}{|Synsets(verb(F))|}$ calculates the overlap between the synsets for the verb in $h$ and the synsets for the verb in $F$ over the number of synsets for the verb in $F$.[3]

We introduced the syntactic and synset scores in order to account for a frequent phenomenon in our data: the partial matches between the values of the features in $F$ and in $k$.

### 3.2 Selectional preferences

The clustering algorithm defines the set of constructions in which the generalization step over unseen cases is performed. SPs are defined as semantic profiles, that is, probability distributions over the semantic properties, i. e. LWN nodes. For example, we get the probability of the node *actio* 'act' in the position 'A_(in)Obj[acc]' for *eo* 'go'.

If $s$ is a semantic property and $a$ an argument position for a verb $v$, the semantic profile $P_a(s|v)$ is the sum of $P_a(s, k|v)$ over all constructions $k$ containing $v$ or a WN-synonym of $v$, i. e. a verb contained in one or more synsets for $v$. $P_a(s, k|v)$ is approximated as $\frac{P(k,v)P_a(s|k,v)}{P(v)}$, where $P(k, v)$ is estimated as $\frac{n_k \cdot freq(k,v)}{\sum_{k'} n_{k'} \cdot freq(k',v)}$

To estimate $P_a(s|k, v)$ we consider each frame $h$ in $k$ and account for: a) the similarity between $v$ and the verb in $h$; b) the similarity between $s$ and the fillers of $h$. This is achieved by calculating a *similarity score* between $h$, $v$, $a$ and $s$, defined as:

$$syns\_score(v, V(h)) \cdot \frac{\sum_f |s \cap S(f)|}{N_{fil}(h, a)} \quad (1)$$

where $V(h)$ in (1) contains the verbs of $h$, $N_{fil}(h, a)$ counts the $a$-fillers in $h$, $f$ ranges in the set of $a$-fillers in $h$, $S(f)$ contains the semantic properties for $f$ and $|s\cap S(f)|$ is 1 when $s$ appears in $S(f)$ and 0 otherwise.

$P_a(s|k, v)$ is thus obtained by normalizing the sum of these similarity scores over all frames in $k$, divided by the total number of frames in $k$ containing $v$ or its synonyms.

The similarity scores weight the contributions of the synonyms of $v$, whose fillers play a role in the generalization step. This is our innovation with respect to Alishahi (2008)'s system. It was introduced because of the sparseness of our data, where

[3] The algorithm uses smoothed versions of all the previous formulae by adding a very small constant so that the probabilities are never 0.

| $k$ | $h$ |
|---|---|
| 1 | induco + P_Sb[acc]{forma}<br>introduco + P_Sb{PR}<br>introduco + P_Sb{forma}<br>addo +P_Sb{praesidium} |
| 2 | induco + A_Obj[acc]{forma}<br>immitto + A_Obj[acc]{PR},Obj[dat]{antrum}<br>introduco + A_Obj[acc]{NP} |
| 3 | introduco + A_(in)Obj[acc]{finis},Obj[acc]{copia},Sb{NP}<br>induco + A_(in)Obj[acc]{effectus},Obj[acc]{forma} |
| 4 | introduco + A_Obj[acc]{forma}<br>induco + A_Obj[acc]{perfectio},Sb[nom]{PR} |
| 5 | induco + A_Obj[acc]{forma}n<br>immitto + A_Obj[acc]{PR},Obj[dat]{antrum}<br>introduco + A_Obj[acc]{NP} |

Table 1: Constructions ($k$) for the frames ($h$) containing the verb *introduco* 'bring in'.

many verbs are hapaxes, which makes the generalization from their fillers difficult.

## 4 Results and evaluation

The clustering algorithm was run on 15509 frames and it generated 7105 constructions. Table 1 displays the 5 constructions assigned to the 9 frames where the verb *introduco* 'bring in, introduce' occurs. Note the semantic similarity between *addo* 'add to, bring to', *immitto* 'send against, insert', *induco* 'bring forward, introduce' and *introduco*, and the similarity between the syntactic patterns and the argument fillers within the same construction. For example, *finis* 'end, borders' and *effectus* 'result' share the semantic properties ATTRIBUTE, COGNITIO 'cognition', CONSCIENTIA 'conscience', EVENTUM 'event', among others.

The vast majority of constructions contain less than 4 frames. This contrasts with the more general constructions found by Alishahi (2008) and can be explained by several factors. First, the coverage of LWN is quite low with respect to the fillers in our dataset. In fact, 782 fillers out of 2408 could not be assigned to any LWN synset; for these lemmas the semantic scores with all the other nouns are 0, causing probabilities lower than the baseline; this results in assigning the frame to the singleton construction consisting of the frame itself. The same happens for fillers consisting of verbal lemmas, participles, pronouns and named entities, which amount to a third of the total number. Furthermore, the data are not tagged by sense and the system deals with noun ambiguity by listing together all synsets of a word $n$ (and their hypernyms) to form the semantic properties for $n$: consequently, each sense contributes to the semantic description of $n$ in relation to the number of hypernyms it carries, rather than to its observed frequency. Finally, a common problem in SP acquisition systems is the noise in the data, including tagging and metaphorical usages. This problem is even greater in our case, where the small size of the data underestimates the variance and therefore overestimates the contribution of noisy observations. Metaphorical and abstract usages are especially frequent in the data from the IT-TB, due to the philosophical domain of the texts.

| semantic property | probability |
|---|---|
| *actio* 'act' | 0.0089 |
| *actus* 'act' | 0.0089 |
| *pars* 'part' | 0.0089 |
| *object* | 0.0088 |
| *physical object* | 0.0088 |
| *instrumentality* | 0.0088 |
| *instrumentation* | 0.0088 |
| *location* | 0.0088 |
| *populus* 'people' | 0.0088 |
| *plaga* 'region' | 0.0088 |
| *regio* 'region' | 0.0088 |
| *arvum* 'area' | 0.0088 |
| *orbis* 'area' | 0.0088 |
| *external body part* ' | 0.0088 |
| *nympha* 'nymph', 'water' | 0.0088 |
| *latex* 'water' | 0.0088 |
| *lympha* 'water' | 0.0088 |
| *intercapedo* 'gap, break' | 0.0088 |
| *orificium* 'opening' | 0.0088 |

Table 2: Top 20 semantic properties in the semantic profile for *ascendo* 'ascend' + A_(de)Obj[abl].

As to the SP acquisition, we ran the system on all constructions generated by the clustering. We excluded the pronouns occurring as argument fillers, and manually tagged the named entities. For each verb lemma and slot we obtained a probability distribution over the 6608 LWN noun nodes.

Table 2 displays the 20 semantic properties with the highest SP probabilities as ablative arguments of *ascendo* 'ascend' introduced by *de* 'down from', 'out of'. This semantic profile was created from the following fillers for the verbs contained in the constructions for *ascendo* and its synonyms: *abyssus* 'abyss', *fumus* 'smoke', *lacus* 'lake', *machina* 'machine', *manus* 'hand', *negotiatio* 'business', *mare* 'sea', *os* 'mouth', *templum* 'temple', *terra* 'land'. These nouns are well represented by the semantic properties related to water and physical places. Note also the high rank of general properties like *actio* 'act', which are associated to a large number of fillers and thus generally get a high probability.

Regarding evaluation, we are interested in testing two properties of our model: calibration and discrimination. Calibration is related to the model's ability to distinguish between high and low probabilities. We verify that our model is adequately calibrated, since its SP distribution is always very skewed (cf. figure 1). Therefore, the model is able to assign a high probability to a small set of nouns (preferred nouns) and a low probability to a large set of nouns (the rest), thus performing better than the baseline model, defined as the model that assigns the uniform distribution over all nouns (4724 LWN leaf nodes). Moreover, our model's entropy is always lower than the baseline: 12.2 vs. the 6.9-11.3 range; by the maximum entropy principle, this confirms that the system uses some information for estimating the probabilities: LWN structure, co-occurrence frequency, syntactic patterns. However, we have no guarantee that the model uses this information sensibly. For this, we test the system's discrimination potential, i. e. its ability to correctly estimate the SP probability of each single LWN node.

| noun | SP probability |
|---|---|
| *pars* 'part' | 0.0029 |
| *locus* 'place' | 0.0026 |
| *forma* 'form' | 0.0023 |
| *ratio* 'account' 'reason', 'opinion' | 0.0023 |
| *respectus* 'consideration' | 0.0022 |
| *caput* 'head', 'origin' | 0.0022 |
| *anima* 'soul' | 0.0021 |
| *animus* 'soul', 'spirit' | 0.0020 |
| *figura* 'form', 'figure' | 0.0020 |
| *spiritus* 'spirit' | 0.0020 |
| *causa* cause' ' | 0.0020 |
| *corpus* 'body' | 0.0019 |
| *sententia* 'judgement' | 0.0019 |
| *finitio* 'limit', 'definition' | 0.0019 |
| *species* 'sight', 'appearance' | 0.0019 |

Table 3: 15 nouns with the highest probabilities as accusative objects of *dico* 'say'.

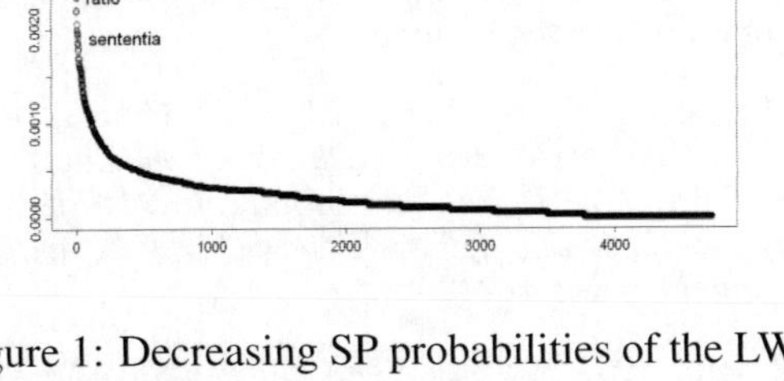


Figure 1: Decreasing SP probabilities of the LWN leaf nodes for the objects of *dico* 'say'.

Table 3 displays the 15 nouns with the highest probabilities as direct objects for *dico* 'say'. From table 3 – and the rest of the distribution, represented in figure 1 – we see that the model assigns a high probability to most seen fillers for *dico* in the corpus: *anima* 'soul', *corpus* 'body', *locus* 'place', *pars* 'part', etc.

For what concerns evaluating the SP probability assigned to nouns unseen in the training set, Alishahi (2008) follows the approach suggested by Resnik (1993), using human plausibility judgements on verb-noun pairs. Given the absence of native speakers of Latin, we used random occurrences in corpora, considered as positive examples of plausible argument fillers; on the other hand, we cannot extract non-plausible fillers from a corpus unless we use a frequency-based criterion. However, we can measure how well our system predicts the probability of these unseen events.

As a preliminary evaluation experiment, we randomly selected from our corpora a list of 19 high-frequency verbs (freq.>51) and 7 medium-frequency verbs (11<freq.<50), for each of which we chose an interesting argument slot. Then we randomly extracted one filler for each such pair from two collections of Latin texts (*Perseus Digital Library* and *Corpus Thomisticum*), provided that it was not in the training set. The semantic score in equation 1 on page 3 is then calculated between the set of semantic properties of $n$ and that for $f$, to obtain the probability of finding the random filler $n$ as an argument for a verb $v$.

For each of the 26 (verb, slot) pairs, we looked at three measures of central tendency: mean, median and the value of the third quantile, which were compared with the probability assigned by the model to the random filler. If this probability was higher than the measure, the outcome was considered a success. The successes were 22 for the mean, 25 for the median and 19 for the third quartile.[4] For all three measures a binomial test found the success rate to be statistically significant at the 5% level. For example, table 3 and figure 1 show that the filler for *dico*+A_Obj[acc] in the evaluation set – *sententia* 'judgement' – is ranked 13th within the verb's semantic profile.

## 5 Conclusion and future work

We proposed a method for automatically acquiring probabilistic SP for Latin verbs from a small corpus using the WN hierarchy; we suggested some

[4]The dataset consists of all LWN leaf nodes $n$, for which we calculated $P_a(n|v)$. By definition, if we divide the dataset in four equal-sized parts (*quartiles*), 25% of the leaf nodes have a probability higher than the value at the third quartile. Therefore, in 19 cases out of 26 the random fillers are placed in the high-probability quarter of the plot, which is a good result, since this is where the preferred arguments gather.

new strategies for tackling the data sparseness in the crucial generalization step over unseen cases. Our work also contributes to the state of the art in semantic processing of Latin by integrating syntactic information from annotated corpora with the lexical resource LWN. This demonstrates the usefulness of the method for small corpora and the relevance of computational approaches for historical linguistics.

In order to measure the impact of the frame clusters for the SP acquisition, we plan to run the system for SP acquisition without performing the clustering step, thus defining all constructions as singleton sets containing one frame each. Finally, an extensive evaluation will require a more comprehensive set, composed of a higher number of unseen argument fillers; from the frequencies of these nouns, it will be possible to directly compare plausible arguments (high frequency) and implausible ones (low frequency). For this, a larger automatically parsed corpus will be necessary.

## 6 Acknowledgements

We wish to thank Afra Alishahi, Stefano Minozzi and three anonymous reviewers.

## References

E. Agirre and D. Martinez. 2001. Learning class-to-class selectional preferences. In *Proceedings of the ACL/EACL 2001 Workshop on Computational Natural Language Learning (CoNLL-2001)*, pages 1–8.

A. Alishahi. 2008. *A probabilistic model of early argument structure acquisition*. Ph.D. thesis, Department of Computer Science, University of Toronto.

D. Bamman and G. Crane. 2006. The design and use of a Latin dependency treebank. In *Proceedings of the Fifth International Workshop on Treebanks and Linguistic Theories*, pages 67–78. ÚFAL MFF UK.

D. Bamman and G. Crane. 2008. Building a dynamic lexicon from a digital library. In *Proceedings of the 8th ACM/IEEE-CS Joint Conference on Digital Libraries*, pages 11–20.

L. Bentivogli, P. Forner, and and Pianta E. Magnini, B. 2004. Revising wordnet domains hierarchy: Semantics, coverage, and balancing. In *Proceedings of COLING Workshop on Multilingual Linguistic Resources*, pages 101–108.

S. Clark and D. Weir. 1999. An iterative approach to estimating frequencies over a semantic hierarchy. In *Proceedings of the Joint SIGDAT Conference on Empirical Methods in Natural Language Processing and Very Large Corpora. University of Maryland*, pages 258–265.

K. Erk. 2007. A simple, similarity-based model for selectional preferences. In *Proceedings of the 45th Annual Meeting of the Association for Computational Linguistics*, pages 216–223.

D. T. T. Haug and M. L. Jøndal. 2008. Creating a parallel treebank of the old Indo-European Bible translations. In *Proceedings of Language Technologies for Cultural Heritage Workshop*, pages 27–34.

H. Li and N. Abe. 1998. Generalizing case frames using a thesaurus and the MDL principle. *Computational Linguistics*, 24(2):217–244.

B. McGillivray and M. Passarotti. 2009. The development of the *Index Thomisticus* Treebank Valency Lexicon. In *Proceedings of the Workshop on Language Technology and Resources for Cultural Heritage, Social Sciences, Humanities, and Education*, pages 33–40.

B. McGillivray, M. Passarotti, and P. Ruffolo. 2009. The *Index Thomisticus* treebank project: Annotation, parsing and valency lexicon. *TAL*, 50(2):103–127.

B. McGillivray. 2009. Selectional Preferences from a Latin treebank. In Przepiórkowski A. Passarotti, M., S. Raynaud, and F. van Eynde, editors, *Proceedings of the Eigth International Workshop on Treebanks and Linguistic Theories (TLT8)*, pages 131–136. EDUCatt.

S. Minozzi. 2009. The Latin Wordnet project. In P. Anreiter and M. Kienpointner, editors, *Proceedings of the 15th International Colloquium on Latin Linguistics (ICLL)*, Innsbrucker Beitraege zur Sprachwissenschaft.

M. Passarotti and P. Ruffolo. forthcoming. Parsing the *Index Thomisticus Treebank*. some preliminary results. In P. Anreiter and M. Kienpointner, editors, *Proceedings of the 15th International Colloquium on Latin Linguistics*, Innsbrucker Beiträge zur Sprachwissenschaft.

M. Passarotti. 2007. Verso il Lessico Tomistico Biculturale. La treebank dell'*Index Thomisticus*. In R. Petrilli and D. Femia, editors, *Atti del XIII Congresso Nazionale della Società di Filosofia del Linguaggio*, pages 187–205.

P. Resnik. 1993. *Selection and Information: A Class-Based Approach to Lexical Relationships*. Ph.D. thesis, University of Pennsylvania.

M. Rooth, S. Riezler, D. Prescher, G. Carroll, and F. Beil. 1999. Inducing a semantically annotated lexicon via EM-based clustering. In *Proceedings of the 37th Annual Meeting of the Association for Computational Linguistics*, pages 104–111.

# Edit Tree Distance alignments for Semantic Role Labelling

**Hector-Hugo Franco-Penya**
Trinity College Dublin
Dublin, Ireland.
francoph@cs.tcd.ie

## Abstract

"Tree SRL system" is a Semantic Role Labelling supervised system based on a tree-distance algorithm and a simple k-NN implementation. The novelty of the system lies in comparing the sentences as tree structures with multiple relations instead of extracting vectors of features for each relation and classifying them. The system was tested with the English CoNLL-2009 shared task data set where 79% accuracy was obtained.

## 1 Introduction

Semantic Role Labelling (SRL) is a natural language processing task which deals with semantic analysis at sentence-level. SRL is the task of identifying arguments for a certain predicate and labelling them. The predicates are usually verbs. They establish "what happened". The arguments determine events such as "who", "whom", "where", etc, with reference to one predicate. The possible semantic roles are pre-defined for each predicate. The set of roles depends on the corpora.

SRL is becoming an important tool for information extraction, text summarization, machine translation and question answering (Màrquez, et al, 2008).

## 2 The data

The data set I used is taken from the CoNLL-2009 shared task (Hajič et al., 2009) and is part of Propbank. Propbank (Palmer et al, 2005) is a hand-annotated corpus. It transforms sentences into propositions. It adds a semantic layer to the Penn TreeBank (Marcus et al, 1994) and defines a set of semantic roles for each predicate.

It is difficult to define universal semantic roles for all predicates. That is why PropBank defines a set of semantic roles for each possible sense of each predicate (frame) [See a sample of the frame "raise" on the Figure 1 caption].

| | Sentences | predicates | arguments | Predicates per sentence | arguments per sub-tree | File size in Mb |
|---|---|---|---|---|---|---|
| Tra | 39279 | 179014 | 393699 | 4.55 | 2.20 | 56.2 |
| Dev | 1334 | 6390 | 13865 | 4.79 | 2.17 | 1.97 |
| Evl | 2399 | 10498 | 23286 | 4.38 | 2.22 | 3.41 |

**Table 1:** The data

The data set is divided into three files: training (Tra), development (Dev) and evaluation (Evl). The following table describes the number of sentences, sub-trees and labels contained in them, and the ratios of sub-trees per sentences and relations per sub-tree.

The core arguments are labelled by numbers. Adjuncts, which are common to all predicates, have their own labels, like: AM-LOC, TMP, NEG, etc. The four most frequent labels in the data set are: A1:35%, A0:20.86%, A2:7.88% and AM-TMP: 7.72%

Propbank was originally built using constituent tree structures, but here only the dependency tree structure version was used. Note that dependency tree structures have labels on the arrows. The tree distance algorithm cannot work with these labelled arrows and so they are moved to the child node as an extra label.

The task performed by the Tree SRL system consists of labelling the relations (predicate arguments) which are assumed to be already identified.

## 3 Tree Distance

The tree distance algorithm has already been applied to text entailment (Kouylekov & Magnini, 2005) and question answering (Punyakanok et al, 2004; Emms, 2006) with positive results.

The main contribution of this piece of work to the SRL field is the inclusion of the tree distance algorithm into an SRL system, working with tree structures in contrast to the classical "feature extraction" and "classification". Kim et al (2009) developed a similar system for Information Extraction.



*Proceedings of the ACL 2010 Student Research Workshop*, pages 79–84,
Uppsala, Sweden, 13 July 2010. 

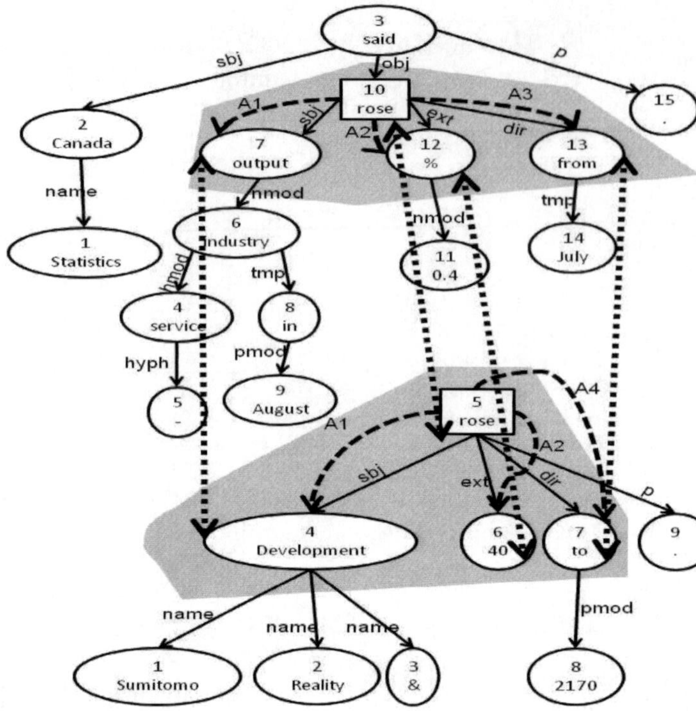


**Figure 1:** Alignment sample
A two sentence sample, in a dependency tree representation. In each node, the word form and the position of the word in the sentence are shown. Straight arrows represent syntactic dependencies. The label of the dependency is not shown. The square node represent the predicate that is going to be analyzed, (there can be multiple predicates in a single sentence). Semi-dotted arrows between a square node and an ellipse node represent a semantic relation. This arrow has a semantic tag (A1, A2, A3 and A4).

The grey shadow contains all the nodes of the sub tree for the "rose" predicate.
The dotted double arrows between the nodes of both sentences represent the tree distance alignment for both sub-trees. In this particular case every single node is matched.

Both predicate nodes are samples of the frame "raise" sense 01 (which means "go up quantifiably") where the core arguments are:
**A0**: Agent, causer of motion **A1**: Logical subject, patient, thing rising
**A2**: EXT, amount raised **A3**: Start point **A4:** End point **AM**: Medium

Tai (1979) introduced a criterion for matching nodes between tree representations (or converting one tree into another one) and (Shasha & Zhang, 1990; Zhang & Shasha, 1989) developed an algorithm that finds an optimal matching tree solution for any given pair of trees. The advantage of this algorithm is that its computational cost is low. The optimal matching depends on the defined atomic cost of matching two nodes.

## 4 Tree SRL system architecture

For the training and testing data set, all possible sub-trees were extracted. Figure 3 and Figure 5 describe the process. Then, using the tree distance algorithm, the test sub-trees are labelled using the training ones. Finally, the predicted labels get assembled on the original sentence where the test sub-tree came from. Figure 2 describes the process.

A sub-tree extracted from a sentence, contains a predicate node, all its argument nodes and all the ancestors up to the first common ancestor of all nodes. (Figure 1 shows two samples of sub-tree extraction. Figure 3 describes how sub trees are obtained)

**Input**: training data set (labelled)
**Input**: testing data set (unlabelled)
**Output**: testing data set (labelled)
Load training and testing data;
Adapt the trees for the tree distance algorithm;
**foreach** sentence (training & testing data) **do**
    obtain each minimal sub-tree for each predicate;
**end**
**foreach** sub-tree T from the testing data **do**
    calculate the distance and the alignment from T to each training sub-tree;
    sort the list of alignments by ascending tree distance;
    use the list to label the sub-tree T;
    Assemble T labels on the original sentence
**End**

**Figure 2:** Tree SRL system pseudo code

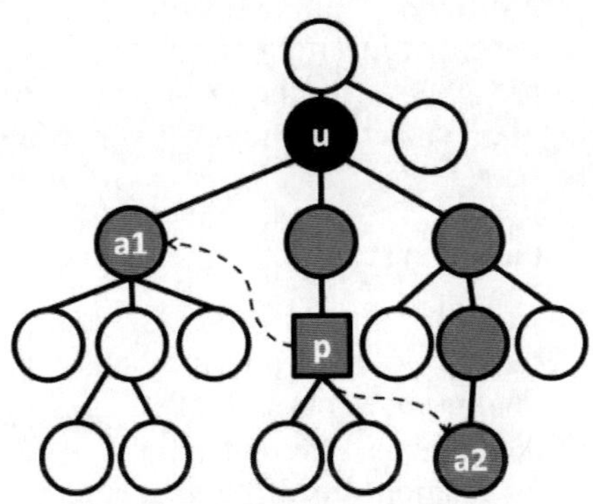


**Figure 3:** Sub-tree extraction sample. Assuming that "p" (the square node) is a predicate node and the nodes "a1" and "a2" are its arguments (the arguments are defined by the semantic relations. In this case, the semi-doted arrows.), the sub-tree extracted from the above sentence will contain the nodes: "a1", "a2", "p", all ancestors of "a1","a2" and "p" up to the first common one, in this case node "u", which is also included in the sub-tree. All of the white nodes are not included in the sub-tree. The straight lines represent syntactic dependency relations.

## 5 Labelling

Suppose that in Figure 1, the bottom sentence is the query, where the grey shadow contains the sub-tree to be labelled and the top sentence contains the sub-tree sample chosen to label the query. Then, an alignment between the sample sub-tree and the query sub-tree suggests labelling the query sub-tree with A1, A2 and A3, where the first two labels are right but the last label, A4, is predicted as A3, so it is wrong.

**Input**: A sub-tree to be labelled
**Input:** list of alignments sorted by ascending tree distance
**Output:** labelled sub-tree
**foreach** argument(a) in T **do**
  **foreach** alignment (ali) in the sorted list **do**
    **if** there is a semantic relation (ali.function(p),ali.function(a))
      **Then** break loop;
    **end**
  **end**
  label relation p-a with the label of the relation (ali.function(p),ali.function(a));
**end**
**p** is the node predicate.
**a** is a node argument.
**ali** is an alignment between the sub-tree that has to be labelled and a sub-tree in the training dataset.
The method function is explained in Figure 3.

**Figure 4:** Labelling a relation. (approach A)

**Input**: T: tree structure labelled in post order traversal
**Input**: L: list of nodes to be on the sub-tree in post order traversal
**Output**: T: Sub-Tree
**foreach** node x in the list **do**
  mark x as part of the sub-tree;
**end**
**while** L contains more than 2 unique values **do**
  [minValue , position]=min(L);
  Value = parent(minValue);
  Mark value as part of the sub-tree;
  L[position] = value;
**end**
Remove all nodes that are not marked as part of the sub-tree;

**Figure 5:** Sub-tree extraction

It is not necessary to label a whole sub-tree (query) using just a single sub-tree sample. However, if the whole query is labelled using a single answer sample, the prediction is guaranteed to be consistent (no repeated argument labels).

Some possible ways to label the semantic relation using a sorted list of alignments (with each sub-tree of the training data set) is discussed ahead. Each sub-tree contains one predicate and several semantic relations, one for each argument node.

### 5.1 Treating relations independently

In this sub-section, the neighbouring sub-trees for one relation of a sub-tree T refers to the nearest sub-trees with which the match with T produces a match between two predicate nodes and two argument nodes. A label from the nearest neighbour(s) can be transferred to T for labelling the relation.

The current implementation **(Approach A),** described in more detail in Figure 4, labels a relation using the first nearest neighbour from a list ordered by ascending tree distance. If there are several nearest neighbours, the first one on the list is used. This is a naive implementation of the k-NN algorithm where in case of multiple nearest neighbours only one is used and the others get ignored.

A negative aspect of this strategy is that it can select a different sub-tree based on the input order. This makes the algorithm indeterministic. A way to make it deterministic can be by extending the parameter "k" in case of multiple cases at the same distance or a tie in the voting **(Approach B)**.

### 5.2 Treating relations dependently

In this section, a sample refers to a sub-tree containing all arguments and its labels. The arguments for a certain predicate are related.

Some strategies can lead to non-consistent structures (core argument labels cannot appear twice in the same sub-tree). **Approach B** treats the relations independently. It does not have any mechanism to keep the consistency of the whole predicate structure.

Another way is to find a sample that contains enough information to label the whole sub-tree **(Approach C)**. This approach always generates consistent structures. The limitation of this model is that the required sample may not exist or the tree distance may be very high, making those samples poor predictors. The implemented method **(Approach A)** indirectly attempts to find a training sample sub-tree which contains labels for all the arguments of the predicate.

It is expected for tree distances to be smaller than other sub-trees that do not have information to label all the desired relations.

The system tries to get a consistent structure using a simple algorithm. Only in the case when using the nearest tree does not lead to labelling the whole structure, labels are predicted using multiple samples, thereby, risking the structure consistency.

Future implementations will rank possible candidate labels for each relation (probably using multiple samples).

A "joint scoring algorithm", which is commonly used (Marquez et al, 2008), can be applied for consistency checking after finding the rank probability for all the argument labels for the same predicate **(Approach D)**.

## 6 Experiments: the matching cost

The cost of matching two nodes is crucial to the performance of the system. Different atomic measures (ways to measure the cost of matching two nodes) that were tested are explained ahead. Results for experiments using these atomic measures are given in Table 2.

### 6.1 Binary system

For Binary system, the atomic cost of matching two nodes is one if label POS or dependency relations are different, otherwise the cost is zero. The atomic cost of inserting or deleting a node is always one. Note that the measure is totally based on the syntactic structure (words are not used).

### 6.2 Ternary system

The next intuitive measure is how the system would perform in case of a ternary cost (ternary system). The atomic cost is half if POS **or** dependency relation is different, one if POS **and** dependency relation are different or zero in all other case. For this system, Table 2 shows a very similar accuracy to the binary one.

### 6.3 Hamming system

The atomic cost of matching two nodes is the sum of the following sub costs:

0.25 if POS is different.
0.25 if dependency relation is different.
0.25 if Lemma is different.
0.25 if one node is a predicate but the other is not or if both nodes are predicates but with different lemma.

The cost to create or delete nodes is one. Note that the sum of all costs cannot be greater than one.

### 6.4 Predicate match system

The analysis of results for the previous systems shows that the accuracy is higher for the subtrees that are labelled using sub-trees with the same predicate node. Consequently, this strategy attempts to force the predicate to be the same.

In this system, the atomic cost of matching two nodes is the sum of the following sub costs:

0.3 if POS is different.
0.3 if dependency relation is different.
1 if one is a predicate and the other node is not or both nodes are predicates but with different lemma.

The cost to create or delete nodes is one.

### 6.5 Complex system

This strategy attempts to improve the accuracy by adding an extra label to the argument nodes and using it.

The atomic cost of matching two nodes is the sum of the following sub costs:

0.1 for each different label (dependency relation or POS or lemma).
0.1 for each pair of different labels (dependency relation or POS or lemma).
0.4 if one node is a predicate and the other is not.
0.4 if both nodes are predicates and lemma is different.
2 if one node is marked as an argument and the other is not or one node is marked as a predicate and the other is not.

The atomic cost of deleting or inserting a node is: two if the node is an argument or predicate node and one in any other case.

## 7 Results

Table 2 shows the accuracy of all the systems. The validation data set is added to the training data set when the system is labelling the evaluation data set. This is a common methodology followed in CoNLL2009 (Li et al, 2009).

| System | Evaluation | Development |
|---|---|---|
| Binary | 64.36% | 61.12% |
| Ternary | 64.88% | 61.28% |
| Hamming | 78.01% | |
| Predicate Match | 76.98% | |
| Complex | 78.98% | |

**Table 2:** System accuracy

Accuracy is measured as the percentage of semantic labels correctly predicted.

The implementation of the Tree SRL system takes several days to run a single experiment. It makes non viable the idea of using the development data set for adjusting parameters and that is why, for the last three systems (Hamming, Predicate Match and Complex), the accuracy over the development data set is not measured. The same reason supports adding the development data set to the training data set without over fitting the system, because the development data set is not really used for adjusting parameters.

However, the observations of the system on the development data set shows:

1. If the complexity gets increased (Ternary), the number of cases having the multiple nearest sub-trees gets reduced.
2. The output of the system only contains five per cent of inconsistent structures (Binary and Ternary), which is lower than expected. 0.5% of inconsistent sub-trees were detected in the training data-set.
3. Higher accuracy for the relations where a sub-tree is labelled using a sub-tree sample which has the same predicate node. This has led to the design of the "predicate match" and the "complex" systems.
4. Some sub-trees are very small (just one node). This resulted in low accuracy for they predicted labels due to multiple nearest neighbours.

It is surprising that the hamming measure reaches higher accuracy than the "predicate match", which uses more information, and is also surprising that the accuracies for "Hamming", "Predicate Match" and "Complex" systems are very similar.

The CoNLL-2009 SRL shared task was evaluated on multiple languages: Catalan, Chinese, Czech, English, German, Japanese and Spanish. Some results for those languages using "Tree SRL System Binary" are shown in Table 3.

| Language | Accuracy on evaluation | Training data set size in Mb |
|---|---|---|
| English | 64.36% | 56 |
| Spanish | 57.86% | 46 |
| Catalan | 58.49% | 43 |
| Japanese | 50.71% | 8 |
| German | These languages had been excluded from the experiments because some of the sentences did not follow a dependency tree structure. | |
| Czech | | |
| Chinese | | |

**Table 3:** Accuracy for other languages (Binary system)

The accuracy results for multiple languages suggest that the size of the corpora has a strong influence on the results of the system performance.

The results are not comparable with the rest of the CoNLL-2009 systems because the task is different. This system does not identify arguments and does not perform predicate sense disambiguation.

## 8 Conclusion

The tree distance algorithm has been applied successfully to build a SRL system. Future work will focus on improving the performance of the system by: a) trying to extend the sub-trees which will contain more contextual information, b) using different approaches to label semantic relations discussed in Section 5. Also, the system will be expanded to identify arguments using a tree distance algorithm.

Evaluating the task of identifying the arguments and labelling the relations separately will assist in determining which systems to combine to create an hybrid system with better performance.

**Acknowledgments**
This research is supported by the Science Foundation Ireland (Grant 07/CE/I1142) as part of the Centre for Next Generation Localisation (www.cngl.ie) at Trinity College Dublin.

Thanks are due to Dr Martin Emms for his support on the development of this project.

## References

Martin Emms. 2006. Variants of Tree Similarity in a Question Answering Task. *In Proceedings of the Workshop on Linguistic Distances, held in conjunction with COLING 2006,* 100—108, Sydney, Australia, Asociation for Computational Linguistics.

Jan Hajič, Massimiliano Ciaramita, Richard Johansson, Daisuke Ka-wahara, Maria Antonia Martí, Luis Màrquez, Adam Meyers, Joakim Nivre, Sebastian Padó, Jan Štěpánek, Pavel Stravnák, Mihai Surdeanu, Nianwen Xue and Yi Zhang. 2009. The CoNLL-2009 shared task: syntactic and semantic dependencies in multiple languages. *In CoNLL '09: Proceedings of the Thirteenth Conference on Computational Natural Language Learning* (pp. 1-18). Morristown, NJ, USA: Association for Computational Linguistics.

Seokhwan Kim, Minwoo Jeong and Gary Geunbae Lee. 2009. A Local Tree Alignment-based Soft Pattern Matching Approach for Information Extraction. *Proceedings of NAAACL HLT*, 169-172. Boulder, Colorado, June 2009

Milen Kouylekov and Bernardo Magnini. 2005. Recognizing textual entailment with tree edit distance algorithms. *In Recognizing Textual Entailment* (pp. 17-20). Southampton, U.K.

Baoli Li, Martin Emms, Saturnino Luz and Carl Vogel. 2009. Exploring multilingual semantic role labeling. *In CoNLL '09: Proceedings of the Thirteenth Conference on Computational Natural Language Learning* (pp. 73-78). Morristown, NJ, USA: Association for Computational Linguistics.

Mitchell Marcus, Beatrice Santorini and Mary Ann Marcinkiewicz. 1994. Building a large annotated corpus of Eng-lish: The Penn Treebank. *Computational linguistics*, 19(2), 313–330.

Alessandro Moschitti, Daniele Pighin and Roberto Basili. 2008. Tree kernels for semantic role labeling. *Computational Linguistics,* 34(2), 193-224. Cambridge, MA, USA: MIT Press.

Lluis Màrquez, Xavier Carreras, Kenneth. C. Litkowski and Suzanne Stevenson. 2008. Semantic Role Labeling: An Introduction to the Special Issue. *Computational Linguistics*, 34(2), 145-159.

Martha Palmer, Paul Kingsbury and Daniel Gildea. 2005. The Proposition Bank: An Annotated Corpus of Semantic Roles. *Computational Linguistics*, 31(1), 71-106.

Vasin Punyakanok, Dan Roth and Wen-tau Yih. 2004. Mapping dependencies trees: An application to question answering. *In Proceedings of AI\&Math* 2004 (pp. 1-10). Ford.

Dennis Shasha and Kaizhong Zhang. 1990. Fast algorithms for the unit cost editing distance between trees. *J. Algorithms*, 11(4), 581-621. Duluth, MN, USA: Academic Press, Inc.

Kuo-Chung Tai. 1979. The Tree-to-Tree Correction Problem. *J. ACM,* 26(3), 422-433. New York, NY, USA: ACM.

Kaizhong Zhang and Dennis Shasha. 1989. Simple fast algorithms for the editing distance between trees and related problems. SIAM *J. Comput.*, 18(6), 1245-1262. Philadelphia, PA, USA: Society for Industrial and Applied Mathematics.

# Automatic Sanskrit Segmentizer Using Finite State Transducers

**Vipul Mittal**
Language Technologies Research Center, IIIT-H,
Gachibowli, Hyderabad, India.
vipulmittal@research.iiit.ac.in

## Abstract

In this paper, we propose a novel method for automatic segmentation of a Sanskrit string into different words. The input for our segmentizer is a Sanskrit string either encoded as a Unicode string or as a Roman transliterated string and the output is a set of possible splits with weights associated with each of them. We followed two different approaches to segment a Sanskrit text using *sandhi*[1] rules extracted from a parallel corpus of manually sandhi split text. While the first approach augments the finite state transducer used to analyze Sanskrit morphology and traverse it to segment a word, the second approach generates all possible segmentations and validates each constituent using a morph analyzer.

## 1 Introduction

Sanskrit has a rich tradition of oral transmission of texts and this process causes the text to undergo euphonic changes at the word boundaries. In oral transmission, the text is predominantly spoken as a continuous speech. However, continuous speech makes the text ambiguous. To overcome this problem, there is also a tradition of reciting the pada-pāṭha (recitation of words) in addition to the recitation of a saṃhitā (a continuous sandhied text). In the written form, because of the dominance of oral transmission, the text is written as a continuous string of letters rather than a sequence of words. Thus, the Sanskrit texts consist of a very long sequence of phonemes, with the word boundaries having undergone euphonic changes. This makes it difficult to split a continuous string into words and process the text automatically.

Sanskrit words are mostly analyzed by building a finite state transducer (Beesley, 1998). In the first approach, this transducer was modified by linking the final states to appropriate intermediate states incorporating the sandhi rules. This approach then allows one to traverse the string from left to right and generate all and only possible splits that are morphologically valid. The second approach is very closely based on the *Optimality Theory* (Prince and Smolensky, 1993) where we generate all the possible splits for a word and validate each using a morphological analyzer. We use one of the fastest morphological analyzers available viz. the one developed by *Apertium* group[2]. The splits that are not validated are pruned out. Based on the number of times the first answer is correct, we achieved an accuracy of around 92% using the second approach while the first approach performed with around 71% accuracy.

## 2 Issues involved in Sanskrit Processing

The segmentizer is an important component of an NLP system. Especially, languages such as Chinese (Badino, 2004), Japanese, Thai (Haruechaiyasak, 2008) or Vietnamese (Thang et al. , 2008) which do not mark word boundaries explicitly or highly agglutinative languages like Turkish need segmentizers. In all these languages, there are no explicit delimiters to specify the word boundaries. In Thai, each syllable is transcribed using several characters and there is no space in the text between syllables. So the problem of segmentation is basically twofold: (1) syllable segmentation followed by (2) word segmentation itself. A sentence in these languages

[1] *Sandhi* means euphony transformation of words when they are consecutively pronounced. Typically when a word $w_1$ is followed by a word $w_2$, some terminal segment of $w_1$ merges with some initial segment of $w_2$ to be replaced by a "smoothed" phonetic interpolation, corresponding to minimizing the energy necessary to reconfigurate the vocal organs at the juncture between the words.

[2] http://wiki.apertium.org/wiki/lttoolbox; It processes around 50,000 words per sec.



*Proceedings of the ACL 2010 Student Research Workshop*, pages 85–90,
Uppsala, Sweden, 13 July 2010. 

is segmented by predicting the word boundaries, where euphonic changes do not occur across the word boundaries and it is more like mere concatenation of words. So the task here is just to choose between various combinations of the words in a sentence.

However, in Sanskrit, euphonic changes occur across word boundaries leading to addition and deletion of some original part of the combining words. These euphonic changes in Sanskrit introduce non-determinism in the segmentation. This makes the segmentation process in Sanskrit more complex than in Chinese or Japanese. In case of highly agglutinative languages like Turkish, the components are related to each other semantically involving dependency analysis. Whereas in Sanskrit, only the compounds involve a certain level of dependency analysis, while sandhi is just gluing of words together, without the need for words to be related semantically. For example, consider the following part of a verse,

San: *nāradam paripapraccha vālmīkirmunipuṅgavam*
gloss: to_the_Narada asked Valmiki-to_the_wisest_among_sages
Eng: Valmiki asked the Narada, the wisest among the sages.

In the above verse, the words *vālmīkiḥ* and *munipuṅgavam* (wisest among the sages - an adjective of Narada) are not related semantically, but still undergo euphonic change and are glued together as *vālmīkirmunipuṅgavam.*

Further, the split need not be unique. Here is an example, where a string *māturājñāmparipālaya* may be decomposed in two different ways after undergoing euphonic changes across word boundaries.

- *mātuh ājñām paripālaya* (obey the order of mother) and,
- *mā āturājñām paripālaya* (do not obey the order of the diseased).

There are special cases where the sandhied forms are not necessarily written together. In such cases, the white space that physically marks the boundary of the words, logically refers to a single sandhied form. Thus, the white space is deceptive, and if treated as a word boundary, the morphological analyzer fails to recognize the word. For example, consider

*śrutvā ca nārado vacaḥ.*

In this example, the space between *śrutvā* and *ca* represent a proper word boundary and the word *śrutvā* is recognized by the morphological analyzer whereas the space between *nārado* and *vacaḥ* does not mark the word boundary making it deceptive. Because of the word *vacaḥ*, *nāradaḥ* has undergone a phonetic change and is rendered as *nārado*. In unsandhied form, it would be written as,

San: *śrutvā ca nāradaḥ vacaḥ.*
gloss: after_listening and Narada's speech
Eng: And after listening to Narada's speech

The third factor aggravating Sanskrit segmentation is productive compound formation. Unlike English, where either the components of a compound are written as distinct words or are separated by a hyphen, the components of compounds in Sanskrit are always written together. Moreover, before these components are joined, they undergo the euphonic changes. The components of a compound typically do not carry inflection or in other words they are the bound morphemes used only in compounds. This forces a need of a special module to recognize compounds.

Assuming that a sandhi handler to handle the sandhi involving spaces is available and a bound morpheme recognizer is available, we discuss the development of sandhi splitter or a segmentizer that splits a continuous string of letters into meaningful words. To illustrate this point, we give an example.
Consider the text,

*śrutvā caitattrilokajño vālmīkernārado vacaḥ.*

We assume that the sandhi handler handling the sandhi involving spaces is available and it splits the above string as,

*śrutvā caitattrilokajñaḥ vālmīkernāradaḥ vacaḥ.*

The sandhi splitter or segmentizer is supposed to split this into *śrutvā ca etat triloka-jñaḥ vālmīkeḥ nāradaḥ vacaḥ.*

This presupposes the availability of rules corresponding to euphonic changes and a good coverage morphological analyzer that can also analyze the bound morphemes in compounds.

A segmentizer for Sanskrit developed by Huet (Huet, 2009), decorates the final states of its finite state transducer handling Sanskrit morphology with the possible sandhi rules. However, it is still not clear how one can prioritize various splits with this approach. Further, this system in current state demands some more work before the sandhi splitter of this system can be used as a standalone system allowing plugging in of different morphological analyzers. With a variety of morphological analyzers being developed by various researchers[3], at times with complementary abilities, it would be worth to experiment with various morphological analyzers for splitting a sandhied text. Hence, we thought of exploring other alternatives and present two approaches, both of which assume the existence of a good coverage morphological analyzer. Before we describe our approaches, we first define the scoring matrix used to prioritize various analyses followed by the baseline system.

## 3 Scoring Matrix

Just as in the case of any NLP systems, with the sandhi splitter being no exception, it is always desirable to produce the most likely output when a machine produces multiple outputs. To ensure that the correct output is not deeply buried down the pile of incorrect answers, it is natural to prioritize solutions based on some frequencies. A Parallel corpus of Sanskrit text in sandhied and sandhi split form is being developed as a part of the Consortium project in India. The corpus contains texts from various fields ranging from children stories, dramas to Ayurveda texts. Around 100K words of such a parallel corpus is available from which around 25,000 parallel strings of unsandhied and corresponding sandhied texts were extracted. The same corpus was also used to extract a total of 2650 sandhi rules including the cases of mere concatenation, and the frequency distribution of these sandhi rules. Each sandhi rule is a triple $(x, y, z)$ where $y$ is the last letter of the first primitive, $z$ is the first letter of the second primitive, and $x$ is the letter sequence created by euphonic combination. We define the estimated probability of the occurrence of a sandhi rule as follows:

Let $R_i$ denote the $i^{th}$ rule with $f_{R_i}$ as the frequency of occurrence in the manually split parallel text. The probability of rule $R_i$ is:

$$P_{R_i} = \frac{f_{R_i}}{\sum_{i=1}^{n} f_{R_i}}$$

where $n$ denotes the total number of sandhi rules found in the corpus.

Let a word be split into a candidate $S_j$ with $k$ constituents as $< c_1, c_2, ..c_k >$ by applying $k-1$ sandhi rules $< R_1, R_2, ..R_{k-1} >$ in between the constituents. It should be noted here that the rules $R_1, ..R_{k-1}$ and the constituents $c_1, ..c_k$ are interdependent since a different rule sequence will result in a different constituents sequence. Also, except $c_1$ and $c_k$, all intermediate constituents take part in two segmentations, one as the right word and one as the left.

The weight of the split $S_j$ is defined as:

$$W_{S_j} = \frac{\prod_{x=1}^{k-1}(P_{c_x} + P_{c_{x+1}}) * P_{R_x}}{k}$$

where $P_{c_x}$ is the probability of occurrence of the word $c_x$ in the corpus. The factor of $k$ was introduced to give more preference to the split with less number of segments than the one with more segments.

## 4 Baseline System

We define our own baseline system which assumes that each Sanskrit word can be segmented only in two constituents. A word is traversed from left to right and is segmented by applying the first applicable rule provided both the constituents are valid morphs. Using the 2,650 rules, on a test data of 2,510 words parallel corpus, the baseline performance of the system was around 52.7% where the first answer was correct.

## 5 Two Approaches

We now present the two approaches we explored for sandhi splitting.

### 5.1 Augmenting FST with Sandhi rules

In this approach, we build an FST, using OpenFst (Allauzen et al., 2007) toolkit, incorporating

[3] http://sanskrit.uohyd.ernet.in, http://www.sanskritlibrary.org, http://sanskrit.jnu.ernet.in

sandhi rules in the FST itself and traverse it to find the sandhi splittings.

We illustrate the augmentation of a sandhi rule with an example. Let the two strings be *xaXi* (dadhi)[4] and *awra* (atra). The initial FST without considering any sandhi rules is shown in Figure 1.

### 5.1.1 Results

The performance of this system measured in terms of the number of times the highest ranked segmentation is correct, with around 500 sandhi rules, and only noun morphology tested on the same test data used for testing baseline system gave the following rank-wise distribution presented in Table 1.

| Rank | % of output |
|---|---|
| 1 | 71.2509 |
| 2 | 5.64543 |
| 3 | 3.85324 |
| 4 | 3.35651 |
| 5 | 1.56123 |
| >5 | 14.33268 |

Table 1: Rank-wise Distribution for Approach-1.

The system was slow consuming, on an average, around 10 seconds per string of 15 letters.[5].

With the increase in the sandhi rules, though system's performance was better, it slowed down the system further. Moreover, this was tested only with the inflection morphology of nouns. The verb inflection morphology and the derivational morphology were not used at all. Since, the system is supposed to be part of a real time application viz. machine translation, we decided to explore other possibilities.

### 5.2 Approach based on Optimality Theory

Our second approach follows optimality theory(OT) which proposes that the observed forms of a language are a result of the interaction between the conflicting constraints. The three basic components of the theory are:

1. GEN - generates all possible outputs, or candidates.

2. CON - provides the criteria and the constraints that will be used to decide between candidates.

3. EVAL - chooses the optimal candidate based on the conflicts on the constraints.

OT assumes that these components are universal and the grammars differ in the way they rank the universal constraint set, CON. The grammar of each language ranks the constraints in some dominance order in such a way that every constraint must have outperformed every lower ranked constraint. Thus a candidate A is optimal if it performs better than some other candidate B on a higher ranking constraint even if A has more violations of a lower ranked constraint than B.

The GEN function produces every possible segmentation by applying the rules wherever applicable. The rules tokenize the input surface form into individual constituents. This might contain some insignificant words that will be eventually pruned out using the morphological analyser in the EVAL function thus leaving the winning candidate. Therefore, the approach followed is very closely based on optimality theory. The morph analyser has no role in the generation of the candidates but only during their validation thus composing the back-end of the segmentizer. In original OT, the winning candidate need not satisfy all the constraints but it must outperform all the other candidates on some higher ranked constraint. While in our scenario, the winning candidate must satisfy all the constraints and therefore there could be more than one winning candidates.

Currently we are applying only two constraints. We are planning to introduce some more constraints. The constraints applied are:

- C1 : All the constituents of a split must be valid morphs.

- C2 : Select the split with maximum weight, as defined in section 3.

The basic outline of the algorithm is:

1: Recursively break a word at every possible position applying a sandhi rule and generate all possible candidates for the input.
2: Pass the constituents of all the candidates through the morph analyzer.
3: Declare the candidate as a valid candidate, if all its constituents are recognized by the morphological analyzer.
4: Assign weights to the accepted candidates and sort them based on the weights.
5: The optimal solution will be the one with the highest salience.

### 5.2.1 Results

The current morphological analyzer can recognize around 140 million words. Using the 2650 rules

[5] Tested on a system with 2.93GHz Core 2 Duo processor and 2GB RAM

and the same test data used for previous approach, we obtained the following results:

- Almost 93% of the times, the highest ranked segmentation is correct. And in almost 98% of the cases, the correct split was among the top 3 possible splits.
- The system consumes around 0.04 seconds per string of 15 letters on an average.

The complete rank wise distribution is given in Table 2.

| | % of output | |
|---|---|---|
| **Rank** | **Approach-1** | **Approach-2** |
| 1 | 71.2509 | **92.8771** |
| 2 | 5.64543 | 5.44693 |
| 3 | 3.85324 | 1.07076 |
| 4 | 3.35651 | 0.41899 |
| 5 | 1.56123 | 0.09311 |
| >5 | 14.33268 | 0.0931 |

Table 2: Complete rank-wise Distribution.

## 6 Conclusion

We presented two methods to automatically segment a Sanskrit word into its morphologically valid constituents. Though both the approaches outperformed the baseline system, the approach that is close to optimality theory gives better results both in terms of time consumption and segmentations. The results are encouraging. But the real test of this system will be when it is integrated with some real application such as a machine translation system. This sandhi splitter being modular, wherein one can plug in different morphological analyzer and different set of sandhi rules, the splitter can also be used for segmentization of other languages.

**Future Work** The major task would be to explore ways to shift rank 2 and rank 3 segmentations more towards rank 1. We are also exploring the possibility of including some semantic information about the words while defining weights. The sandhi with white spaces also needs to be handled.

## Acknowledgments

I would like to express my gratitude to Amba Kulkarni and Rajeev Sangal for their guidance and support.

## References

Akshar Bharati, Amba P. Kulkarni, and V Sheeba. 2006. *Building a wide coverage Sanskrit morphological analyzer: A practical approach.* The First National Symposium on Modelling and Shallow Parsing of Indian Languages, IIT-Bombay.

Alan Prince and Paul Smolensky. 1993. *Optimality Theory: Constraint Interaction in Generative Grammar.* RuCCS Technical Report 2 at Center for Cognitive Science, Rutgers University, Piscataway.

Amba Kulkarni and Devanand Shukla. 2009. *Sanskrit Morphological analyzer: Some Issues.* To appear in Bh.K Festschrift volume by LSI.

Choochart Haruechaiyasak, Sarawoot Kongyoung, and Matthew N. Dailey. 2008. *A Comparative Study on Thai Word Segmentation Approaches.* ECTI-CON, Krabi.

Cyril Allauzen, Michael Riley, Johan Schalkwyk, Wojciech Skut, and Mehryar Mohri. 2007. *OpenFst: A General and Efficient Weighted Finite-State Transducer Library.* CIAA'07, Prague, Czech Republic.

Deniz Yuret and Ergun Biçici. 2009. *Modeling Morphologically Rich Languages Using Split Words and Unstructured Dependencies.* ACL-IJCNLP'09, Singapore.

DINH Q. Thang, LE H. Phuong, NGUYEN T. M. Huyen, NGUYEN C. Tu, Mathias Rossignol, and VU X. Luong. 2008. *Word Segmentation of Vietnamese Texts: a Comparison of Approaches.* LREC'08, Marrakech, Morocco.

Gérard Huet. 2009. *Formal structure of Sanskrit text: Requirements analysis for a mechanical Sanskrit processor.* Sanskrit Computational Linguistics 1 & 2, pages 266-277, Springer-Verlag LNAI 5402.

John C. J. Hoeks and Petra Hendriks. 2005. *Optimality Theory and Human Sentence Processing: The Case of Coordination.* Proceedings of the 27th Annual Meeting of the Cognitive Science Society, Erlbaum, Mahwah, NJ, pp. 959–964.

Kenneth R. Beesley. 1998. *Arabic morphology using only finite-state operations* Proceedings of the ACL Workshop on Computational Approaches to Semitic Languages, Montréal, Québec.

Leonardo Badino. 2004. *Chinese Text Word-Segmentation Considering Semantic Links among Sentences.* INTERSPEECH 2004 - ICSLP , Jeju, Korea.

# Adapting Self-training for Semantic Role Labeling

**Rasoul Samad Zadeh Kaljahi**
FCSIT, University of Malaya
50406, Kuala Lumpur, Malaysia.
rsk7945@perdana.um.edu.my

## Abstract

Supervised semantic role labeling (SRL) systems trained on hand-crafted annotated corpora have recently achieved state-of-the-art performance. However, creating such corpora is tedious and costly, with the resulting corpora not sufficiently representative of the language. This paper describes a part of an ongoing work on applying bootstrapping methods to SRL to deal with this problem. Previous work shows that, due to the complexity of SRL, this task is not straight forward. One major difficulty is the propagation of classification noise into the successive iterations. We address this problem by employing *balancing* and *preselection* methods for self-training, as a bootstrapping algorithm. The proposed methods could achieve improvement over the base line, which do not use these methods.

## 1 Introduction

Semantic role labeling has been an active research field of computational linguistics since its introduction by Gildea and Jurafsky (2002). It reveals the event structure encoded in the sentence, which is useful for other NLP tasks or applications such as information extraction, question answering, and machine translation (Surdeanu et al., 2003). Several CoNLL shared tasks (Carreras and Marquez, 2005; Surdeanu et al., 2008) dedicated to semantic role labeling affirm the increasing attention to this field.

One important supportive factor of studying *supervised* statistical SRL has been the existence of hand-annotated semantic corpora for training SRL systems. *FrameNet* (Baker et al., 1998) was the first such resource, which made the emergence of this research field possible by the seminal work of Gildea and Jurafsky (2002). However, this corpus only exemplifies the semantic role assignment by selecting some illustrative examples for annotation. This questions its suitability for statistical learning. *Propbank* was started by Kingsbury and Palmer (2002) aiming at developing a more representative resource of English, appropriate for statistical SRL study.

Propbank has been used as the learning framework by the majority of SRL work and competitions like CoNLL shared tasks. However, it only covers the newswire text from a specific genre and also deals only with verb predicates.

All state-of-the-art SRL systems show a dramatic drop in performance when tested on a new text domain (Punyakanok et al., 2008). This evince the infeasibility of building a comprehensive hand-crafted corpus of natural language useful for training a robust semantic role labeler.

A possible relief for this problem is the utility of *semi-supervised* learning methods along with the existence of huge amount of natural language text available at a low cost. Semi-supervised methods compensate the scarcity of labeled data by utilizing an additional and much larger amount of unlabeled data via a variety of algorithms.

*Self-training* (Yarowsky, 1995) is a semi-supervised algorithm which has been well studied in the NLP area and gained promising result. It iteratively extend its training set by labeling the unlabeled data using a base classifier trained on the labeled data. Although the algorithm is theoretically straightforward, it involves a large number of parameters, highly influenced by the specifications of the underlying task. Thus to achieve the best-performing parameter set or even to investigate the usefulness of these algorithms for a learning task such as SRL, a thorough experiment is required. This work investigates its application to the SRL problem.

## 2 Related Work

The algorithm proposed by Yarowsky (1995) for the problem of word sense disambiguation has been cited as the origination of self-training. In that work, he bootstrapped a ruleset from a



*Proceedings of the ACL 2010 Student Research Workshop*, pages 91–96,
Uppsala, Sweden, 13 July 2010. 

| Feature Name | Description |
|---|---|
| Phrase Type | Phrase type of the constituent |
| Position+Predicate Voice | Concatenation of constituent position relative to verb and verb voice |
| Predicate Lemma | Lemma of the predicate |
| Predicate POS | POS tag of the predicate |
| Path | Tree path of non-terminals from predicate to constituent |
| Head Word Lemma | Lemma of the head word of the constituent |
| Content Word Lemma | Lemma of the content word of the constituent |
| Head Word POS | POS tag of the head word of the constituent |
| Content Word POS | POS tag of the head word of the constituent |
| Governing Category | The first VP or S ancestor of a NP constituent |
| Predicate Subcategorization | Rule expanding the predicate's parent |
| Constituent Subcategorization * | Rule expanding the constituent's parent |
| Clause+VP+NP Count in Path | Number of clauses, NPs and VPs in the path |
| Constituent and Predicate Distance | Number of words between constituent and predicate |
| Compound Verb Identifier | Verb predicate structure type: simple, compound, or discontinuous compound |
| Head Word Location in Constituent * | Location of head word inside the constituent based on the number of words in its right and left |

Table 1: Features

small number of seed words extracted from an online dictionary using a corpus of unannotated English text and gained a comparable accuracy to fully supervised approaches.

Subsequently, several studies applied the algorithm to other domains of NLP. Reference resolution (Ng and Cardie 2003), POS tagging (Clark et al., 2003), and parsing (McClosky et al., 2006) were shown to be benefited from self-training. These studies show that the performance of self-training is tied with its several parameters and the specifications of the underlying task.

In SRL field, He and Gildea (2006) used self-training to address the problem of unseen frames when using FrameNet as the underlying training corpus. They generalized FrameNet frame elements to 15 thematic roles to control the complexity of the process. The improvement gained by the progress of self-training was small and inconsistent. They reported that the NULL label (non-argument) had often dominated other labels in the examples added to the training set.

Lee et al. (2007) attacked another SRL learning problem using self-training. Using Propbank instead of FrameNet, they aimed at increasing the performance of supervised SRL system by exploiting a large amount of unlabeled data (about 7 times more than labeled data). The algorithm variation was similar to that of He and Gildea (2006), but it only dealt with core arguments of the Propbank. They achieved a minor improvement too and credited it to the relatively poor performance of their base classifier and the insufficiency of the unlabeled data.

## 3 SRL System

To have enough control over entire the system and thus a flexible experimental framework, we developed our own SRL system instead of using a third-party system. The system works with PropBank-style annotation and is described here.

**Syntactic Formalism:** A Penn Treebank constituent-based approach for SRL is taken. Syntactic parse trees are produced by the reranking parser of Charniak and Johnson (2005).

**Architecture:** A two-stage pipeline architecture is used, where in the first stage less-probable argument candidates (samples) in the parse tree are pruned, and in the next stage, final arguments are identified and assigned a semantic role. However, for unlabeled data, a preprocessing stage identifies the verb predicates based on the POS tag assigned by the parser. The joint argument identification and classification is chosen to decrease the complexity of self-training process.

**Features:** Features are listed in table 1. We tried to avoid features like named entity tags to less depend on extra annotation. Features marked with * are used in addition to common features in the literature, due to their impact on the performance in feature selection process.

**Classifier:** We chose a *Maximum Entropy* classifier for its efficient training time and also its built-in multi-classification capability. Moreover, the probability score that it assigns to labels is useful in selection process in self-training. The *Maxent Toolkit*[1] was used for this purpose.

[1]http://homepages.inf.ed.ac.uk/lzhang10/maxent_toolkit.html

1- Add the seed example set ***L*** to currently empty training set ***T***.
2- Train the base classifier ***C*** with training set ***T***.
3- Iterate the following steps until the stop criterion ***S*** is met.
   a- **Select *p*** examples from ***U*** into pool ***P***.
   b- Label pool ***P*** with classifier ***C***
   c- **Select *n*** labeled examples with the highest confidence score whose score meets a certain threshold ***t*** and **add** to training set ***T***.
   d- Retrain the classifier ***C*** with new training set.

Figure 1: Self-training Algorithm

| | WSJ Test | | | Brown Test | | |
|---|---|---|---|---|---|---|
| | P | R | F1 | P | R | F1 |
| **Cur** | 77.43 | 68.15 | **72.50** | 69.14 | 57.01 | **62.49** |
| **Pun** | 82.28 | 76.78 | **79.44** | 73.38 | 62.93 | **67.75** |

Table 2: Performances of the current system (Cur) and the state-of-the-art (**Pun**yakanok et al., 2008)

## 4 Self-training

### 4.1 The Algorithm

While the general theme of the self-training algorithm is almost identical in different implementations, variations of it are developed based on the characteristics of the task in hand, mainly by customizing several involved parameters. Figure 1 shows the algorithm with highlighted parameters.

The size of seed labeled data set **L** and unlabeled data **U**, and their ratio are the fundamental parameters in any semi-supervised learning. The data used in this work is explained in section 5.1.

In addition to performance, efficiency of the classifier (**C**) is important for self-training, which is computationally expensive. Our classifier is a compromise between performance and efficiency. Table 2 shows its performance compared to the state-of-the-art (Punyakanok et al. 2008) when trained on the whole labeled training set.

Stop criterion (**S**) can be set to a predetermined number of iterations, finishing all of the unlabeled data, or convergence of the process in terms of improvement. We use the second option for all experiments here.

In each iteration, one can label entire the unlabeled data or only a portion of it. In the latter case, a number of unlaleled examples (**p**) are selected and loaded into a *pool* (**P**). The selection can be based on a specific strategy, known as *preselection* (Abney, 2008) or simply done according to the original order of the unlabeled data. We investigate preselection in this work.

After labeling the **p** unlabeled data, training set is augmented by adding the newly labeled data. Two main parameters are involved in this step: *selection* of labeled examples to be added to training set and *addition* of them to that set.

Selection is the crucial point of self-training, in which the propagation of labeling noise into upcoming iterations is the major concern. One can select all of labeled examples, but usually only a number of them (**n**), known as *growth size*, based on a quality measure is selected. This measure is often the confidence score assigned by the classifier. To prevent poor labelings diminishing the quality of training set, a threshold (**t**) is set on this confidence score. Selection is also influenced by other factors, one of which being the balance between selected labels, which is explored in this study and explained in detail in the section 4.3.

The selected labeled examples can be retained in unlabeled set to be labeled again in next iterations (*delibility*) or moved so that they are labeled only once (*indelibility*). We choose the second approach here.

### 4.2 Preselection

While using a pool can improve the efficiency of the self-training process, there can be two other motivations behind it, concerned with the performance of the process.

One idea is that when all data is labeled, since the growth size is often much smaller than the labeled size, a uniform set of examples preferred by the classifier is chosen in each iteration. This leads to a biased classifier like the one discussed in previous section. Limiting the labeling size to a pool and at the same time (pre)selecting divergence examples into it can remedy the problem.

The other motivation is originated from the fact that the base classifier is relatively weak due to small seed size, thus its predictions, as the measure of confidence in selection process, may not be reliable. Preselecting a set of unlabeled examples more probable to be correctly labeled by the classifier in initial steps seems to be a useful strategy against this fact.

We examine both ideas here, by a random preselection for the first case and a measure of simplicity for the second case. Random preselection is built into our system, since we use randomized training data. As the measure of simplicity, we propose the number of samples extracted from each sentence; that is we sort unlabeled sentences in ascending order based on the number of samples and load the pool from the beginning.

### 4.3 Selection Balancing

Most of the previous self-training problems involve a binary classification. Semantic role labeling is a multi-class classification problem with an unbalanced distribution of classes in a given text. For example, the frequency of A1 as the most frequent role in CoNLL training set is 84,917, while the frequency of 21 roles is less than 20. The situation becomes worse when the dominant label NULL (for non-arguments) is added for argument identification purpose in a joint architecture. This biases the classifiers towards the frequent classes, and the impact is magnified as self-training proceeds.

In previous work, although they used a reduced set of roles (yet not balanced), He and Gildea (2006) and Lee et al. (2007), did not discriminate between roles when selecting high-confidence labeled samples. The former study reports that the majority of labels assigned to samples were NULL and argument labels appeared only in last iterations.

To attack this problem, we propose a natural way of balancing, in which instead of labeling and selection based on argument samples, we perform a sentence-based selection and labeling. The idea is that argument roles are distributed over the sentences. As the measure for selecting a labeled sentence, the average of the probabilities assigned by the classifier to all argument samples extracted from the sentence is used.

## 5 Experiments and Results

In these experiments, we target two main problems addressed by semi-supervised methods: the performance of the algorithm in exploiting unlabeled data when labeled data is scarce and the domain-generalizability of the algorithm by using an out-of-domain unlabeled data.

We use the CoNLL 2005 shared task data and setting for testing and evaluation purpose. The evaluation metrics include *precision*, *recall*, and their harmonic mean, *F1*.

### 5.1 The Data

The labeled data are selected from Propbank corpus prepared for CoNLL 2005 shared task. Our learning curve experiments on varying size of labeled data shows that the steepest increase in F1 is achieved by $1/10^{th}$ of CoNLL training data. Therefore, for training a base classifier as high-performance as possible, while simulating the labeled data scarcity with a reasonably small amount of it, 4000 sentence are selected randomly from the total 39,832 training sentences as seed data (L). These sentences contain 71,400 argument samples covering 38 semantic roles out of 52 roles present in the total training set.

We use one unlabeled training set (U) for in-domain and another for out-of-domain experiments. The former is the remaining portion of CoNLL training data and contains 35,832 sentences (698,567 samples). The out-of-domain set was extracted from Open American National Corpus [2] (OANC), a 14-million words multi-genre corpus of American English. The whole corpus was preprocessed to prune some problematic sentences. We also excluded the *biomed* section due to its large size to retain the domain balance of the data. Finally, 304,711 sentences with the length between 3 and 100 were parsed by the syntactic parser. Out of these, 35,832 sentences were randomly selected for the experiments reported here (832,795 samples).

Two points are worth noting about the results in advance. First, we do not exclude the argument roles not present in seed data when evaluating the results. Second, we observed that our predicate-identification method is not reliable, since it is solely based on POS tags assigned by parser which is error-prone. Experiments with gold predicates confirmed this conclusion.

### 5.2 The Effect of Balanced Selection

Figures 2 and 3 depict the results of using unbalanced and balanced selection with WSJ and OANC data respectively. To be comparable with previous work (He and Gildea, 2006), the growth size (n) for unbalanced method is 7000 samples and for balanced method is 350 sentences, since each sentence roughly contains 20 samples. A probability threshold (t) of 0.70 is used for both cases. The F1 of base classifier, best-performed classifier, and final classifier are marked.

When trained on WSJ unlabeled set, the balanced method outperforms the other in both WSJ (68.53 vs. 67.96) and Brown test sets (59.62 vs. 58.95). A two-tail t-test based on different random selection of training data confirms the statistical significance of this improvement at $p<=0.05$ level. Also, the self-training trend is

[2] http://www.americannationalcorpus.org/OANC

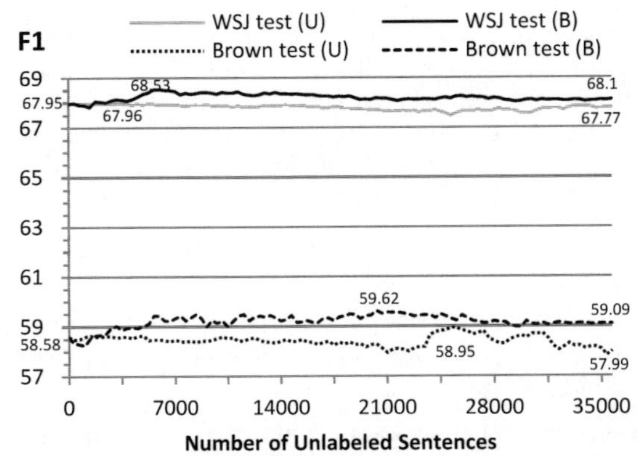


Figure 2: Balanced (B) and Unbalanced (U) Selection with WSJ Unlabeled Data

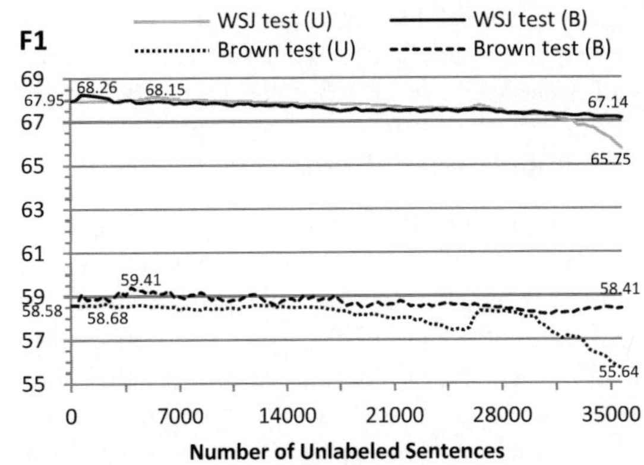


Figure 3: Balanced (B) and Unbalanced (U) Selection with OANC Unlabeled Data

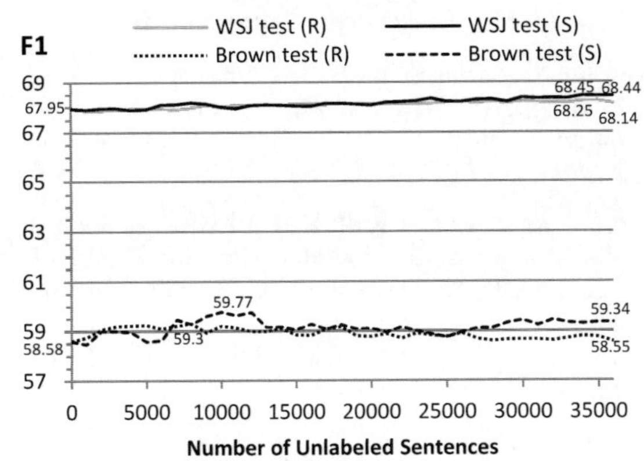


Figure 4: Random (R) and Simplicity (S) Pre-selection with WSJ Unlabeled Data

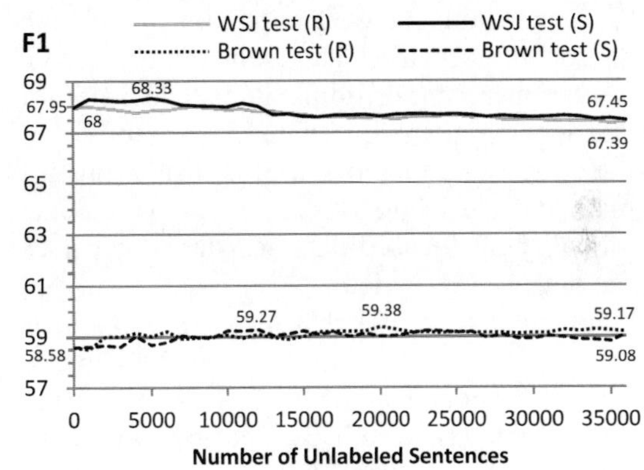


Figure 5: Random (R) and Simplicity (S) Pre-selection with OANC Unlabeled Data

more promising with both test sets. When trained on OANC, the F1 degrades with both methods as self-training progress. However, for both test sets, the best classifier is achieved by the balanced selection (68.26 vs. 68.15 and 59.41 vs. 58.68). Moreover, balanced selection shows a more normal behavior, while the other degrades the performance sharply in the last iterations (due to a swift drop of recall).

Consistent with previous work, with unbalanced selection, non-NULL-labeled unlabeled samples are selected only after the middle of the process. But, with the balanced method, selection is more evenly distributed over the roles.

A comparison between the results on Brown test set with each of unlabeled sets shows that in-domain data generalizes even better than out-of-domain data (59.62 vs. 59.41 and also note the trend). One apparent reason is that the classifier cannot accurately label the out-of-domain unlabeled data successively used for training. The lower quality of our out-of-domain data can be another reason for this behavior. Furthermore, the parser we used was trained on WSJ, so it negatively affected the OANC parses and consequently its SRL results.

### 5.3 The Effect of Preselection

Figures 4 and 5 show the results of using pool with random and simplicity-based preselection with WSJ and OANC data respectively. The pool size (p) is 2000, and growth size (n) is 1000 sentences. The probability threshold (t) used is 0.5.

Comparing these figures with the previous figures shows that preselection improves the self-training trend, so that more unlabeled data can still be useful. This observation was consistent with various random selection of training data.

Between the two strategies, simplicity-based method outperforms the random method in both self-training trend and best classifier F1 (68.45 vs. 68.25 and 59.77 vs. 59.3 with WSJ and 68.33 vs. 68 with OANC), though the t-test shows that the F1 difference is not significant at $p<=0.05$. This improvement does not apply to the case of using OANC data when tested with Brown data

(59.27 vs. 59.38), where, however, the difference is not statistically significant. The same conclusion to the section 5.2 can be made here.

## 6 Conclusion and Future Work

This work studies the application of self-training in learning semantic role labeling with the use of unlabeled data. We used a balancing method for selecting newly labeled examples for augmenting the training set in each iteration of the self-training process. The idea was to reduce the effect of unbalanced distribution of semantic roles in training data. We also used a pool and examined two preselection methods for loading unlabeled data into it.

These methods showed improvement in both classifier performance and self-training trend. However, using out-of-domain unlabeled data for increasing the domain generalization ability of the system was not more useful than using in-domain data. Among possible reasons are the low quality of the used data and the poor parses of the out-of-domain data.

Another major factor that may affect the self-training behavior here is the poor performance of the base classifier compared to the state-of-the-art (see Table 2), which exploits more complicated SRL architecture. Due to high computational cost of self-training approach, bootstrapping experiments with such complex SRL approaches are difficult and time-consuming.

Moreover, parameter tuning process shows that other parameters such as pool-size, growth number and probability threshold are very effective. Therefore, more comprehensive parameter tuning experiments than what was done here is required and may yield better results.

We are currently planning to port this setting to co-training, another bootstrapping algorithm. One direction for future work can be adapting the architecture of the SRL system to better match with the bootstrapping process. Another direction can be adapting bootstrapping parameters to fit the semantic role labeling complexity.

## References

Abney, S. 2008. *Semisupervised Learning for Computational Linguistics.* Chapman and Hall, London.

Baker, F., Fillmore, C. and Lowe, J. 1998. The Berkeley FrameNet project. In *Proceedings of COLING-ACL*, pages 86-90.

Charniak, E. and Johnson, M. 2005. Coarse-to-fine n-best parsing and MaxEnt discriminative reranking. In *Proceedings of the 43rd Annual Meeting of the ACL*, pages 173-180.

Carreras, X. and Marquez, L. 2005. Introduction to the CoNLL-2005 shared task: Semantic role labeling. In *Proceedings of the 9th Conference on Natural Language Learning (CoNLL)*, pages. 152-164.

Clark S., Curran, R. J. and Osborne M. 2003. Bootstrapping POS taggers using Unlabeled Data. In *Proceedings of the 7th Conference on Natural Language Learning At HLT-NAACL 2003,* pages 49-55.

Gildea, D. and Jurafsky, D. 2002. Automatic labeling of semantic roles. *CL*, 28(3):245-288.

He, S. and Gildea, H. 2006. Self-training and Co-training for Semantic Role Labeling: Primary Report. TR 891, University of Colorado at Boulder

Kingsbury, P. and Palmer, M. 2002. From Treebank to PropBank. In *Proceedings of the 3rd International Conference on Language Resources and Evaluation (LREC-2002).*

Lee, J., Song, Y. and Rim, H. 2007. Investigation of Weakly Supervised Learning for Semantic Role Labeling. In *Proceedings of the Sixth international Conference on Advanced Language Processing and Web information Technology (ALPIT 2007)*, pages 165-170.

McClosky, D., Charniak, E., and Johnson, M. 2006. Effective self-training for parsing. In *Proceedings of the Main Conference on Human Language Technology Conference of the North American Chapter of the ACL*, pages 152-159.

Ng, V. and Cardie, C. 2003. Weakly supervised natural language learning without redundant views. In *Proceedings of the 2003 Conference of the North American Chapter of the ACL on Human Language Technology,* pages 94-101.

Punyakanok, V., Roth, D. and Yi, W. 2008. The Importance of Syntactic Parsing and Inference in Semantic Role Labeling. *CL*, 34(2):257-287.

Surdeanu, M., Harabagiu, S., Williams, J. and Aarseth, P. 2003. Using predicate argument structures for information extraction. In *Proceedings of the 41st Annual Meeting of the ACL*, pages 8-15.

Surdeanu, M., Johansson, R., Meyers, A., Marquez, L. and Nivre, J. 2008. The CoNLL 2008 shared task on joint parsing of syntactic and semantic dependencies. In *Proceedings of the 12th Conference on Natural Language Learning (CoNLL)*, pages 159-177.

Yarowsky, E. 1995. Unsupervised Word Sense Disambiguation Rivaling Supervised Methods. In *proceeding of the 33rd Annual Meeting of ACL*, pages 189-196.

# Weakly Supervised Learning of Presupposition Relations between Verbs

**Galina Tremper**
Department of Computational Linguistics
Heidelberg University, Germany
tremper@cl.uni-heidelberg.de

**Abstract**

Presupposition relations between verbs are not very well covered in existing lexical semantic resources. We propose a weakly supervised algorithm for learning presupposition relations between verbs that distinguishes five semantic relations: presupposition, entailment, temporal inclusion, antonymy and other/no relation. We start with a number of seed verb pairs selected manually for each semantic relation and classify unseen verb pairs. Our algorithm achieves an overall accuracy of 36% for type-based classification.

## 1 Introduction

A main characteristics of natural language is that significant portions of content conveyed in a message may not be overtly realized. This is the case for presuppositions: e.g, the utterance *Columbus didn't manage to reach India.* presupposes that *Columbus had tried to reach India.* This presupposition does not need to be stated, but is implicitly understood. Determining the presuppositions of events reported in texts can be exploited to improve the quality of many natural language processing applications, such as information extraction, text understanding, text summarization, question-answering or machine translation.

The phenomenon of presupposition has been throughly investigated by philosophers and linguists (i.a. Stalnaker, 1974; van der Sandt, 1992). There are only few attempts for practical implementations of presupposition in computational linguistics (e.g. Bos, 2003). Especially, presupposition is understudied in the field of corpus-based learning of semantic relations. Machine learning methods have been previously applied to determine semantic relations such as *is-a* and *part-of*, also *succession*, *reaction* and *production* (Pantel and Pennacchiotti, 2006). Chklovski and Pantel (2004) explored classification of fine-grained verb semantic relations, such as *similarity*, *strength*, *antonymy*, *enablement* and *happens-before*. For the task of entailment recognition, learning of entailment relations was attempted (Pekar, 2008). None of the previous work investigated subclassifying semantic relations including presupposition and entailment, two relations that are closely related, but behave differently in context.

In particular, the inferential behaviour of presuppositions and entailments crucially differs in special semantic contexts. E.g., while presuppositions are preserved under negation (as in *Columbus managed/didn't manage to reach India* the presupposition *tried to*), entailments do not survive under negation (*John F. Kennedy has been/has not been killed*). Here the entailment *died* only survives in the positive sentence. Such differences are crucial for both analysis and generation-oriented NLP tasks.

This paper presents a weakly supervised algorithm for learning presupposition relations between verbs cast as a discriminative classification problem. The structure of the paper is as follows: Section 2 reviews state of the art. Section 3 introduces our task and the learning algorithm. Section 4 reports on experiment organization; the results are presented in Section 5. Finally, we summarise and present objectives for future work.

## 2 Related Work

One of the existing semantic resources related to our paper is WordNet (Fellbaum, 1998). It comprises lexical semantic information about English nouns, verbs, adjectives and adverbs. Among the semantic relations defined specifically for verbs are entailment, hyponymy, troponymy, antonymy and cause. However, not all of them are well covered, for example, there are only few entries for presupposition and entailment in WordNet.



*Proceedings of the ACL 2010 Student Research Workshop*, pages 97–102,
Uppsala, Sweden, 13 July 2010. 

One attempt to acquire fine-grained semantic relations from corpora is VerbOcean (Chklovski and Pantel, 2004). Chklovski and Pantel used a semi-automatic approach for extracting semantic relations between verbs using a list of patterns. The selection of the semantic relations was inspired by WordNet. VerbOcean showed good accuracy values for the *antonymy* (50%), *similarity* (63%) and *strength* (75%) relations. However, VerbOcean doesn't distinguish between *entailment* and *presupposition*; they are conflated in the classes *enablement* and *happens-before*.

A distributional method for extracting highly associated verbs was proposed by Lin and Pantel (2001). This method extracts semantically related words with good precision, but it does not determine the type and symmetry of the relation. However, the method is able to recognize the existence of semantic relations holding between verbs and hence can be used as a basis for finding and further discriminating more detailed semantic relations.

## 3 A Weakly Supervised Approach to Learning Presupposition Relations

We describe a weakly supervised approach for learning semantic relations between verbs including implicit relations such as presupposition. Our aim is to perform a type-based classification of verb pairs. I.e., we determine the class of a verb-pair relation by observing co-occurrences of these verbs in contexts that are indicative for their intrinsic meaning relation. This task differs from a token-based classification, which aims at classifying each verb pair instance as it occurs in context.

**Classified relations.** We distinguish between the five classes of semantic relations presented in Table 1. We chose *entailment*, *temporal inclusion* and *antonymy*, because these relations may be confounded with the *presupposition* relation. A special class *other/no* comprises semantic relations not discussed in this paper (e.g. synonymy) and verb pairs that are not related by a semantic relation. The relations can be subdivided into symmetric and asymmetric relations, and relations that involve temporal sequence, or those that do not involve a temporal order, as displayed in Table 1.

| Semantic Relation | Example | Symmetry | Temporal Sequence |
|---|---|---|---|
| Presupposition | *find - seek, answer - ask* | asymmetric | yes |
| Entailment | *look - see, buy - own* | asymmetric | yes |
| Temporal Inclusion | *walk - step, talk - whisper* | symmetric | no |
| Antonymy | *win - lose, love - hate* | symmetric | no |
| Other/no | *have - own, sing - jump* | undefined | undefined |

Table 1: Selected Semantic Relations

**A Weakly Supervised Learning Approach.** Our algorithm starts with a small number of seed verb pairs selected manually for each relation and iteratively classifies a large set of unseen and unlabeled verb pairs. Each iteration has two phases:

1. **Training the Classifiers** We independently train binary classifiers for each semantic relation using both shallow and deep features.
2. **Ensemble Learning and Ranking** Each of the five classifiers is applied to each sentence from an unlabeled corpus. The predictions of the classifiers are combined using ensemble learning techniques to determine the most confident classification. The obtained list of the classified instances is ranked using pattern scores, in order to select the most reliable candidates for extension of the training set.

**Features.** Both shallow lexical-syntactic and deep syntactic features are used for the classification of semantic relations. They include:

1. the distance between two analyzed verbs and the order of their appearance
2. verb form (tense, aspect, modality, voice), presence of negation and polarity verbs[1]
3. coordinating/subordinating conjunctions
4. adverbial adjuncts
5. PoS-tag-contexts (two words preceding and two words following each verb)
6. the length of the path of grammatical functions relating the two verbs
7. co-reference relation holding between the subjects and objects of the verbs (both verbs have the same subject/object, subject of one verb corresponds to the object of the second or there is no relation between them).

In order to extract these features the training corpus is parsed using a deep parser.

[1]Polarity verbs are taken from the polarity lexicon of Nairn et al. (2006). It encodes whether the complement of proposition embedding verbs is true or false. We used the verbs themselves as a feature without their polarity-tags.

## 4 Experimental Setting

**Initial Subset of Verb Pair Candidates.** Unlike other semi-supervised approaches, we don't use patterns for acquiring new candidates for classification. Candidate verb pairs are obtained from a previously compiled list of highly associated verbs. We use the DIRT Collection (Lin and Pantel, 2001) from which we further extract pairs of highly associated verbs as candidates for classification. The advantage of this resource is that it consists of pairs of verbs which stand in a semantic relation (cf. Section 2). This considerably reduces the number of verb pairs that need to be processed as candidates in our classification task.

DIRT contains 5,604 verb types and 808,764 verb pair types. This still represents a huge number of verb pairs to be processed. We therefore filtered the extracted set by checking verb pair frequency in the first three parts of the ukWAC corpus (Baroni et al., 2009) (UKWAC_1...3) and by applying the PMI test with threshold 2.0. This reduces the number of verb pairs to 199,393.

For each semantic relation we select three verb pairs as seeds. The only exception is *temporal inclusion* for which we selected six verb pairs, due to the low frequency of such verb pairs within a single sentence. These verb pairs were used for building an initial training corpus of verb pairs in context. The remaining verb pairs are used to build the corpus of unlabeled verb pairs in context in the iterative classification process.

**Preprocessing.** Given these verb pairs, we extracted sentences for training and for unlabeled data set from the first three parts of the UKWAC corpus (Baroni et al., 2009). We compiled a set of CQP queries (Evert, 2005) to find sentences that contain both verbs of a verb pair and applied them on UKWAC_1...3 to build the training and unlabeled subcorpora. We filter out sentences with more than 60 words and sentences with a distance between verbs exceeding 20 words. To avoid growing complexity, only sentences with exactly one occurrence of each verb pair are retained. We also remove sentences that trigger wrong candidates, in which the auxiliaries *have* or *do* appear in a candidate verb pair.

The corpus is parsed using the XLE parser (Crouch et al., 2008). Its output contains both the structural and functional information we need to extract the shallow and deep features used in the classification, and to generate patterns.

**Training Corpus.** From this preprocessed corpus, we created a training corpus that contains three different components:

1. *Manually annotated training set.* All sentences containing seed verb pairs extracted from UKWAC_1 are annotated manually with two values *true/false* in order to separate the negative training data.
2. *Automatically annotated training set.* We build an extended, heuristically annotated training set for the seed verb pairs, by extracting further instances from the remaining corpora (UKWAC_2 and UKWAC_3). Using the manual annotations of step 1., we manually compiled a small stoplist of patterns that are used to filter out wrong instances. The constructed stoplist serves as an elementary disambiguation step. For example, the verbs *look* and *see* can stand in an entailment relation if *look* is followed by the prepositions *at, on, in*, but not in case of prepositions *after* or *forward* (e.g. *looking forward to*).
3. *Synonymous verb pairs.* To further enrich the training set of data, synonyms of the verb pairs are manually selected from WordNet. The corresponding verb pairs were extracted from UKWAC_1...3. In order to avoid adding noise, we used only synonyms of unambiguous verbs. The problem of ambiguity of the target verbs wasn't considered at this step.

The overall size of the training set for the first classification step is 15,717 sentences from which 5,032 are manually labeled, 9,918 sentences are automatically labeled and 757 sentences contain synonymous verb pairs. The distribution is unbalanced: *temporal inclusion* e.g. covers only 2%, while *entailment* covers 39% of sentences. We balanced the training set by undersampling *entailment* and *other/no* by 20% and correspondingly oversampling the *temporal inclusion* class.

**Patterns.** Similar to other pattern-based approaches we use a set of seed verb pairs to induce indicative patterns for each semantic relation. We use the induced patterns to restrict the number of the verb pair candidates and to rank the labelled instances in the iterative classification step.

The patterns use information about the verb forms of analyzed verb pairs, modal verbs and the polarity verbs (only if they are related to the analyzed verbs) and coordinating/subordinating conjunctions connecting two verbs. The analyzed verbs in the sentence are substituted with V1 and V2 placeholders in the pattern. For example, for the sentence: *Here we should be careful for there are those who seek and do not find.* and the verb pair *(find,seek)* we induce the following pattern: *V2 and do [not|n't] V1.* The patterns are extracted automatically from deep parses of the training corpus. Examples of the best patterns we determined for semantic relations are presented in Table 2.

| Semantic Relation | Patterns |
|---|---|
| Presupposition | V2-ed * though * was * V1-ed, V2-ed * but was [not\|n't] V1-ed, V2-ing * might V1 |
| Entailment | if * V1 * V2, V1-ing * [shall\|will\|'ll] V2, V2 * by V1-ing |
| Temporal Inclusion | V2 * V1-ing, V1-ing and V2-ing, when V2 * V1 |
| Antonymy | V1 or * V2, either * V1 or * V2, V1-ed * but V2-ed |
| Other/no | V1 * V2, V1-ing * V2-ing, V2-ed * and * V1-ed |

Table 2: Patterns for Selected Semantic Relations

Pattern ranks are used to compute the reliability score for instances, as proposed by Pantel and Pennacchiotti (2006). The pattern reliability is calculated as follows:

$$r_\pi(p) = \frac{1}{|I|} \sum_{i \in I} \frac{pmi(i,p)}{max_{pmi}} \times r_i(i) \quad (1)$$

where:
$pmi(i,p)$ - pointwise mutual information (PMI) between the instance $i$ and the pattern $p$;
$max_{pmi}$ - maximum PMI between all patterns and all instances;
$r_i(i)$ - reliability of an instance $i$. For seeds $r_i(i) = 1$ (they are selected manually), for the next iterations the instance reliability is:

$$r_i(i) = \frac{1}{|P|} \sum_{p \in P} \frac{pmi(i,p)}{max_{pmi}} \times r_\pi(p) \quad (2)$$

We also consider using the patterns as a feature for classification, in case they turn out to be sufficiently discriminative.

**Training Binary Classifiers.** We independently train 5 binary classifiers, one for each semantic relation, using the J48 decision tree algorithm (Witten and Frank, 2005).

**Data Sets.** As the primary goal of this paper is to classify semantic relations on the type level, we elaborated a first gold standard dataset for type-based classification. We used a small sample of 100 verb pairs randomly selected from the automatically labeled corpus. This sample was manually annotated by two judges after we had eliminated the system annotations in order not to influence the judges' decisions. The judges had the possibility to select more than one annotation, if necessary. We measured inter-annotator agreement was 61% ($k \approx 0.21$). The low agreement shows the difficulty of decision in the annotation of fine-grained semantic relations.[2]

While the first gold standard dataset of verb pairs was annotated *out of context*, we constructed a second gold standard of verb pairs annotated at the token level, i.e. in context. This second data set can be used to evaluate a token-based classifier (a task not attempted in the present paper). It also offers a ground truth for type-based classification, in that it controls for contextual ambiguity effects. I.e., we can extract a type-based gold standard on the basis of the token-annotated data.[3] We proposed to one judge to annotate the same 100 verb pair types as in the previous annotation task, this time in context. For this purpose we randomly selected 10 instances for each verb pair type (for rare verb pair types only 5). We compared the gold standards elaborated by the same judge for type-based and token-based classification:

- 62% of verb pair types were annotated with the same labels on both levels, indicating correct annotation
- 10% of verb pair types were assigned conflicting labels, indicating wrong annotation
- 28% of verb pair types were assigned labels not present on the type level, or the type level label was not assigned in context

The figures show that for the most part the type-based annotation conforms with the ground truth obtained from token-based annotation. Only 10% of verb pair types were established as conflicting with the ground truth. The remaining 28% can be considered as potentially correct: either the annotated data does not contain the appropriate context for a given type label or the type-level anno-

[2]Data inspection revealed that one annotator was more experienced in semantic annotation tasks. We evaluate our system using the annotations of only one judge.

[3]This option was not pursued in the present paper.

tation, performed without context, does not foresee an existing relation. This points to a general difficulty, namely to acquire representative data sets for token-level annotation, and also to perform type-level annotations without context for the present task.

**Combining Classifiers in Ensemble Learning.** Both token-based and type-based classification starts with determining of the most confident classification for instances. Each instance of the corpus of unlabeled verb pairs is classified by the individual binary classifiers. In order to select the most confident classification we compare the votes of the individual classifiers as follows:

1. If an instance is classified by one of the classifiers as *true* with confidence less than 0.75, we discard this classification.
2. If an instance is classified as *true* by more than one classifier, we consider only the classification with the highest confidence.[4]

In contrast to token-based classification that accepts only one semantic relation, for type-based classification we allow the existence of more than one semantic relation for a verb pair. To avoid the unreliable classifications, we apply several filters:

1. If less than 10% of the instances for a verb pair are classified with some specific semantic relation, this classification is considered to be unconfident and is discarded.
2. If a verb pair is classified as positive for more than three semantic relations, this verb pair remains unclassified.
3. If a verb pair is classified with up to three semantic relations and if more than 10% of the examples are classified with any of these relations, the verb pair is labeled with all of them.

**Iteration and Stopping Criterion.** After determining the most confident classification we rank the instances, following the ranking procedure of Pantel and Pennacchiotti (2006). Instances that exceed a reliability threshold (0.3 for our experiment) are selected for the extended training set. The remainining instances are returned to the unlabeled set. The algorithm stops if the average reliability score is smaller than a threshold value. In our paper we concentrate on the first iteration. Extension of the training set and re-ranking of patterns will be reported in future work.

[4]We assume that within a given context a verb pair can exhibit only one relation.

| Semantic relation (Count1/Count2) | Majority | Without NONE | Baseline |
|---|---|---|---|
| Presupposition (12/22) | 67% | 36% | 18% |
| Entailment (9/20) | 67% | 35% | 8% |
| Temp. Inclusion (7/11) | 71% | 36% | 19% |
| Antonymy (11/24) | 72% | 42% | 12% |
| NONE (61/29) | 49% | 31% | 43% |
| Macro-Average | 56% | 36% | |
| Micro-Average | 65% | 36% | |

Table 3: Accuracy for type-based classification

## 5 Evaluation Results

**Results for type-based classification.** We evaluate the accuracy of classification based on two alternative measures:

1. *Majority* - the semantic relation with which the majority of the sentences containing a verb pair have been annotated.
2. *Without NONE* - as in 1., but after removing the label *NONE* from all relation assignments except for those cases where NONE is the only label assigned to a verb pair.[5]

We computed accuracy as the number of verb pairs which were correctly labeled by the system divided by the total number of system labels. We compare our results against a baseline of random assignment, taking the distribution found in the manually labeled gold standard as the underlying verb relation distribution. Table 3 shows the accuracy results for each semantic relation[6].

**Results for token-based classification.** We also evaluate the accuracy of classification for token-based classification as the number of instances which were correctly labeled by the system divided by the total number of system labels. As the baseline we took the relation distribution on the token level. Table 4 shows the accuracy results for each semantic relation.

**Discussion.** The results obtained for type-based classification are well above the baseline with one exception. The best performance is achieved by *antonymy* (72% and 42% respectively for both

[5]The second measure was used because in many cases the relation NONE has been determined to be the majority class.

[6]Count1 is the total number of system labels for the Majority measure and Count2 is the total number of system labels for the Without NONE measure.

| Semantic relation | Count | Accuracy | Baseline |
|---|---|---|---|
| Presupposition | 43 | 21% | 8% |
| Entailment | 39 | 15% | 5% |
| Temp. Inclusion | 15 | 13% | 3% |
| Antonymy | 34 | 29% | 5% |
| NONE | 511 | 81% | 79% |
| Macro-Average | | 61% | |
| Micro-Average | | 31% | |

Table 4: Accuracy for token-based classification

measures), followed by *temporal inclusion*, *presupposition* and *entailment*. Accuracy scores for token-based classification (excluding NONE) are lower at 29% to 13%. Error analysis of randomly selected false positives shows that the main reason for lower accuracy on the token level is that the context is not always significant enough to determine the correct relation.

**Comparison to Related Work.** Other projects such as VerbOcean (Chklovski and Pantel, 2004) report higher accuracy: the average accuracy is 65.5% if at least one tag is correct and 53% for the correct preferred tag. However, we cannot objectively compare the results of VerbOcean to our system because of the difference in the set of relation classes and evaluation procedures. Similar to us, Chklovski and Pantel (2004) evaluated VerbOcean using a small sample of data which was presented to two judges for manual evaluation. In contrast to our setup, they didn't remove the system annotations from the evaluation data set. Given the difficulty of the classification we suspect that correction of system output relations for establishing a gold standard bears a strong risk in favouring system classifications.

## 6 Conclusion and Future Work

The results achieved in our experiment show that weakly supervised methods can be applied for learning presupposition relations between verbs. Our work also shows that they are more difficult to classify than other typical lexical semantic relations, such as antonymy. Error analysis suggests that many errors can be avoided if verbs are disambiguated in context. It would be interesting to test our algorithm with different amounts of manually annotated training sets and different combinations of manually and automatically annotated training sets to determine the minimal amount of data needed to assure good accuracy.

In future work we will integrate word sense disambiguation as well as information about predicate-argument structure. Also, we are going to analyze the influence of single features on the classification and determining optimal feature sets, as well as the question of including patterns in the feature set. In this paper we used the same combination of features for all classifiers.

## 7 Acknowledgements

I would like to thank Anette Frank for supervision of this work, Dekang Lin and Patrick Pantel for sharing the DIRT resource and Carina Silberer and Christine Neupert creation of the gold standard.

## References

Baroni, M., Bernardini, S., Ferraresi, A., Zanchetta, E.: The WaCky Wide Web: a collection of very large linguistically processed web-crawled corpora. Journal of Language Resources and Evaluation, Vol.43 (3), 209–226 (2009)

Bos, J.: Implementing the Binding and Accommodation Theory for Anaphora Resolution and Presupposition Projection. Computational Linguistics, Vol.29 (2), 179–210 (2003)

Chklovski, T., Pantel, P.: Verbocean: Mining the web for fine-grained semantic verb relations. Proceedings of EMNLP 2004, 33–40, Barcelona (2004)

Crouch, D., Dalrymple, M., Kaplan, R., King, T., Maxwell, J., Newman, P.: XLE Documentation. Palo Alto Research Center (2008)

Evert, S.: The CQP Query Language Tutorial (CWB Version 2.2.b90). IMS, Stuttgart (2005)

Fellbaum, C.: WordNet: An Electronic Lexical Database. 1st edition, MIT Press (1998)

Lin, D., Pantel, P.: Discovery of Inference Rules for Question Answering. Natural Language Engineering, Vol.7, 343–360 (2001)

Nairn, R., Condoravdi, C., Karttunen, L.: Computing Relative Polarity for Textual Inference. Proc. of ICoS-5, Buxton, UK (2006)

Pantel, P., Pennacchiotti, M.: Espresso: Leveraging Generic Patterns for Automatically Harvesting Semantic Relations. COLING 2006, 113-120 (2006)

Pekar, V.: Discovery of event entailment knowledge from text corpora. Computer Speech & Language, Vol.22 (1), 1–16 (2008)

Stalnaker, R.C.: Pragmatic Presuppositions. Semantics and Philosophy, New York: Univ. Press (1974)

van der Sandt, R.: Presupposition Projection as Anaphora Resolution. Journal of Semantics, Vol.9, 333–377 (1992)

Witten, I., Frank, E.: Data Mining: Practical Machine Learning Tools and Techniques. (2005)

# Importance of linguistic constraints in statistical dependency parsing

**Bharat Ram Ambati**
Language Technologies Research Centre, IIIT-Hyderabad,
Gachibowli, Hyderabad, India – 500032.
ambati@research.iiit.ac.in

## Abstract

Statistical systems with high accuracy are very useful in real-world applications. If these systems can capture basic linguistic information, then the usefulness of these statistical systems improve a lot. This paper is an attempt at incorporating linguistic constraints in statistical dependency parsing. We consider a simple linguistic constraint that a verb should not have multiple subjects/objects as its children in the dependency tree. We first describe the importance of this constraint considering Machine Translation systems which use dependency parser output, as an example application. We then show how the current state-of-the-art dependency parsers violate this constraint. We present two new methods to handle this constraint. We evaluate our methods on the state-of-the-art dependency parsers for Hindi and Czech.

## 1 Introduction

Parsing is one of the major tasks which helps in understanding the natural language. It is useful in several natural language applications. Machine translation, anaphora resolution, word sense disambiguation, question answering, summarization are few of them. This led to the development of grammar-driven, data-driven and hybrid parsers. Due to the availability of annotated corpora in recent years, data driven parsing has achieved considerable success. The availability of phrase structure treebank for English (Marcus et al., 1993) has seen the development of many efficient parsers. Using the dependency analysis, a similar large scale annotation effort for Czech, has been the Prague Dependency Treebank (Hajicova, 1998). Unlike English, Czech is a free-word-order language and is also morphologically very rich. It has been suggested that free-word-order languages can be handled better using the dependency based framework than the constituency based one (Hudson, 1984; Shieber, 1985; Mel'čuk, 1988, Bharati et al., 1995). The basic difference between a constituent based representation and a dependency representation is the lack of nonterminal nodes in the latter. It has also been noted that use of appropriate edge labels gives a level of semantics. It is perhaps due to these reasons that the recent past has seen a surge in the development of dependency based treebanks.

Due to the availability of dependency treebanks, there are several recent attempts at building dependency parsers. Two CoNLL shared tasks (Buchholz and Marsi, 2006; Nivre et al., 2007a) were held aiming at building state-of-the-art dependency parsers for different languages. Recently in NLP Tools Contest in ICON-2009 (Husain, 2009 and references therein), rule-based, constraint based, statistical and hybrid approaches were explored towards building dependency parsers for three Indian languages namely, Telugu, Hindi and Bangla. In all these efforts, state-of-the-art accuracies are obtained by two data-driven parsers, namely, Malt (Nivre et al., 2007b) and MST (McDonald et al., 2006). The major limitation of both these parsers is that they won't take linguistic constraints into account explicitly. But, in real-world applications of the parsers, some basic linguistic constraints are very useful. If we can make these parsers handle linguistic constraints also, then they become very useful in real-world applications.

This paper is an effort towards incorporating linguistic constraints in statistical dependency parser. We consider a simple constraint that a verb should not have multiple subjects/objects as its children. In section 2, we take machine translation using dependency parser as an example and explain the need of this linguistic constraint. In section 3, we propose two approaches to handle this case. We evaluate our approaches on the state-of-the-art dependency parsers for Hindi and Czech and analyze the results in section 4. General discussion and future directions of the work are presented in section 5. We conclude our paper in section 6.



*Proceedings of the ACL 2010 Student Research Workshop*, pages 103–108,
Uppsala, Sweden, 13 July 2010. ©2010 Association for Computational Linguistics

## 2 Motivation

In this section we take Machine Translation (MT) systems that use dependency parser output as an example and explain the need of linguistic constraints. We take a simple constraint that a verb should not have multiple subjects/objects as its children in the dependency tree. Indian Language to Indian Language Machine Transtion System[1] is one such MT system which uses dependency parser output. In this system the general framework has three major components. a) dependency analysis of the source sentence. b) transfer from source dependency tree to target dependency tree, and c) sentence generation from the target dependency tree. In the transfer part several rules are framed based on the source language dependency tree. For instance, for Telugu to Hindi MT system, based on the dependency labels of the Telugu sentence post-positions markers that need to be added to the words are decided. Consider the following example,

(1)

**Telugu:** raamu oka pamdu tinnaadu
*'Ramu' 'one' 'fruit' 'ate'*

**Hindi:** raamu ne eka phala khaayaa
*'Ramu' 'ERG' 'one' 'fruit' 'ate'*

**English:** "Ramu ate a fruit".

In the above Telugu sentence, '*raamu*' is the subject of the verb '*tinnaadu*'. While translating this sentence to Hindi, the post-position marker '*ne*' is added to the subject. If the dependency parser marks two subjects, both the words will have '*ne*' marker. This affects the comprehensibility. If we can avoid such instances, then the output of the MT system will be improved.

This problem is not due to morphological richness or free-word-order nature of the target language. Consider an example of free-word-order language to fixed-word-order language MT system like Hindi to English MT system. The dependency labels help in identifying the position of the word in the target sentence. Consider the example sentences given below.

(2a) *raama seba khaatha hai*
'Ram' 'apple' 'eats' 'is'
*'Ram eats an apple'*

(2b) *seba raama khaatha hai*
'apple' 'Ram' 'eats' 'is'
*'Ram eats an apple'*

Though the source sentence is different, the target sentence is same. Even though the source sentences are different, the dependency tree is same for both the sentences. In both the cases, '*raama*' is the subject and '*seba*' is the object of the verb '*khaatha*'. This information helps in getting the correct translation. If the parser for the source sentence assigns the label 'subject' to both '*raama*' and '*seba*', the MT system can not give the correct output.

There were some attempts at handling these kind of linguistic constraints using integer programming approaches (Riedel et al., 2006; Bharati et al., 2008). In these approaches dependency parsing is formulated as solving an integer program as McDonald et al. (2006) has formulated dependency parsing as MST problem. All the linguistic constraints are encoded as constraints while solving the integer program. In other words, all the parses that violate these constraints are removed from the solution list. The parse with satisfies all the constraints is considered as the dependency tree for the sentence. In the following section, we describe two new approaches to avoid multiple subjects/objects for a verb.

## 3 Approaches

In this section, we describe the two different approaches for avoiding the cases of a verb having multiple subjects/objects as its children in the dependency tree.

### 3.1 Naive Approach (NA)

In this approach we first run a parser on the input sentence. Instead of first best dependency label, we extract the k-best labels for each token in the sentence. For each verb in the sentence, we check if there are multiple children with the dependency label 'subject'. If there are any such cases, we extract the list of all the children with label 'subject'. we find the node in this list which appears left most in the sentence with respect to other nodes. We assign 'subject' to this node. For the rest of the nodes in this list we assign the second best label and remove the first best label from their respective k-best list of labels. We check recursively, till all such instances are

[1] http://sampark.iiit.ac.in/

avoided. We repeat the same procedure for 'object'.

Main criterion to avoid multiple subjects/objects in this approach is position of the node in the sentence. Consider the following example,

Eg. 3: *raama seba khaatha hai*
'Ram' 'apple' 'eats' 'is'
'Ram eats an apple'

Suppose the parser assigns the label 'subject' to both the nouns, '*raama*' and '*seba*'. Then naive approach assigns the label subject to '*raama*' and second best label to '*seba*' as '*raama*' precedes '*seba*'.

In this manner we can avoid a verb having multiple children with dependency labels subject/object.

Limitation to this approach is word-order. The algorithm described here works well for fixed word order languages. For example, consider a language with fixed word order like English. English is a SVO (Subject, Verb, Object) language. Subject always occurs before the object. So, if a verb has multiple subjects, based on position we can say that the node that occurs first will be the subject. But if we consider a free-word order language like Hindi, this approach wouldn't work always.

Consider (2a) and (2b). In both these examples, '*raama*' is the subject of the verb '*khaatha*' and '*seba*' is the object of the verb '*khaatha*'. The only difference in these two sentences is the order of the word. In (2a), subject precedes object. Whereas in (2b), object precedes subject. Suppose the parser identifies both '*raama*' and '*seba*' as subjects. NA can correctly identify '*raama*' as the subject in case of (2a). But in case of (2b), '*seba*' is identified as the subject. To handle these kind of instances, we use a probabilistic approach.

### 3.2 Probabilistic Approach (PA)

The probabilistic approach is similar to naive approach except that the main criterion to avoid multiple subjects/objects in this approach is probability of the node having a particular label. Whereas in naive approach, position of the node is the main criterion to avoid multiple subjects/objects. In this approach, for each node in the sentence, we extract the k-best labels along with their probabilities. Similar to NA, we first check for each verb if there are multiple children with the dependency label 'subject'. If there are any such cases, we extract the list of all the children with label 'subject'. We find the node in this list which has the highest probability value. We assign 'subject' to this node. For the rest of the nodes in this list we assign the second best label and remove the first best label from their respective k-best list of labels. We check recursively, till all such instances are avoided. We repeat the same procedure for 'object'.

Consider (2a) and (2b). Suppose the parser identifies both '*raama*' and '*seba*' as subjects. Probability of '*raama*' being a subject will be more than '*seba*' being a subject. So, the probabilistic approach correctly marks '*raama*' as subject in both (2a) and (2b). But, NA couldn't identify '*raama*' as subject in (2b).

## 4 Experiments

We evaluate our approaches on the state-of-the-art parsers for two languages namely, Hindi and Czech. First we calculate the instances of multiple subjects/objects in the output of the state-of-the-art parsers for these two languages. Then we apply our approaches and analyze the results.

### 4.1 Hindi

Recently in NLP Tools Contest in ICON-2009 (Husain, 2009 and references herein), rule-based, constraint based, statistical and hybrid approaches were explored for parsing Hindi. All these attempts were at finding the inter-chunk dependency relations, given gold-standard POS and chunk tags. The state-of-the-art accuracy of 74.48% LAS (Labeled Attachment Score) is achieved by Ambati et al. (2009) for Hindi. They used two well-known data-driven parsers, Malt[2] (Nivre et al., 2007b), and MST[3] (McDonald et al., 2006) for their experiments. As the accuracy of the labeler of MST parser is very low, they used maximum entropy classification algorithm, MAXENT[4] for labeling.

For Hindi, dependency annotation is done using paninian framework (Begum et al., 2008; Bharati et al., 1995). So, in Hindi, the equivalent labels for subject and object are '*karta (k1)*' and '*karma (k2)*'. '*karta*' and '*karma*' are syntactico-semantic labels which have some properties of both grammatical roles and thematic roles. *k1* behaves similar to subject and agent. *k2* behaves similar to object and patient (Bharati et al., 1995; Bharati et al., 2009). Here, by object we mean

---

[2] Malt Version 1.3.1
[3] MST Version 0.4b
[4]http://homepages.inf.ed.ac.uk/lzhang10/maxent_toolkit.htm
l

only direct object. Thus we consider only *k1* and *k2* labels which are equivalent of subject and direct object. Annotation scheme is such that there wouldn't be multiple subjects/objects for a verb in any case (Bharati et al., 2009). For example, even in case of coordination, coordinating conjunction is the head and conjuncts are children of the coordinating conjunction. The coordinating conjunction is attached to the verb with k1/k2 label and the conjuncts get attached to the coordinating conjunction with a dependency label '*ccof*'.

We replicated the experiments of Ambati et al. (2009) on test set (150 sentences) of Hindi and analyzed the outputs of Malt and MST+MaxEnt. We consider this as the baseline. In the output of Malt, there are 39 instances of multiple subjects/objects. There are 51 such instances in the output of MST+MAXENT.

Malt is good at short distance labeling and MST is good at long distance labeling (McDonald and Nivre, 2007). As '*k1*' and '*k2*' are short distance labels, Malt could able predict these labels more accurately than MST. Because of this output of MST has higher number of instances of multiple subjects/objects than Malt.

| | *Total Instances* |
|---|---|
| *Malt* | **39** |
| *MST + MAXENT* | **51** |

Table 1: Number of instances of multiple subjects or objects in the output of the state-of-the-art parsers for Hindi

Both the parsers output first best label for each node in the sentence. In case of Malt, we modified the implementation to extract all the possible dependency labels with their scores. As Malt uses libsvm for learning, we couldn't able to get the probabilities. Though interpreting the scores provided by libsvm as probabilities is not the correct way, that is the only option currently available with Malt. In case of MST+MAXENT, labeling is performed by MAXENT. We used a java version of MAXENT[5] to extract all possible tags with their scores. We applied both the naive and probabilistic approaches to avoid multiple subjects/objects. We evaluated our experiments based on unlabeled attachment score (UAS), labeled attachment score (LAS) and labeled score (LS) (Nivre et al., 2007a). Results are presented in Table 2.

As expected, PA performs better than NA. With PA we got an improvement of 0.26% in LAS over the previous best results for Malt. In case of MST+MAXENT we got an improvement of 0.61% in LAS over the previous best results. Note that in case of MST+MAXENT, the slight difference between state-of-the-art results of Ambati et al. (2009) and our baseline accuracy is due different MAXENT package used.

| | *Malt* | | | *MST+MAXENT* | | |
|---|---|---|---|---|---|---|
| | *UAS* | *LAS* | *LS* | *UAS* | *LAS* | *LS* |
| *Baseline* | 90.14 | 74.48 | 76.38 | 91.26 | 72.75 | 75.26 |
| *NA* | 90.14 | 74.57 | 76.38 | 91.26 | 72.84 | 75.26 |
| *PA* | **90.14** | **74.74** | **76.56** | **91.26** | **73.36** | **75.87** |

Table 2: Comparison of NA and PA with previous best results for Hindi

Improvement in case of MST+MAXENT is greater than that of Malt. One reason is because of more number of instances of multiple subjects/objects in case of MST+MAXENT. Other reason is use of probabilities in case MST+MAXENT. Whereas in case of Malt, we interpreted the scores as probabilities which is not a good way to do. But, in case of Malt, that is the only option available.

### 4.2 Czech

In case of Czech, we replicated the experiments of Hall et al. (2007) using latest version of Malt (version 1.3.1) and analyzed the output. We consider this as the baseline. The minor variation of the baseline results from the results of CoNLL-2007 shared task is due to different version Malt parser being used. Due to practical reasons we couldn't use the older version. In the output of Malt, there are 39 instances of multiple subjects/objects out of 286 sentences in the testing data. In case of Czech, the equivalent labels for subject and object are 'agent' and 'theme'.

Czech is a free-word-order language similar to Hindi. So as expected, PA performed better than NA. Interestingly, accuracy of PA is lower than the baseline. Main reason for this is scores of libsvm of Malt. We explain the reason for this using the following example, consider a verb 'V' has two children 'C1' and 'C2' with dependency label subject. Assume that the label for 'C1' is subject and the label of 'C2' is object in the gold-data. As the parser marked 'C1' with subject, this

[5] http://maxent.sourceforge.net/

adds to the accuracy of the parser. While avoiding multiple subjects, if 'C1' is marked as subject, then the accuracy doesn't drop. If 'C2' is marked as object then the accuracy increases. But, if 'C2' is marked as subject and 'C1' is marked as object then the accuracy drops. This could happen if probability of 'C1' having subject as label is lower than 'C1' having subject as the label. This is because of two reasons, (a) parser itself wrongly predicted the probabilities, and (b) parser predicted correctly, but due to the limitation of libsvm, we couldn't get the scores correctly.

| | *UAS* | *LAS* | *LS* |
|---|---|---|---|
| *Baseline* | **82.92** | **76.32** | **83.69** |
| *NA* | 82.92 | 75.92 | 83.35 |
| *PA* | *82.92* | *75.97* | *83.40* |

Table 3: Comparison of NA and PA with previous best results for Czech

## 5 Discussion and Future Work

Results show that the probabilistic approach performs consistently better than the naive approach. For Hindi, we could able to achieve an improvement 0.26% and 0.61% in LAS over the previous best results using Malt and MST respectively. We couldn't able to achieve any improvement in case of Czech due to the limitation of libsvm learner used in Malt.

We plan to evaluate our approaches on all the data-sets of CoNLL-X and CoNLL-2007 shared tasks using Malt. Settings of MST parser are available only for CoNLL-X shared task data sets. So, we plan to evaluate our approaches on CoNLL-X shared task data using MST also. Malt has the limitation for extracting probabilities due to libsvm learner. Latest version of Malt (version 1.3.1) provides option for liblinear learner also. Liblinear provides option for extracting probabilities. So we can also use liblinear learning algorithm for Malt and explore the usefulness of our approaches. Currently, we are handling only two labels, subject and object. Apart from subject and object there can be other labels for which multiple instances for a single verb is not valid. We can extend our approaches to handle such labels also. We tried to incorporate one simple linguistic constraint in the statistical dependency parsers. We can also explore the ways of incorporating other useful linguistic constraints.

## 6 Conclusion

Statistical systems with high accuracy are very useful in practical applications. If these systems can capture basic linguistic information, then the usefulness of the statistical system improves a lot. In this paper, we presented a new method of incorporating linguistic constraints into the statistical dependency parsers. We took a simple constraint that a verb should not have multiple subjects/objects as its children. We proposed two approaches, one based on position and the other based on probabilities to handle this. We evaluated our approaches on state-of-the-art dependency parsers for Hindi and Czech.

**Acknowledgments**

I would like to express my gratitude to Prof. Joakim Nivre and Prof. Rajeev Sangal for their guidance and support. I would also like to thank Mr. Samar Husain for his valuable suggestions.

## References

B. R. Ambati, P. Gadde and K. Jindal. 2009. Experiments in Indian Language Dependency Parsing. In *Proceedings of the ICON09 NLP Tools Contest: Indian Language Dependency Parsing,* pp 32-37.

R. Begum, S. Husain, A. Dhwaj, D. Sharma, L. Bai, and R. Sangal. 2008. Dependency annotation scheme for Indian languages. In *Proceedings of IJCNLP-2008.*

A. Bharati, V. Chaitanya and R. Sangal. 1995. *Natural Language Processing: A Paninian Perspective*, Prentice-Hall of India, New Delhi, pp. 65-106.

A. Bharati, S. Husain, D. M. Sharma, and R. Sangal. 2008. A Two-Stage Constraint Based Dependency Parser for Free Word Order Languages. In *Proceedings of the COLIPS International Conference on Asian Language Processing 2008 (IALP).* Chiang Mai, Thailand.

S. Buchholz and E. Marsi. 2006. CoNLL-X shared task on multilingual dependency parsing. In *Proc. of the Tenth Conf. on Computational Natural Language Learning (CoNLL).*

E. Hajicova. 1998. Prague Dependency Treebank: From Analytic to Tectogrammatical Annotation. In *Proc. TSD'98.*

J. Hall, J. Nilsson, J. Nivre, G. Eryigit, B. Megyesi, M. Nilsson and M. Saers. 2007. Single Malt or Blended? A Study in Multilingual Parser Optimization. In *Proceedings of the CoNLL Shared Task Session of EMNLP-CoNLL.*

R. Hudson. 1984. *Word Grammar*, Basil Blackwell, 108 Cowley Rd, Oxford, OX4 1JF, England.

S. Husain. 2009. Dependency Parsers for Indian Languages. In *Proceedings of ICON09 NLP Tools Contest: Indian Language Dependency Parsing.* Hyderabad, India.

M. Marcus, B. Santorini, and M.A. Marcinkiewicz. 1993. Building a large annotated corpus of English: The Penn Treebank, *Computational Linguistics 1993.*

I. A. Mel'čuk. 1988. *Dependency Syntax: Theory and Practice*, State University, Press of New York.

R. McDonald, K. Lerman, and F. Pereira. 2006. Multilingual dependency analysis with a two-stage discriminative parser. In *Proceedings of the Tenth Conference on Computational Natural Language Learning (CoNLL-X)*, pp. 216–220.

R. McDonald and J. Nivre. 2007. Characterizing the errors of data-driven dependency parsing models. *In Proc. of EMNLP-CoNLL.*

J. Nivre, J. Hall, S. Kubler, R. McDonald, J. Nilsson, S. Riedel and D. Yuret. 2007a. The CoNLL 2007 Shared Task on Dependency Parsing. In *Proceedings of EMNLP/CoNLL-2007.*

J. Nivre, J. Hall, J. Nilsson, A. Chanev, G. Eryigit, S. Kübler, S. Marinov and E Marsi. 2007b. *MaltParser: A language-independent system for data-driven dependency parsing. Natural Language Engineering*, 13(2), 95-135.

S. Riedel, Ruket Çakıcı and Ivan Meza-Ruiz. 2006. Multi-lingual Dependency Parsing with Incremental Integer Linear Programming. In *Proceedings of the Tenth Conference on Computational Natural Language Learning (CoNLL-X).*

S. M. Shieber. 1985. Evidence against the context-freeness of natural language. In *Linguistics and Philosophy*, p. 8, 334–343.

# The use of formal language models in the typology of the morphology of Amerindian languages

**Andrés Osvaldo Porta**
Universidad de Buenos Aires
hugporta@yahoo.com.ar

## Abstract

The aim of this work is to present some preliminary results of an investigation in course on the typology of the morphology of the native South American languages from the point of view of the formal language theory. With this object, we give two contrasting examples of descriptions of two Aboriginal languages finite verb forms morphology: Argentinean Quechua (quichua santiagueño) and Toba. The description of the morphology of the finite verb forms of Argentinean quechua, uses finite automata and finite transducers. In this case the construction is straightforward using two level morphology and then, describes in a very natural way the Argentinean Quechua morphology using a regular language. On the contrary, the Toba verbs morphology, with a system that simultaneously uses prefixes and suffixes, has not a natural description as regular language. Toba has a complex system of causative suffixes, whose successive applications determinate the use of prefixes belonging different person marking prefix sets. We adopt the solution of Creider et al. (1995) to naturally deal with this and other similar morphological processes which involve interactions between prefixes and suffixes and then we describe the toba morphology using linear context-free languages.[1].

## 1 Introduction

It has been proved (Johnson, 1972; Kaplan and Kay, 1994) that regular models have an expressive power equal to the noncyclic components of generative grammmars representing the morphophonology of natural languages. However, these works make no considerations about what class of formal languages is the natural for describing the morphology of one particular language. On the other hand, the criteria of classification of Amerindian languages, do not involve complexity criteria. In order to establish criteria that take into account the complexity of the description we present two contrasting examples in two Argentinean native languages: toba and quichua santiagueño. While the quichua has a natural representation in terms of a regular language using two level morphology, we will show that the Toba morphology has a more natural representation in terms of linear context-free languages.

## 2 Quichua Santiagueño

The quichua santiagueño is a language of the Quechua language family. It is spoken in the Santiago del Estero state, Argentina. Typologically is an agglutinative language and its structure is almost exclusively based on the use of suffixes and is extremely regular. The morphology takes a dominant part in this language with a rich set of validation suffixes. The quichua santiagueño has a much simpler phonologic system that other languages of this family: for example it has no series of aspirated or glottalized stops.

Since the description of the verbal morphology is rich enough for our aim to expose the regular nature of quichua santiagueño morphology, we have restricted our study to the morphology of finite verbs forms. We use the two level morphology paradigm to express with finite regular transducers the rules that clearly illustrate how naturally this language phonology is regular. The construction uses the descriptive works of Alderetes (2001) and Nardi (Albarracín et. al, 2002)

[1]This work is part of the undergraduate thesis Finite state morphology: The Koskenniemi's two level morphology model and its application to describing the morphosyntaxis of two native Argentinean languages



*Proceedings of the ACL 2010 Student Research Workshop*, pages 109–114,
Uppsala, Sweden, 13 July 2010. ©2010 Association for Computational Linguistics

### 2.1 Phonological two level rules for the quichua santiagueño

In this section we present the alphabet of the quichua santiagueño with which we have implemented the quichua phonological rules in the paradigm of two level morphology. The subsets abbreviations are: V (vowel), Vlng (underlying vowel).Valt (high vowel),VMed (median vowel), Vbaj (bass vowel) , Ftr (trasparent to medialization phonema), Cpos (posterior consonant).

```
ALPHABET
  a e i o u p t ch k q s sh ll m
  n l r w y b d g gg f h x r rr
  A E I O U W N Q Y + '
NULL 0
ANY @
BOUNDARY #
SUBSET C        p t ch k q s sh ll m
                n l r w y b d f h
                x r rr h Q
SUBSET V        i e a o u A E I O U
SUBSET Vlng     I E A O U
SUBSET Valt     u i U I
SUBSET VMed     e o E O
SUBSET Vbaj     a A
SUBSET Ftr      n y r Y N
SUBSET Cpos     gg q Q
```

With the aim of showing the simplicity of the phonologic rules we transcribe the two-level rules we have implemeted with the transducers in the thesis. R1-R4 model the medialization vowels procesess, R5-R7 are elision and ephentesis procesess with very specific contexts and R7 represents a diachornic phonological process with a subjacent form present in others quechua dialects.

```
Rules

R1 i:i /<= CPos:@ __

R2 i:i /<=  __ Ftr:@ CPos:@

R3 u:u /<= CPos:@ __

R4 u:u /<=  __ Ftr:@ CPos:@

R5  W:w <=> a:a a:a +:0__a:a +:0

R6 U:0 <=> m:m __+:0 p:p u:u +:0

R7 N:0 <=> ___+:0 r:@ Q:@ a:a +:0
```

### 2.2 Quichua Santigueño morphology

The grammar that models the agglutination order is showed with a non deterministic finite automata. This implemented automata is presented in Figure 1. This description of the morphophonology was implemented using PC-KIMMO (Antworth, 1990)

## 3 The Toba morphology

The Toba language belongs, with the languages pilaga, mocovi and kaduveo, to the guaycuru language family (Messineo, 2003; Klein, 1978). The toba is spoken in the Gran Chaco region (which is comprised between Argentina, Bolivia and Paraguay) and in some reduced settlements near Buenos Aires, Argentina. From the point of view of the morphologic typology it presents characteristics of a polysynthetic agglutinative language. In this language the verb is the morphologically more complex wordclass. The grammatical category of person is prefixed to the verbal theme. There are suffixes to indicate plurals and other grammatical categories as aspect, location-direction, reflexive and reciprocal and desiderative mode. The verb has no mark of time. As an example of a typical verb we can considerate the *sanadatema*:

**Example 1** .

| | | | | |
|---|---|---|---|---|
| *s-* | *anat(a)* | *-d* | *-em* | *-a* |
| *1Act-* | *advice* | *2 dat* | *ben* | [2] |
| *" I* | *advice* | *you"* | | |

One of the characteristics of the toba verb morphology is a system of markation active-inactive on the verbal prefixes (Messineo, 2003; Klein, 1978). There are in this language two sets or verbal prefixes that mark action:

1. Class I (In):codifies inactive participants, objects of transitive verbs and pacients of intransitive verbs. .

2. Class II(Act): codifies active participants, subjects of transitive and intransitive verbs.

[2]abrev: Act:active, ben:benefactive, dat:dative,inst: intrumental,Med: Median voice, pos: Posessor, refl: reflexive

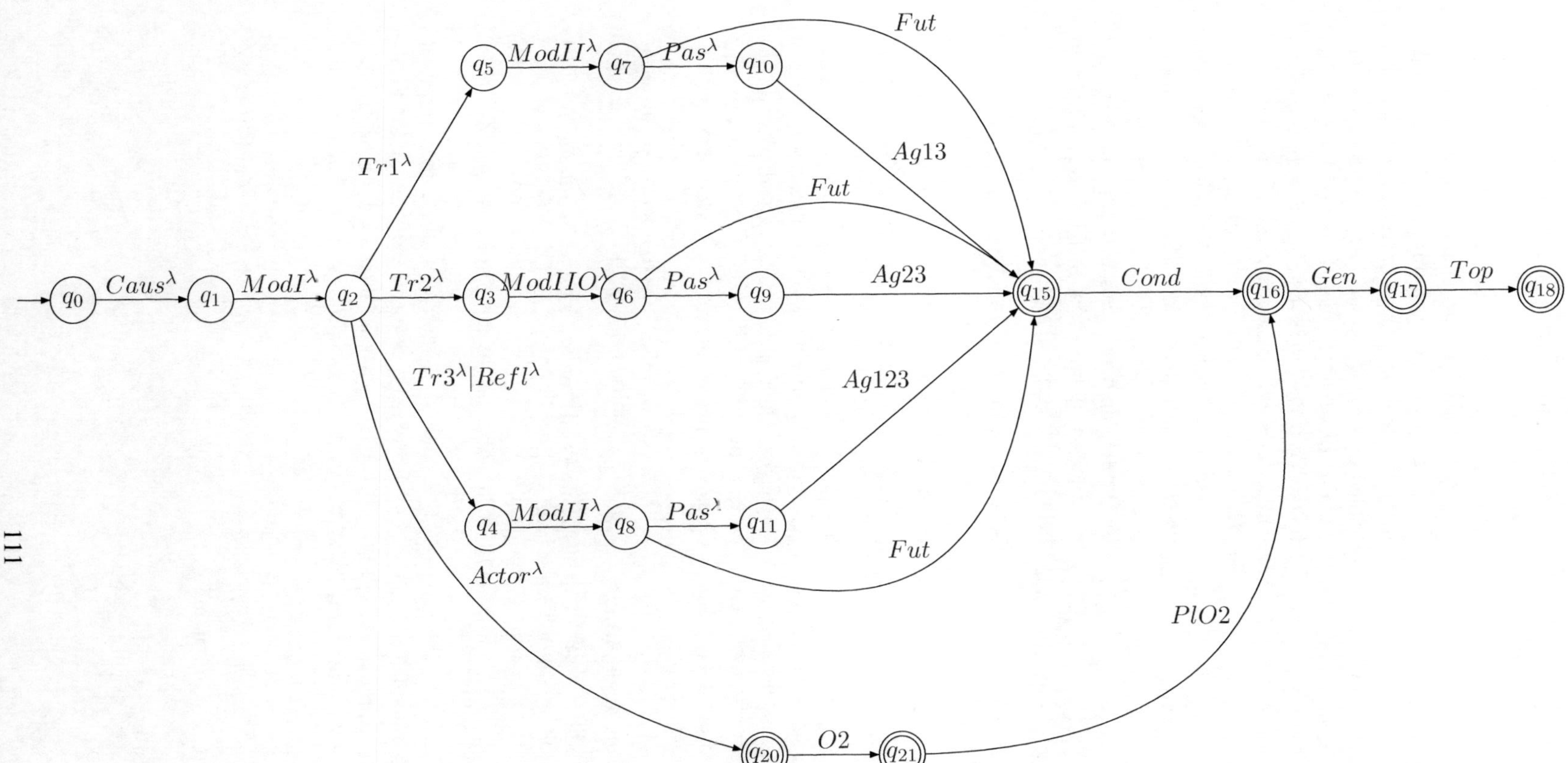


Figure 1: Schema of the verbal morphology of the quichua santiagueño. The supra indices $\lambda$ indicate possible null transitions.
Abrev.: Caus: Causative suffixes.ModI: Set I of Modal Suffixes.Tri : i th. person trasition Suffixes.ModII: Set II of modal suffixes .Pas: Past suffixes. Ag: AgentSuffix , in this case, for example, Ag1, indicates the agent suffix for the 1st person. Ag12 is an abbreviator for $A1 \cup A2$. Cond : Conditional Suffixes. Gen : General Suffixes. Fut: future suffixes.Top : Topicaliser suffixes. O2: Object 2nd person Suffixes. PLO2: Plural of Object 2nd person Suffixes.

Active affected(Medium voice, Med): codifies the presence of an active participant affected by the action that the verb codifies. .

The toba has a great quantity of morphological processes that involve interactions between suffixes and prefixes. In the next example the suffixation of the reflexive ($-l'at$) forces the use of the active person with prefixes of the voice medium class because the agent is affected by the action.

**Example 2** .

| | | | |
|---|---|---|---|
| *(a)* | *y-* | *alawat* | |
| | *3Activa* | *-kill* | |
| | *" He* | *kills"* | |
| *(b)* | *n-* | *alawat* | *-l'at* |
| | *3Med-* | *kill* | *-refl* |
| | *" He kills* | *himself"* | |

The agglutination of this suffix occurs in the last suffix box (after locatives, directional and other derivational suffixes). Then, if we model this process using finite automata we will add many items to the lexicon (Sproat, 1992). The derivation of names from verbs is very productive. There are many nominalizer suffixes. The resulting names use obligatory possessing person nominal prefixes.

**Example 3** .

| | | |
|---|---|---|
| *l-* | *edaGan* | *-at* |
| *3pos* | *write* | *instr* |
| | *"his pencil"* | |

The toba language also presents a complex system of causative suffixes that act as switching the transitivity of the verb. Transitivity is specially appreciable in the switching of the 3rd person prefix mark. In section 3.2 we will use this process to show how linear context free grammars are a better than regular grammars for modeling agglutination in this language, but first we will present the former class of languages and its acceptor automata.

### 3.1 Linear context free languages and two-taped nondeterministic finite-state automata

A linear context-free language is a language generated by a grammar context-free grammars G in which every production has one of the three forms (Creider et al., 1995):

1. $A \rightarrow a$, with $a$ terminal symbol
2. $A \rightarrow aB$, with $B$ a non terminal symbol and $a$ a terminal symbol.
3. $A \rightarrow Ba$, with $B$ a non terminal symbol and $a$ a terminal symbol.

Linear context-free grammars have been studied by Rosenberg (1967) who showed that there is an equivalence between them and two-taped nondeterministic finite-state automata. Informally, a two-head nondeterministic finite-state automata could be thought as a generalization of a usual nondeterministic finite-state automata which has two read heads that independently reads in two different tapes, and at each transition only one tape moves. When both tapes have been processed, if the automata is at a final state, the parsing is successful. In the ambit that we are studying we can think that if a word is a string of prefixes, a stem and suffixes, one automata head will read will the prefixes and the other the suffixes. Taking into account that linear grammars are in Rosenberg's terms: " The lowest class of nonregular context-free grammars", Creider et al. (1995) have taken this formal language class as the optimal to model morphological processes that involve interaction between prefixes and suffixes.

### 3.2 Analysis of the third person verbal paradigm

In this section we model the morphology of the third person of transitive verbs using two-taped finite nondeterministics automata. The modeling of this person is enough to show this description advantages with respect to others in terms of regular languages. The transitivity of the verb plays an important role in the selection of the person marker Class. The person markers are (Messineo, 2003):

1. i-/y- for transitive verbs y and some intrasitive subjects (Pr AcT).
2. d(Vowel) for verbs typically intransitives (Pr ActI).
3. n: subjets of medium voice (Pr ActM).

The successive application of the causative seems to act here, as was interpreted by Buckwalter (2001), like making the switch in the original verb transitivity as is shown en Example 4 in the next page.

**Example 4** .

| | | | | |
|---|---|---|---|---|
| *IV* | *de-* | *que'e* | | *he eats* |
| *TV* | *i-* | *qui'* | *-aGan* | *he eats(something)* |
| *IV* | *de-* | *qui'* | *-aGanataGan* | *he feeds* |
| *TV* | *i-* | *qui'* | *-aGanataGanaGan* | *he feeds(a person)* |
| *IV* | *de* | *qui'* | *-aGanaGanataGan* | *he command to feed* |

If we want to model this morphological process using finite automata again we must enlarge the lexicon size. The resulting grammar, althought capable of modeling the morphology of the toba, would not work effectively. The effectiveness of a grammar is a measure of their productivity (Heintz, 1991). Taking into account the productivity of causative and reflexive verbal derivation we will prefer a description in terms of a context-free linear grammar with high effectivity than another using regular languages with low effectivity.

To model the behavior of causative agglutination and the interaction with person prefixes using the two-head automata, we define two paths determined by the parity of the causative suffixes wich have been agglutinated to the verb. We have also to take into consideration the optative posterior aglutination of reflexive and reciprocal suffixes wich forces the use of medium voice person prefix. From the third person is also formed the third person indefinite actor from a prefix, $qa$ -, which is at left and adjacent to the usual mark of the third person and after the mark of negation $sa$- . Therefore, their agglutination is reserved to the last transitions. The resulting two-typed automata showed in Figure 2 also takes into account the relative order of the boxes and so the mutual restrictions between them (Klein, 1978).

## 4 Future Research

It is interesting to note that phonological rules in toba can be naturally expressed by regular Finite Transducers. There are, however, many South American native languages that presents morphological processes analogous to the Toba and some can present phonological processes that will have a more natural expression using Linear Finite Transducers. For example the Guarani language presents nasal harmony which expands from the root to both suffixes and prefixes (Krivoshein, 1994). This kind of characterization can have some value in language classification and the modeling of the great diversity of South American languages morphology can allow to obtain a formal concept of natural description of a language.

## References


Lelia Albarracín, Mario Tebes y Jorge Alderetes(eds.) 2002. *Introducción al quichua santiagueño por Ricardo L.J. Nardi*. Editorial DUNKEN: Buenos Aires, Argentina.

Jorge Ricardo Alderetes 2002. *El quichua de Santiago del Estero. Gramática y vocabulario.*. Tucumán: Facultad de Filosofía y Letras, UNT:Buenos Aires, Argentina.

Evan L. Antworth 1990. *PC-KIMMO: a two-level processor for morphological analysis.No. 16 in Occasional publications in academic computing*. No. 16 in Occasional publications in academic computing. Dallas: Summer Institute of Linguistics.

Alberto Buckwalter 2001. *Vocabulario toba*. Formosa / Indiana, Equipo Menonita.

Chet Creider, Jorge Hankamer, and Derick Wood. 1995. Preset two-head automata and morphological analysis of natural language . *International Journal of Computer Mathematics*, Volume 58, Issue 1, pp. 1-18.

Joos Heintz y Claus Schönig 1991. Turcic Morphology as Regular Language. *Central Asiatic Journal*, 1-2, pp 96-122.

C. Douglas Johnson 1972. *Formal Aspects of Phonological Description*. The Hague:Mouton.

Ronald M. Kaplan and Martin Kay. 1994. Regular models of phonological rule systems . *Computational Linguistics*, 20(3):331-378.

Harriet Manelis Klein 1978. *Una gramática de la lengua toba: morfología verbal y nominal*. Universidad de la República, Montevideo, Uruguay.

Natalia Krivoshein de Canese 1994. *Gramática de la lengua guaraní*. Colección Nemity, Asunción, Paraguay.

María Cristina Messineo 2003. *Lengua toba (guaycurú). Aspectos gramaticales y discursivos*. LINCOM Studies in Native American Linguistics 48. München: LINCOM EUROPA Academic Publisher.

A.L Rosenberg 1967 A Machine Realization of the linear Context-Free Languages. *Information and Control*, 10: 177-188.

Richard Sproat 1992. *Morphology and Computation*. The MIT Press.

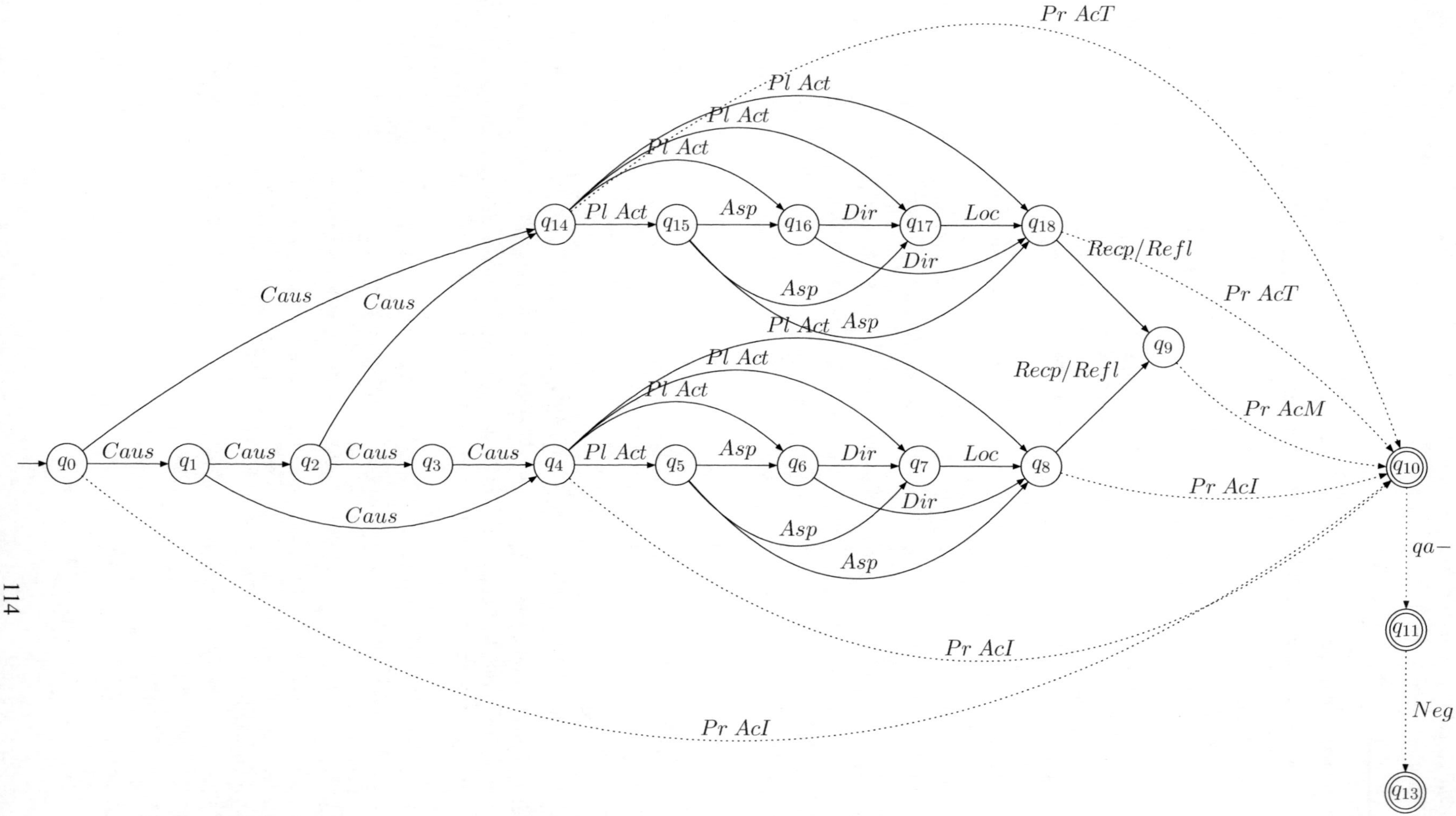




Figure 2: Schema of the 3rd person intransitive verb morphology of the toba .
The entire and dotted lines indicating transitions of the sufix and preffix tape, respectively
Abrev: Caus: Causative suffix. Pl Act: plural actors suffix. Asp: aspectual suffix. Dir: directive suffix. Loc: locative suffix. Recp: reciprocal action suffix. Refl: reflexive suffix. Pr.Ac: acting person prefix(T: transitive, I: intransitive, M: medium) *qa-*: indeterminate person prefix. Neg: negation prefix

# Author Index

**Association for Computational Linguistics**
209 N. Eighth Street
Stroudsburg, Pennsylvania 18360

CURRAN ASSOCIATES INC
proceedings.com